The Vest-Pocket

CEO

Decision-Making Tools for Executives

ALEXANDER HIAM

PRENTICE HALL
Englewood Cliffs, New Jersey 07632

Prentice-Hall International (UK) Limited, *London*
Prentice-Hall of Australia Pty. Limited, *Sydney*
Prentice-Hall Canada, Inc., *Toronto*
Prentice-Hall Hispanoamericana, S.A., *Mexico*
Prentice-Hall of India Private Limited, *New Delhi*
Prentice-Hall of Japan, Inc., *Tokyo*
Simon & Schuster Asia Pte. Ltd., *Singapore*
Editora Prentice-Hall do Brasil, Ltda., *Rio de Janeiro*

© 1990 *by*

PRENTICE-HALL, Inc.

Englewood Cliffs, NJ

10   9   8   7   6   5   4   3   2   1

This publication is designed to provide accurate and authoritative information in regard to the subject matter covered. It is sold with the understanding that the publisher is
not engaged in rendering legal, accounting, or other professional service. If legal advice or other expert assistance is
required, the services of a competent professional person
should be sought.
…From the Declaration of Principles jointly adopted by a Commit-
tee of the American Bar Association and a Committee of Publishers
and Associations.

Library of Congress Cataloging-in-Publication Data

Hiam, Alexander.
    The vest-pocket CEO: decision-making tools for execu-
tives / Alexander Hiam.
    p   cm.
    ISBN 0-13-941691-9
1. Industrial management—Decision-making—Handbooks,
manuals, etc.   2. Executives—Handbooks, manuals,
etc.   I. Title.
HD30.23.H53   1990
658.4'03—dc20   89-22805
                                                            CIP

ISBN 0-13-941691-9

PRENTICE HALL
BUSINESS & PROFESSIONAL DIVISION
A division of Simon & Schuster
Englewood Cliffs, New Jersey 07632

Printed in the United States of America

This book is dedicated to the memory of Bette Schwartzberg, whose editorial vision is in large part responsible for this and many other fine titles for Prentice Hall's Business & Professional Book Division. She held her authors to a standard of clarity and usefulness that ought to be applied to all business reference books.

ABOUT THE AUTHOR

Alexander Hiam's Amherst, Massachusetts-based management consulting firm specializes in business development and decision-making. His writings on management have appeared in American Marketing Association publications, the *Harvard Business Review, Business Digest,* and elsewhere, and he is the winner of a 1989 *Amex Bank Review* book award. Educated at Harvard and the University of California at Berkeley, Mr. Hiam has an MBA in Marketing and Strategic Planning and teaches graduate and undergraduate management courses at Western New England College. He has management experience in transportation, electronics, and biotechnology, and has worked with clients in financial services, retail, manufacturing, publishing, and other industries. His experience in applying decision-making tools for clients formed the basis of this book. Mr. Hiam is currently working on a collection of methods for stimulating revenue growth that is based on his popular *Breakthrough Management* workshop.

HOW THIS BOOK WILL HELP YOU

Executives need fast solutions to many diverse and pressing business challenges. *The Vest-Pocket CEO* is a unique collection of the best decision-making techniques used today by America's leading companies.

Now you too can benefit from the expertise and insight of hundreds of top executives who helped develop these practical tools for dealing with urgent management needs in nine key areas:

- financial decisions
- leadership skills
- manufacturing and operations
- marketing
- organization and human resources
- product development and innovation
- sales management
- strategic planning
- general decision-making

You'll find innovative approaches used by other top executives that can be put to work for your own organization in anywhere from an hour to a few days...ideas that are taken from some of the most successful companies in the country!

Here are just a few of the powerful techniques discussed in this book:

- The Boston Consulting Group Growth Share Matrix, which enables diversified companies to maximize their portfolio performance

- IBM's Process Quality Management, a practical method for helping a group to agree on goals and finish a complex project expediently

- Stanford University's Stress Analysis, a controversial, simple device for identifying causes of stress and developing strategies for reducing them.

- Price-Waterhouse's successful application of Kawasaki Heavy Industries' "just-in-time" production system, featuring a fast and effective walkthrough facility tour

- Ernst & Whinney's customer service checklist for measuring how effectively your firm manages customer service and identifying areas in need of improvement.

- Honeywell's seven tactics for managing a product development team

- The Delphi technique developed by the Rand Corporation for greater accuracy in forecasting sales

In all, there are 101 to-the-point solutions for decision making, problem solving, and performance improvement. Each method starts with a quick summary of the applications and procedures so you can quickly find the right tool for your specific need. A detailed, step-by-step description of how to use the method is included, as well as any ideas or warnings you should note. You'll also find many examples of how these methods have been successfully applied by other companies. If you need further information, a reference section will guide you to the authoritative sources. And as a further aid, the methods are listed alphabetically within each of the nine sections and cross-referenced when applicable.

Whether you're the CEO of a leading corporation or the manager of a small- to medium-size business, you'll find these proven techniques an invaluable guide for making decisions quickly without extensive research or number-crunching. You'll want to keep *The Vest-Pocket CEO* near at hand for practical advice at a glance as you tackle the challenging problems of a busy executive.

CONTENTS

Marketing Decisions, 133

Organization and Human Resources, 197

Product Development & Innovation, 245

Sales Management Decisions, 299

Strategic Planning Decisions, 347

General Decision-Making Tools, 431

PART 1

FINANCIAL DECISIONS

ALTMAN'S Z-SCORE FAILURE FORECAST

Applications

- Predicting bankruptcy in manufacturing companies as far as two years in advance with accuracy.
- Reviewing acquisition candidates, suppliers, and other companies to detect financial problems that may affect your business.
- Measuring an organization's financial health from balance sheet and income statement information.

Procedures

1. Calculate financial ratios from the financial statements of the company or companies you wish to analyze.
2. Compute Z by multiplying the ratios by weighting factors and summing them according to the formula.
3. Analyze the result. A low score indicates a high probability of failure and vice versa.
4. Track trends in the Z scores of suppliers, competitors, customers, acquisition candidates, and others of interest to your company. Use a falling Z score as an indicator of companies that need closer examination.

Cross-Reference

Strategic Planning Devices

The Z-score formula uses ratios that are derived from standard financial statements, so it can be applied to publicly traded competitors, acquisition candidates, suppliers, customers, and other companies of interest. The Z score may also be useful for establishing trends in the financial condition of your own company. Sometimes a Z-score analysis is needed to convince management of the seriousness of a company's condition so that turnaround efforts can be initiated.

INSTRUCTIONS

1. Calculate the following five ratios:

Symbol	Ratio and comments
$X1$	Working Capital / Total Assets
	The difference between current assets and current liabilities divided by the total book value.
$X2$	Retained Earnings / Total Assets
	Note that this ratio is lower for younger companies since retained earnings accrue over the lifetime of a company. This penalty for youth reflects the higher probability of failure among younger companies.
$X3$	Earnings Before Interest and Taxes / Total Assets
	Also referred to as return on capital employed, this ratio incorporates all capital employed, both debt and equity.
$X4$	Market Value of Equity / Book Value of Total Debt
	Stock market capitalization is used in this ratio (sum the current value of all classes of stock). For the divisor, combine both short-term and long-term debt.
$X5$	Sales / Total Assets
	A simple measure of capital turnover. (Use annual sales from the income statement.)

2. Multiply each ratio by its weighting factor, given in the following formula, and sum to calculate Z:

$$Z = (1.2)X1 + (1.4)X2 + (3.3)X3 + (0.6)X4 + X5$$

3. Assess the Z score. Scores below 1.81 indicate a high likelihood of bankruptcy. Scores above 3.00 indicate a low likelihood of failure. Scores in the middle of this range are not clear indicators, but they are less likely to be associated with failure than low scores.

Altman calculated the probability of an accurate prediction by using historical data from D&B reports for a sample of 85 failed companies. 95% of bankrupt firms in his sample had Z scores below 1.81 a year before failure, and 72% did two years before. However, only 4% did three years prior to bankruptcy, suggesting the Z-score method is not particularly useful for forecasts of more than two years.

Warning: The Z score will not be accurate even one year in advance if the company cooks its books!

4. Repeat the analysis periodically and plot Z scores for companies of interest on a graph with Z scores on the vertical axis and time on the horizontal. Significant downward trends in Z scores signal a potential problem, and even if the Z score does not fall below 1.81 the source of the problem should be identified and evaluated. Look at trends within the component ratios to see why the Z score is falling and decide whether it represents a serious problem.

Example: A major supplier's Z score falls for two years in a row. Analysis points to declines in working capital and reduced earnings as the major causes. Further analysis can focus on why earnings are falling, whether this is creating cost-cutting pressures that could affect the quality of parts supplied by the company, and whether the company is significantly more leveraged than others in its industry. Rapid expansion might prove to be the explanation, and the response might be to reduce reliance on this supplier until it has recovered from the expansion program.

Altman did not track Z scores over time, but many companies may find it useful to do this for the dozens or even hundreds of firms they have relationships with through purchasing and distribution, and the various companies they may track for competitor analysis or as acquisition candidates. A routine quarterly or annual spreadsheet analysis can be used to compute and plot Z scores along with other ratios and statistics that financial analysts already track at your company.

Private companies

What if you want to analyze a company that is not publicly traded? You will not be able to compute ratio $X4$ for the Z-score formula. Many companies use smaller suppliers and sell to smaller customers that are privately held. Although Altman did not extend his study to these companies, the other four ratios can be computed from D&B reports and a partial Z computed by dropping $X4$. This measure will tend to be lower than the standard Z score, and no research exists to associate specific probabilities of failure with ranges in this score. Therefore, it is best used as a long-term tracking mechanism, with significant declines considered a flag requiring closer examination as in step 4.

References

Edward Altman. "Financial Ratios, Discriminant Analysis and the Prediction of Corporate Bankruptcy." *Journal of Finance* (September 1968).

Donald Bibeault. *Corporate Turnaround: How Managers Turn Losers Into Winners.* New York: McGraw-Hill, 1982.

ARMCO PREAPPROVAL AUDIT

Applications

- Obtaining an objective second opinion on large capital expenditure requests prior to approval.
- Identifying and evaluating key assumptions behind the projections in a capital expenditure request.
- Improving the quality and carefulness of capital expenditure requests.

Procedures

1. Form an audit team to evaluate a capital expenditure proposal.
2. The team identifies and evaluates key assumptions.
3. The team alerts the proposal's authors to any problems, giving them an opportunity to revise the proposal.
4. The team prepares a report describing and evaluating key assumptions.
5. The team leader reviews the report with the project's proposers, then delivers it to upper management.

Cross-Reference

Manufacturing and Operations

This method originated at Armco in response to a $50 million capital expenditure request from a division. Management wanted to verify the division's projections and formed a team to identify and analyze underlying assumptions. Since then the method has been formalized and refined. In several cases it has led to reworking of proposals, which has produced better, more realistic capital expenditure requests. This method was reported to *Harvard Business Review* readers in 1984 by Robert Lambrix, then Armco's treasurer, and Surendra Singhvi, manager of financial planning at Armco.

INSTRUCTIONS

1. Form an audit team.

To evaluate a capital expenditure request or proposal, form an audit team of three to five representatives from multiple areas, such as marketing, engineering, and finance. Appoint one chairperson. Give the team at least five weeks to complete the audit. Do *not* include members of top management or other interested parties.

Note: The team should not be formed until a formal proposal for a capital expenditure has been completed.

2. Identify and evaluate key assumptions.

The team should review the proposal's key assumptions with an eye to validity and reasonableness. Assumptions in the following areas are generally key at Armco:

Area	Assumptions
Capital Investment	Cost estimate
	Process feasibility
	Capacity
Market	Served market size
	Positioning
	Price
	Competitor activities
	Consistency with other programs and forecasts
Financial	Cost and margin projections
	Consistency with corporate policies and standards

Area	Assumptions
Strategy	Market penetration strategy
	Fit with division and corporate strategies
Risk and Sensitivity Analysis	Appropriateness
	Interpretation of results

Use these categories as an indication of where the team should focus its attention.

Note: The team should scrutinize documentation of existing business and examine all other material supporting the forecasts. Make sure all claims are documented. Bring in outside sources of information when possible to verify forecasts.

3. Discussion of problems.

If substantial problems are identified by the audit team, it should meet with the proposal's authors to try to resolve differences. In some cases the authors elect to modify their proposal when made aware of unreasonable assumptions in it.

4. Preparation of audit report.

Coordinated by the audit committee chairman, a short report is prepared which identifies the key assumptions and evaluates their reasonableness. Any important disagreements concerning project assumptions should be highlighted, but the report should *not* recommend approval or disapproval of the project.

5. Review and delivery.

The committee chairman reviews the audit report with the head of the proposal's originating division or subsidiary. The report is then delivered to upper management at least one week in advance of the decision deadline. After delivering its report, the committee is disbanded.

Reference

Robert J. Lambrix and Surendra S. Singhvi. "Pre-approval Audits of Capital Projects." *Harvard Business Review* (March–April 1984): 12–14.

ARTHUR YOUNG SUSTAINABLE-GROWTH ANALYSIS

Applications

- Using an expanded formula for sustainable growth as an aid to financial planning.
- Understanding and modeling the impact of changes in financial and operating variables on sustainable-growth rate.
- Evaluating strategies to increase a company's sustainable-growth rate.

Procedures

1. Compute your firm's sustainable-growth rate using the expanded financial planning formula.
2. Modify the formula to reflect different categories of debt if necessary.
3. Use the formula for decision making and analysis, especially when you need to evaluate alternatives for increasing the sustainable-growth rate in order to achieve strategic goals.

Cross-Reference

Strategic Planning Decisions

Charles Kyd, a consultant with Arthur Young and Co., recommends calculating sustainable-growth rate using an expanded formula. The formula shows the individual components of g, sustainable growth, and therefore gives management information of use in planning decisions by showing how dividends, income taxes, interest rates, and operating performance affect financial growth. In essence, the formula is treated as a model of the firm's financial performance and is used as an aid to financial decisions.

Note: The concept behind sustainable growth is that growth in revenues must be balanced by growth in assets in order for the firm to be able to support the sales growth.

INSTRUCTIONS

1. Compute the expanded formula for your company.

The financial planning formula for sustainable growth rate is:

$$g = b \times (1 - \text{Tax Rate}) \times$$

$$\left[\text{EOA} + \frac{\text{Debt}}{\text{Equity}} \times (\text{EOA} - \text{Average Interest Rate})\right]$$

> b = earnings retention ratio = (earnings after dividends)/dividends
>
> EOA = EBIT on assets = (earnings before interest and taxes)/beginning-of-period assets

Note that EOA represents earnings on assets before interest and taxes. The formula adds EOA, the rate of earnings on assets, to the company's net pretax benefit to return on equity from the use of debt. This second rate is computed by dividing debt by equity and multiplying the result by EOA minus average interest rate (the last term of the formula).

After adding these two rates, the formula multiplies the sum by two ratios for earnings retention, one representing earnings retained after dividends and the other after taxes. These are the first and second terms of the formula.

2. Expand the formula further to reflect different types of debt.

If your firm uses different types of debt with significantly different interest rates, it may be desirable to expand the formula to show the individual impact of each category of debt. Expand the last term of the formula as follows to reflect as many categories of debt as necessary:

$$[EOA +$$

$$\frac{Debt\ A}{Equity} \times (EOA - Interest\ Rate\ of\ Debt\ A) +$$

$$\frac{Debt\ B}{Equity} \times (EOA - Interest\ Rate\ of\ Debt\ B) +$$

$$\frac{Debt\ C}{Equity} \times (EOA - Interest\ Rate\ of\ Debt\ C)\ ]$$

3. Use the formula for decision-making and analysis.

The formula provides considerable insight into the financial status and options of a company. Look at the individual components of the formula for insights into these options or to evaluate the impact of proposed changes.

If g is undesirably low, as is sometimes the case when a company needs to expand to protect or build market share, the formula can be examined to look for ways to increase the sustainable-growth rate.

- Alter debt or equity in the formula to bring g to the desired growth rate and indicate how much outside financing is required.
- Play with operating ratios to alter earnings and identify the operating changes necessary to support a higher sustainable-growth rate without external financing.
- Model different tax rates and dividend policies if there are any options available on these dimensions.

In some cases the formula will highlight other problems. For example, compare EOA with interest rates on debt to see whether the company is earning at a higher rate than the rate at which it borrows money. In some cases EOA is higher than interest rates on existing debt, but (if the firm is already highly leveraged or rates have gone up) new debt will exceed EOA. This imposes a penalty on debt-based strategies for increasing sustainable growth and may lead management to focus on other components of the formula instead.

Idea: A balance sheet–driven spreadsheet on a PC is a useful aid to financial modeling with this formula. The referenced article in *Lotus* magazine gives very clear instructions for creating a simple spreadsheet model of sustainable growth using this formula in either Lotus123 or Symphony. (The magazine is published by Lotus Development Corp. out of Cambridge, Massachusetts.)

Reference

Charles W. Kyd. "Sustainable Growth and the Financial-Planning Formula." *Lotus: Computing for Managers and Professionals* (October 1987): 58–63. Copyright © 1987 Lotus Publishing Corporation. Quoted with permission. All rights reserved.

BANK OF AMERICA'S NINE WARNING SIGNALS

Applications

- Identifying commercial borrowers that are suffering from financial or other business problems.
- Screening customers, suppliers, and other important companies to identify those encountering difficulties.

Procedures

Use the list of warning signals to guide analysis and screening. Consider establishing a formal review process for all companies with which you do business.

This list was developed by a vice-president at Bank of America and is useful in anticipating or discovering problems in a business. Other lenders will benefit from comparing Bank of America's screening method with their own and should use the opportunity to make sure that their screening is as thorough as possible.

While developed initially for analyzing borrowers, it can also be applied as a screen for suppliers, acquisition candidates, subsidiaries, competitors, and even your own company. If your company depends on another company, it makes sense to analyze and track the health of that company as closely as a bank looks at a corporate borrower.

The financial staff of a corporation is in a good position to assess the financial health of suppliers, customers, and other business partners. Although it is currently uncommon for the CFO's staff to be involved in evaluating companies for sales, manufacturing, purchasing, and other departments, it makes good sense to have them play this role. Screening tools such as those used by banks are useful for this purpose.

INSTRUCTIONS

Look for any of these warning signals to identify companies that are at risk and need closer scrutiny. The warning signals are listed in order from most to least common.

Warning Signals

1. *Delays in submitting financial exhibits.*
2. *Declines in deposit balances and a high incidence of overdrafts or returned checks.*
3. *Failure to perform on other obligations.* For example; B of A looks at performance on personal debt by the principals. (Other business obligations may be relevant depending on context.)
4. *An inventory glut.* This can be indicated by financial statements, credit reports, or advice from the organization's suppliers.
5. *Delinquent loan payments; past due periods increasing.* This information is readily available to a lender but is harder for other organizations to obtain unless they have a good business relationship with the banker or access to a current credit report.
6. *Difficulty in arranging meetings and visits.* If it is hard to visit a business, it is usually because they have something to hide.
7. *Legal action against the business.*
8. *Increasing payables or accruals.* This can be indicated in financial statements and information from the business's suppliers.
9. *Negative information from competitors and customers.*

Note: Many of these red flags become apparent before a company fails (or fails to perform adequately), but it is uncommon to track and report them for suppliers, subsidiaries, and other organizations that a company may depend on. A tracking system which provides regular reports based on observed performance and review of credit reports will give management early warning of trouble.

Reference

K.D. Martin. "Problem Loan Signals and Follow-Up." *Journal of Commercial Bank Lending* (September 1973): 39.

ELLSWORTH'S FINANCIAL POLICY ANALYSIS

Applications

- Improving the integration of financial policies and corporate strategy.
- Making financial policy more responsive to operating needs.
- Exploring alternative financial structures that may make the firm more competitive in its product markets and provide better shareholder value in the long run.
- Identifying assumptions behind financial policies and making sure they are consistent with current strategy and objectives.

Procedures

1. Identify assumptions behind current financial policies using the checklist of questions provided.
2. Explore alternative financial policies. Consider their impact on required shareholder returns, actual returns, and growth of returns.
3. Evaluate the role of the chief financial officer.
4. Evaluate the role of operating managers in financial decisions.

Cross-Reference

Strategic planning decisions.

Richard Ellsworth developed this method based on his studies of financial policy as a professor at Harvard Business School and on his previous experience as treasurer of Kaiser Aetna. It addresses the problems many firms experience in integrating financial policy and corporate strategy. Financial policy is rarely optimal from a strategic perspective because financial and operating decisions are separated, dividend and capital structure policies are adopted as organizational goals, and the risk preferences and assumptions of management do not necessarily reflect the company's capital needs. Ellsworth's four-step method identifies limiting assumptions, explores alternatives, and helps integrate financial and business planning.

INSTRUCTIONS

1. Identify the critical assumptions behind financial policies. One way to do this is for the CFO and staff to answer these questions:

- What are the assumptions behind financial policies?
- Are these assumptions imposed by management or by the capital markets?
- Are these assumptions consistent with the organization's opportunities and threats?
- How are financial policies assumed to affect stock value?
- What is the evidence that these assumptions are valid?
- Is there any evidence that they are invalid?

This inquiry produces a list of financial-policy assumptions along with answers to help in understanding the origins and rationale behind each policy.

2. Evaluate alternative financial policies by looking at their impact on the main determinants of shareholder value:

- The minimum return (in dividends and capital gains) required by shareholders given the risk level of each alternative capital structure and investment program.
- The actual return to shareholders associated with each alternative capital structure.

- The growth rate of actual returns to share-holders.

A quantitative model of each alternative can be built (for details see the referenced article), but it requires too many assumptions to be definitive. A simpler approach is to estimate changes for each of the three factors just outlined based on the experience of your firm and its competitors. The following table identifies the variables to consider in making these estimates.

Factor	Affected by:
Required Return	- Nondiversifiable risk, as indicated by betas.
	- Impact of changes in competitive position on financial performance relative to the financial market, and hence on beta.
	- Impact of changes in debt capacity on risk of financial problems, and hence on beta.
Actual Return	- Debt-equity ratio and its impact on cost of capital.
	- Spending-level effects, including:
	a. Ability to respond to challenges and opportunities in product markets.
	b. Ability to undertake additional projects with returns in excess of cost on capital.
	c. Benefits of consistent expenditure levels and organizational costs of stop-start spending.
Growth of Returns	- Impact of increased leverage and decreased dividends on reinvestment and growth.

If you decide to develop quantitative measures of each factor, here is a formula to estimate the percent change in shareholder value from a proposed new policy.

$$\% \text{ change in value} = \left\{ \left(\dfrac{\dfrac{\text{Proposed actual return}}{\text{Proposed required return} - \text{SG}}}{\dfrac{\text{Existing actual return}}{\text{Existing required return} - \text{SG}}} + \dfrac{}{} \left(\dfrac{\text{NPV of investment effects}}{\begin{array}{c}minus\\ \text{NPV of Bank credit cards}\end{array}} \right) - 1 \right) \times 100 \right.$$

SG = sustainable growth rate under respective policies.

NPV = net present value of relevant future cash flows divided by existing shareholder value.

3. Evaluate the role of the chief financial officer. If capital rationing is severe due to policies that do not maximize shareholder value, this may be because of a lack of operational orientation in the CFO's office. Ellsworth suggests several controversial measures to bring the CFO's perspective more in line with corporate strategy.

• Base incentive compensation on corporate performance.

- Identify values and beliefs of CFO and see if they are consistent with the organization's objectives and strategies.
- Select CFO's with operating experience or give the current CFO operating experience.

Example: Dow Chemical uses all of these measures. Their CFO's have operating experience at Dow, own Dow stock and options (which aligns their interests with Dow's), and are exposed to operating needs through membership in the Executive Committee.

4. Evaluate the role of operating managers in financial-policy decisions. Usually this evaluation is simple since operating managers rarely have any role in financial policy. In general, financial policies dictate budget limits, and operational managers have to make strategy decisions within these limits. Here are some measures of operating management's involvement in financial policy:

- Is there communication between financial and operating managers regarding financial policy?
- Is there a formal vehicle for operating managers to express frustrations or concerns with financial policy?
- Do operating managers regularly propose projects whose capital requirements might necessitate changes in financial policy?

If the answers to any of these questions are negative, Ellsworth would argue that the concerns of operating managers are not represented in financial policy and that there is probably an implicit rationing of capital by operating managers that prevents the organization from exploring options.

Who should do the analysis?

Exploring the reasons for existing financial policies is a simple and important task, one the CEO or directors ought to undertake as a routine part of the strategic- and financial-planning cycle. However, the detailed development and comparison of alternative financial structure is time-consuming and requires considerable expertise. It is best performed by the CFO and supporting staff in most cases, with review of assumptions and results by the CEO and board.

Reference

Richard R. Ellsworth. "Subordinate Financial Policy to Corporate Strategy." *Harvard Business Review* (November–December 1983) :170–182.

ERNST GROWTH/LIQUIDITY ANALYSIS

Applications

- Modifying standard balance sheets to provide a clearer picture of trends in liquidity and investments in growth-producing assets.
- Managing cash flow during periods of rapid growth and investment.
- Estimating sustainable-growth rates and external financing needs.
- Developing strategies based on the growth and liquidity position of a firm and its competitors.

Procedures

1. Using balance-sheet figures, combine inventories with long-term assets to measure investment in the long-term growth of the firm.
2. Subtract current liabilities and long-term debt from financial assets to obtain operating liquidity.
3. Look at trends in both growth-producing assets and liquidity over time and compare these values with those of competitors.
4. If needed, plot an operating curve for the firm using annual changes in growth assets and liquidity, normalized by sales.
5. Find operating equilibrium, the limit to internally financed growth, on the graph. Look for an operating gap indicating future liquidity problems.
6. Plot a retained-earnings curve on the graph and use it to identify strategic equilibrium, the limit to externally financed growth.
7. Use the graph to develop strategy and compare financial position with competitors in your industry.

Cross-Reference

Strategic Planning Decisions

Harry Ernst of Compumetrics, a Boston consulting firm, developed this method for a company which had suffered a cash-flow crisis after receiving increased orders then building capacity to meet the increased demand. Management was frustrated by the difficulty of managing growth and liquidity through conventional financial statements and wanted a statement that provided clearer information about liquidity.

This method looks at a company in terms of its liquidity and its investment in growth-producing assets. A firm's investments in assets such as inventory, plant, equipment, and property give it the strength to build sales and profits. Increased investments generally produce growth. They also reduce liquidity by using available cash and short-term assets or by increasing the firm's debt. The trade-off between liquidity and investment in growth is relevant to financial policy and overall strategy, and is useful in competitive analysis as well.

Dr. Ernst has more recently applied this concept to the management of investment portfolios, developing the Growth, Liquidity, and Profitability Method of perimeter investing. The details of this method are beyond the scope of this chapter (but contact Compumetrics if you want a detailed description of it), but the fact that the growth/liquidity balance sheet can be used to predict sales and earnings as reflected in stock prices for a portfolio of stocks lends credence to the use of the method in financial management and competitive strategy decisions within a single firm.

INSTRUCTIONS

1. Restructure the balance sheet to create a growth/liquidity balance sheet. First, combine inventories with long-term assets for the growth side. Subtract this total from stockholder equity (retained earnings plus capital stock) to express as a growth

surplus or deficit the firm's ability to invest in additional growth-producing assets.

THE GROWTH/LIQUIDITY BALANCE SHEET

Growth	Liquidity
Stockholder equity	Cash and receivables (financial assets)
Less	*Less*
Inventories	Current liabilities
Net property, plant, and equipment	Total long-term debt
Other long-term assets	
Equals	*Equals*
Growth surplus or deficit	Operating liquidity

---

2. Subtract all current liabilities and long-term debt from financial assets (such as cash and receivables). The difference is operating liquidity. Restructure the balance sheet with growth to the left and liquidity to the right. Since it uses all the balance-sheet information, this new balance sheet still balances. Growth assets and operating liquidity equal stockholder equity.

3. Look at trends in growth assets and operating liquidity for clues to a company's financial health or to anticipate future behavior. For example, if IBM's 1979 and 1980 balance sheets are analyzed, its operating liquidity drops from -4.4 billion to -6.5 billion. The difference—$2.1 billion—was accounted for in part by heavy investments in physical assets and in part by a failure to account fully for inflation (see Ernst's article, referenced below, in *Harvard Business Review*, page 124). In this period IBM grew at an unsustainable rate according to the growth/liquidity balance sheet.

4. Additional insight may be gained by plotting an operating curve. This is the relationship between yearly changes in operating liquidity and yearly changes in the growth-producing assets.

Prepare growth/liquidity balance sheets for at least five years (using steps 1 through 3). Use successive totals of the growth assets to calculate annual percent change: $(YR2/YR1) - 1$. Also calculate the annual percent changes in operating liquidity. Then divide each year's percent changes in both growth assets and liquidity by the sales figure for the more recent year to normalize them to sales: $[(YR2/YR1) - 1]/YR2$ sales.

Plot the figures on a graph with the investment-capital figures on the horizontal axis and operating-liquidity figures on the vertical axis. Fit a least-squares regression line to the data points to create a downward-sloping line. The slope of the line reflects the trade-off between growth assets and liquidity for a particular firm (and provides clues to management behavior). For example; a slope of -1.0 indicates that liabilities are growing twice as fast as equity, assuming no significant changes in cash and receivables.

OPERATING CURVE

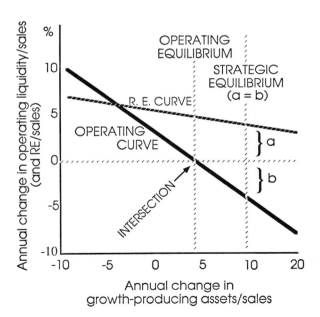

Note: The operating curve will shift up with a rise in either of two ratios: retained earnings to sales or investment capital to sales.

5. Find the point where the operating curve intersects a horizontal line passing through zero on the vertical axis. This point is operating equilibrium, the maximum growth possible *without* external financing. If the company is currently below this point on its operating curve, there is a gap that will have to be filled with long-term financing. If a company falls below its operating curve and drops below the SGR, increasing debt can be expected and investment in growth assets will probably fall until liquidity is restored. A slowing in revenue growth is the likely result.

6. It is also possible to use the graph to identify the maximum growth rate feasible *with* external financing (assuming that the historical relationship between sales growth and the annual change in growth-producing assets will be maintained in the future). First, calculate annual changes in retained earnings divided by sales. Next, plot each year's retained-earnings figure in relation to the annual change in growth-producing assets, just as you plotted the operating curve. Fit a line to these data points. In the graph, this retained-earnings curve is shown as a downward-sloping line, indicating that faster growth would reduce earnings. (This is typical of companies in mature industries, whereas an upward slope is typical of high-growth and new-technology companies.)

Now draw a vertical line on the graph where the distances from the horizontal zero-growth line to the retained-earnings curve and to the operating curve are equal. This vertical line, the strategic equilibrium line, bisects the horizontal axis at an investment growth rate that is consistent with the company's ability to produce sales and profit earnings. If a company moves beyond the strategic-equilibrium line, it will most likely have to compensate with a shift in the other direction in future years.

7. Use the graph for strategic analysis. The operating curve may be compared with those of competitors to see whether operating control is more or less

consistent than the competitors' (as indicated by tightness of fit of the data points to the line). Position on the curve can also be compared to see which firms in an industry have been most aggressive and whether any are over-leveraged or beyond strategic equilibrium. Position on the operating curve might also be relevant to how competitors will perform during a recession or other event that reduces sales growth, the firms that are farther to the right being more vulnerable to these events. An important strategic issue according to Dr. Ernst is "how a company should position itself on the curve to make certain growth continues to be planned rather than forced." Use the operating-curve analysis in annual strategic and financial planning to keep your firm's position within desired limits.

References

Harry B. Ernst. "New Balance Sheet for Managing Liquidity and Growth." *Harvard Business Review* (March–April 1984): 121–136.

"How to Use Balance Sheet Changes to Predict Stock Prices." *GLP Special Report* (September 30, 1988). Ernst Research.

HEEBNER'S SEVEN LAWS OF FORECASTING

Applications

- Evaluating quantitative forecasts.
- Developing a cautious, judgment-oriented philosophy of forecasting.

Procedures

Review the forecasting laws when preparing or interpreting forecasts to avoid false assumptions or over-reliance on quantitative results.

Cross-Reference

Strategic Planning Decisions

Gilbert Heebner, retired chief economist of CoreStates Financial Corp., believes in "reasoned judgment" when it comes to forecasting. His seven laws remind the executive that quantitative forecasts need to be taken with caution, and these laws give specific guidelines for making a qualitative, judgment-based evaluation of any forecast. Many companies rely on the forecasts of their own analysts, the government, and trade organizations, and find them fairly accurate in most years. But occasionally the forecasts are completely off-base, and the firm that applies Heebner's Laws to the development and interpretation of forecasts is more likely to be prepared for these sudden and hard-to-predict changes.

FORECASTING LAWS

1. *History repeats itself; history does not repeat itself.* The future is not random, but it does not repeat itself exactly either.

2. *From time to time major shocks—often unforecastable—throw the economy off course.* Developments from outside the economic system are usually not anticipated by forecasts. But they may be anticipated by experienced observers.

3. *The consensus of economists' forecasts is more often right than wrong.* It is not wise to automatically bet against the consensus.

4. *Adherence to a single economic theory can be dangerous to your forecasting health.* Theories can become less valid as conditions change.

5. *Economic forces work relentlessly but on an uncertain timetable.* This means forecasts are more likely to be correct regarding cause and effect than timing.

6. *Beware when something goes off the drawing board of historical experience.* Abnormalities are always important!

7. *The road is more important than the inn.* The way you arrive at a forecast is more important than the forecast itself. The reasoning behind the forecast is generally eye-opening and is sometimes of more use than the forecast, an argument for greater involvement of executives in the forecasting function.

Reference

Adapted from *Management Briefing: Business Finance* 2(4) (July 1987). The Conference Board.

HOLT/CMA Q RATIO

Applications

- Tracking financial performance of a company from a shareholder perspective.
- Analyzing business units within the company's portfolio to estimate their potential contributions to shareholder value and/or evaluate proposed strategies.

Procedures

1. Calculate the ratio of stock market value (present value for a nonpublic business unit) to the replacement or inflation-adjusted cost of the business's physical assets.
2. Use the ratio as an indication of value creation potential of the firm or of individual business units and their proposed strategies.

Cross-Reference

Manufacturing and Operations (evaluating capital expenditure requests); Strategic Planning Decisions

The Q ratio originated with economist James Tobin in the 1960s but has been applied to problems of investment analysis and business unit planning by the consulting firm Callard, Madden and Associates and by HOLT Planning Associates, a spin-off of CMA. The Q ratio is useful in assessing the potential of a strategy for contributing to the formation of stockholder value. It can also be worthwhile to track the Q ratio of a company over time as a general measure of value creation and more specifically a simple way to relate stock market value to the value of a company's assets. It provides a useful check on ROI,

ROE, and discounted cash-flow analysis of proposals, sometimes leading to different conclusions.

Note: The Q ratio is also utilized in a variety of sophisticated financial models. Contact the consulting firms just mentioned if you want to pursue the subject in depth.

INSTRUCTIONS

1. The Q ratio is defined as the stock market value of a company's physical assets divided by the cost of replacing those assets in today's dollars.

If the stock market value is higher than the replacement cost, the Q ratio is above 1, indicating that the market considers the company able to create value with its assets that exceeds the value of the assets alone. A firm whose Q ratio is higher than 1 has an incentive to invest in additional assets since the stock market will value these new investments at more than their cost to the firm.

In practice, various modifications of the ratio can be made to improve its utility or simplify its calculation. CMA uses as the numerator a firm's market value of equity plus debt and as the denominator the original purchase price of assets, adjusted for inflation to today's equivalent cost. This adjustment is made to each separate asset on the balance sheet. The cost of 20-year-old milling equipment is adjusted to reflect inflation over the last 20 years, but LIFO inventories might only be adjusted by a few years or less.

The CMA version of the ratio is fairly easily calculated for any public company and can be traced over time as one of the measures of financial performance. A downward trend in the ratio should be treated as a warning signal.

2. The Q ratio can also be used in strategic planning for evaluating the contributions of individual business units to the formation of corporate value. But the market value of a business unit is not readily apparent. HOLT and CMA infer it by "discounting the unit's expected stream of net cash receipts over the planning horizon, including its residual value at the end of the planning period,"

according to Bernard Reinmann and Rawley Thomas (senior vice-president of HOLT).

Note: The assumptions made by the financial analyst in discounting future cash flows have a significant impact on the Q ratio. Be sure to make equivalent assumptions when comparing multiple business units. At HOLT and CMA the analysis is based on the assumption that real ROI "is expected to follow a normal life cycle and to approach the constant average of about seven percent over the long term, with a real asset growth rate of about three percent," again according to Reinmann and Thomas.

Q ratios for business units can be used to estimate their potential contribution to the company's stock price. Ratios above 1 are associated with business units that will probably make a positive contribution to stock price in the long run.

Warning: Like any ratio, Q can be misleading and should not be relied on to the exclusion of other forms of analysis. It is likely, for example, to penalize an older business unit whose assets would be costly at current prices. If the assets do not need to be replaced rapidly and the unit is doing well, the unit may make a positive contribution to value despite its low Q ratio. Furthermore, the sale price should also be considered before management decides to divest any business unit with a low Q—the sale price may be even less than the value the business has as part of the firm's portfolio.

Reference

Bernard C. Reimann and Rawley Thomas. "Value-Based Portfolio Planning: Improving Shareholder Returns." *Handbook of Business Strategy: 1986/1987 Yearbook,* ed. William D. Guth (Chapter 21). Warren, Gorham & Lamont, 1986.

MARAKON PROFITABILITY MATRIX

Applications

- Preparing an audit of future profitability for evaluating strategic plans and projections of business units.
- Evaluating a unit's potential future contribution to or drain on a company's financial resources and performance.
- Analyzing and displaying graphically the spread-growth position, share-policy position, and cash-flow position of a business unit based on its current strategy.

Procedures

1. Calculate return on equity for a business unit's projections over the planning period.
2. Determine the cost of equity capital for the unit.
3. Calculate the average growth in revenues per year based on the unit's planned projections. Also estimate the overall growth rate for the unit's market.
4. Calculate the cash-investment ratio for the unit.
5. Plot the ROE and unit growth on a matrix. To plot multiple business units, normalize the axes by using ROE spread and unit growth divided by market growth.

Cross-Reference

Stragetic Planning Decisions

This method is especially useful in evaluating the plans and financial projections of multiple business units. It allows management to assess contributions to cash flow and value at a glance and to compare the growth and share strategies of individual units. It incorporates information on market-share growth, but its emphasis is on the impact each unit's strategy will have on the financial value and performance of the company.

INSTRUCTIONS

1. For a given business unit, identify the company's current equity investment. Using this number, calculate annual ROE (return on equity) projections. (Refer to the unit's strategic or financial plans for projected returns.)

2. Determine the cost of equity capital for the unit. Marakon uses the following formula to calcuate a unit's cost of capital:

Cost of equity capital $= k_e = k + rp$ where k equals return on long-term Treasury bonds and rp equals a risk premium assigned to the unit by management, reflecting the unit's financial leverage and financial policies.

3. Referring again to the unit's financial projections, calculate the average rate of growth in revenues or earnings per year. Marakon designates this g. Now project the average yearly growth in revenues for the business unit's entire market. This market growth rate is designated G.

4. Calculate the cash-investment ratio (CIR) for the business unit. This ratio expresses the business unit's cash needs or surpluses over the planning period and is defined as follows:

CIR $=$ investment of equity capital/earnings

or, for use in calculations,

CIR $= g$/ROE.

Use the average growth rate, g, and the return on equity, ROE, from steps 3 and 1 to calculate the cash investment ratio.

5. Plot the matrix. The simplest form of the matrix is used for comparing alternative strategies

and projections for a single business unit. To prepare the matrix use a graph with the ROE on the vertical axis and g, growth of the unit, on the horizontal axis. Plot each of the alternatives on the graph. Next, place a vertical line on the graph to represent the average market growth for this business unit's market. Now place a horizontal line on the matrix to represent the cost of equity capital. A diagonal line can be added to represent equal returns and growth rates, producing a CIR of 1.

THE MARAKON PROFITABILITY MATRIX

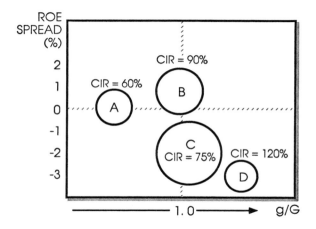

Marakon Associates often uses the matrix to compare multiple business units in a portfolio, and because they have different G's (they are in different markets) and different k_e's (different leverage policies), the matrix must be modified slightly to display all of them at once. Replace "ROE" with "ROE spread"—the difference between each unit's projected ROE and k_e—on the vertical axis. Replace unit growth, "g", with "g/G" (industry growth), on the horizontal axis. Divide the graph into quadrants with lines at g/G equaling 1 and ROE spread equaling 0%. Finally, write the CIR, expressed as a percent, for each unit next to its plot on the graph.

Interpretation

The growth axis provides information about market-share strategies. A build strategy, for example, has a *g/G* ratio above 1. It provides information about units' contribution to a firm's book value. A negative ROE spread, for example, indicates a unit that is making a negative contribution to the value of the company. The CIR figure indicates whether a unit will produce cash or require cash. For example, a CIR of less than 100% indicates a cash producer.

The overall CIR for all the units in the portfolio can also be calculated to see whether the portfolio is balanced from a cash-flow perspective. The overall ROE spread can also be determined to see whether the portfolio adds to or reduces the firm's value over the planning period. These general measures of balance can be used to evaluate individual strategies. If the portfolio is out of balance from a cash, value, or even market-share perspective, changes in the strategies of individual units will be required to solve the problem.

The matrix can also be used to evaluate the strategies of units on their own merit. For example, units which project negative cash flow and a negative ROE spread (high CIR and located in the lower half of the matrix) will probably need to have an aggressive share-building strategy (right side of the matrix) in a market that is attractive to the company in order to justify their place in the portfolio.

References

"The Marakon Profitability Matrix." *Commentary* (April 1981). San Francisco: Marakon Associates.

Ramesh Karnani, "Value-Based Acquisition Planning." March 18, 1986, presentation, Graduate School of Business, University of California at Berkeley. (An interesting extension of the concepts in this model to analysis of prospective acquisition candidates. Contact Marakon for information.)

THE V MATRIX

Applications

- Measuring corporate performance by comparing earning power to cost of capital in order to evaluate the returns offered by the company to its shareholders.
- Evaluating the success of strategies by comparing financial performance of companies.
- Planning financial and operational strategies based on earning power and cost of capital.

Procedures

1. Obtain financial data for companies of interest.
2. Plot the companies on the V Matrix.
3. Interpret and define strategic alternatives based on the widest feasible range of K and ROI for the industry.

Cross-Reference

Strategic Planning Decisions; integrating financial and strategic objectives.

The V Matrix was developed by Patrick McNamee of the University of Ulster in response to the need for strategic planning that maximizes earning power relative to the weighted cost of capital. The theory is that earning power should be kept at or above the cost of capital in order to provide value to the investors. Drawing on an earlier study (the Walsh and Mock paper cited in the references for this section), Professor McNamee developed a matrix that is used for tracking financial performance of companies in an industry. From an investment perspective the matrix is appealing because it relies on financial performance rather than market share, growth, and other common strategic criteria. Another advantage is ease of preparation: All the necessary data comes from standard financial statements in SEC filings or D&B reports.

The *V* in "V Matrix" stands for "valuation factor" and is defined as follows:

$$V = \text{ROI}/K$$

where ROI is the firm's earning power and *K* is its cost of capital.

INSTRUCTIONS

1. Collect the data.

As with most planning matrices, the first step is to collect a time series of data for each company of interest. The V Matrix requires the following information on each company:

- Operating income (*O*)
- Tax rate (*T*)
- Assets at risk (*A*)
- Weighted cost of all funds in the business (*K*)

Operating income, the tax rate, and assets at risk are used to calculate ROI:

$$\text{ROI} = [O(1\text{-}T)]/A.$$

The time series should cover at least three years in most cases, but the matrix can be plotted for a single year's data or a decade worth of data, depending on the needs and interests of the user.

Note: Some users will want to represent either turnover or assets employed by making the size of the circle representing a firm proportional to one of these statistics. If so, collect this information now.

2. Plot the companies on the V matrix.

The cost of capital (*K*) is plotted on the horizontal axis of a graph, and the ROI is plotted on the vertical axis. Scale the axes to cover the range of *K*'s and ROI's found in the data you have collected. Put multiple companies on a single matrix. For a time series, first plot each year's data on a separate matrix, then overlay them to make a summary matrix showing each year's data with arrows indicating directional movement.

If you want to represent the size of the companies, scale circles centered on each data point to the turnover or assets employed. (Use whichever you think is a better representation of size in your industry.)

Complete the matrix by drawing a diagonal line from the origin with a slope of 1—if both axes use the same scale this line divides the matrix in half from lower-left to upper-right corners. Along the line, ROI equals cost of capital. Below it, cost of capital is higher than ROI (an undesirable situation) and above it, ROI exceeds the cost of capital.

3. Interpret the matrix.

The first step is to use the ROI/K ratios to evaluate the performance of the chosen companies. Companies that are well above the diagonal line are performing well. Those well below it are peforming inadequately, and those that fall near the line are sensitive to slight changes in ROI or cost of capital. A helpful option is to draw two more diagonal lines, one for $V = 1.1$ and one for $V = 0.9$. These will form a boundary around the first diagonal line and indicate firms which are in the sensitive zone around the diagonal. Any firms in this area should be watched closely, and management should make it a priority to move them higher on the matrix.

The next step is to relate placement and movement shown by the matrix to corporate strategy. For example, a firm that invests heavily in new plant and equipment may experience a decline in its V statistic despite a rise in ROI if cost of capital increased due to the heavy financing requirements of the strategy. The matrix can be helpful in integrating operational strategy and the financial strategy needed to fund it by focusing on interactions between capital expenditures and the V ratio. Use it not only to track historical performance but also to predict future performance by projecting ROI and cost of capital changes for different strategic options and scenarios.

A third option is to draw the area of feasible strategic alternatives on the matrix. This is a rectangle representing the lowest feasible cost of capital and highest feasible ROI for the industry. Draw a vertical line to represent the lowest feasible cost of capital. One way to determine this figure is to base it on the company in your industry which has the lowest cost of capital. Draw a horizontal line to represent the highest feasible ROI for the industry (based on the company with the highest ROI). These two lines define a realistic upper boundary to *V*. For the lower boundary, draw a horizontal and a vertical line through your current position.

V MATRIX
FIRM A

Adapted and reprinted with permission
from Pergamon Press plc.

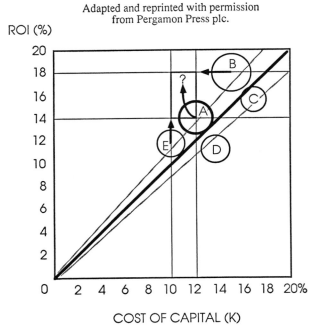

= Firm A's feasible strategies

Example: The exhibit shows a typical V matrix for Company A and its closest competitors, companies B, C, and D. It includes a feasible rectangle based on the ROI's and K's of other competitors. Arrows summarize the movement of competitors over the last three years.

References

Patrick B. McNamee. *Tools and Techniques for Strategic Management.* Elmsford, New York. Pergamon Press, 1985. (See pages 165–173. Also includes a description of the ROI Matrix, which can be used in conjunction with the V Matrix to help identify operational strategies necessary to achieve a desired position on the V Matrix.)

C. Walsh and E. Mock. "Setting Corporate Objectives Using Market Required Earnings." *Long Range Planning* 12 (October 1979): 54–64.

PART 2

LEADERSHIP SKILLS AND METHODS

ALBRECHT & ASSOCIATES
LEADERSHIP MATRIX

Applications

- Understanding your own or someone else's leadership style.
- Diagnosing leadership problems or complaints.
- Anticipating problems you may encounter in a new position due to differences between your style and the style of the previous manager.
- Evaluating leadership style for performance appraisals and management training.

Procedures

1. Observe managers and/or interview their employees.
2. Rank managers based on how much they emphasize shared goals, teamwork, autonomy, and reward in their leadership style.
3. Using your judgment and the Leadership Factor Matrix, decide whether a manager places too much or too little emphasis on specific factors. Use this information in performance appraisals, training, or self-improvement.

Cross-Reference

Organization and Human Resources

Albrecht & Associates, a San Diego consulting firm, specializes in increasing the effectiveness of organizations through organization development. As part of the process, an organization assesses its performance in great detail, looking at everything from administration to innovation. One of the assessment tools Albrecht & Associates uses is a quick device for evaluating leadership style and effectiveness. Its simplicity and ease of use make it a good device for thinking about leadership problems or issues and doing appraisals, and managers will find it well suited to an informal, back-of-the-envelope analysis.

INSTRUCTIONS

The method is based on the assumption that four factors characterize leadership style: goal sharing, teamwork, autonomy (or delegation), and reward.

1. The first step is to collect information about the style of a manager. This may be done through observation, discussion with employees and associates, or both. For example, employees can be asked whether they think their manager gives them too much, too little, or the right amount of responsibility, and the results could be used to assess the effectiveness of the manager's delegation and to rank the manager on the autonomy factor. Formal questionnaires can be used, but in many cases observation or experience alone is sufficient to rank managers on these four factors.

2. Evaluate the observations and information from interviews to rank each manager's style on each factor. This may involve sifting through a variety of complaints and observations to deduce where the manager ranks each factor. For example, if you learn that the manager has not held a staff meeting for six months and find that some employees feel resentment about seemingly arbitrary decisions made by this manager, you would conclude that the manager placed a low emphasis on teamwork.

Note: There is no absolute measure of the right emphasis–the rankings are relative to the standards of the organization or the desires of the executive.

3. Next, use the matrix to map managers based on their leadership style. The matrix summarizes common behaviors for each factor, placing them on a spectrum from low emphasis to high emphasis. This gives a general orientation to the evaluator who wishes to make rankings conform to the norms established by Albrecht & Associates. It also gives some clues to what is considered an ideal emphasis for each factor—clues which may be of use in train-

LEADERSHIP FACTOR MATRIX

Emphasis

Factors	LOW	JUST RIGHT	HIGH
SHARES GOALS	Dictates work	Shares ideas and goal setting with workers	Depends on workers to define tasks
EMPHASIZES TEAMWORK	No group meetings	Goals, assignments, and problem solving in group meetings	Too many group meetings
PERMITS AUTONOMY	Gives workers little freedom or responsibility	Allows workers freedom within established guidelines	Workers confused —no direction from manager
GIVES REWARDS	Criticizes, seldom compliments	Recognizes and demands good work, gives positive feedback	Rewards to gain acceptance, not in response to good work

ing or performance evaluations. Use the evaluation of the manager in placement, appraisal, training, and other leadership decisions.

Idea: If you are in a new position, chart the style on this matrix of the manager you are replacing. Then compare it with your style. Significant differences will be sources of confusion for employees, and a gradual transition may be required on the factors where your style is different.

Reference

Karl Albrecht, *Organization Development.* Englewood Cliffs, NJ: Prentice Hall, © 1983.

CONFERENCE BOARD MANAGEMENT-TRAINING SCORE

Applications

- Evaluating your company's management-training program.
- Identifying training strategies that could improve your company's management training.
- Designing a new management-training program; evaluating alternative training-program designs to see which is most likely to succeed.

Procedures

1. Score your company's management training by counting how many components it includes from the lists provided.
2. Multiply the number of components from each list by a special weighting factor.
3. Calculate an overall score by plugging the resulting numbers into a formula and evaluate the score to see whether your program is likely to be successful or not.

Cross-Reference

Organization and Human Resources

Large U.S. companies are paying increasing attention to management training—looking to the management-training function for competitive advantage and to produce the next generation of senior managers. A wide variety of training programs and techniques are used, both formally and informally. The Conference Board studied management training at 129 organizations to find out which training approaches were most successful. The experiences of these companies were combined to produce a statistical model of management training that can be used to see whether your company's management training shares the success factors identified in the study. If you score high, your firm is doing a better job of management training than most. A low score indicates the need to incorporate different methods into the training program. The method described here will also help identify specific ways to improve your training.

INSTRUCTIONS

1. Score your company's management training by counting how many components it includes from lists A through C.

A. Count those training methods you currently use from this list:

1. On-the-job development through adding responsibilities to or emphasizing responsibilities of the current job.

2. Planned on-the-job development through consultation with acknowledged experts.

3. Planned on-the-job development through temporary task-force or problem-study group assignments.

4. Use of special developmental job assignments.

5. Joint boss-subordinate planning of individualized development.

6. Individualized development through coaching by boss.

7. A formal succession and development-planning program.

8. Individualized feedback regarding the development process.

These are the eight components of job training most often associated with a successful program in the Conference Board study. Add up the number of components used in your company for a total between 0 and 8. Multiply this number by .5020112 and label it "A." You will need it in a moment to compute your score.

B. Count the total number of components you use at your firm from the two following lists:

B1. Planned use of outside educational programs:

1. Specific college or university courses.

2. Advanced degree programs.

3. Special advanced management programs lasting more than four weeks.

4. Other outside programs, conferences, or seminars lasting less than four weeks.

B2. Planned use of in-house educational programs:

1. Inside conferences, seminars, or meetings.

2. Training programs that emphasize basic concepts.

3. Training programs that emphasize various applications of concepts.

4. Training programs that emphasize individual skills practice.

5. Recommended reading programs.

Multiply the total (a number from 0 to 9) by .2746147. Label this statistic "B."

C. Count the total number of components you use at your firm from the following list:

1. Planned changes in management systems involving changes in organization structure associated with management training goals.

2. Changes in the compensation and reward system associated with management training.

3. Changes in the information system associated with management training.

4. Changes in the cultural norms of the organization.

Multiply the total (a number from 0 to 4) by .2134615. Label this statistic "C."

2. If your company's management-training program includes direct involvement of the CEO, you

will need to include a fourth factor, labeled "D." Make D equal .7612833.

3. Compute your training score using the following formula:

$$-.9776179 + A - B + C - D$$

Any score of $-.55$ or lower (a higher negative number) indicates your training program will probably produce disappointing results. Any score above this is good, and a score near or above 0 indicates a strong program that is likely to produce satisfactory results.

Example: Analog Equipment Corp.

They use six of the eight components in step 1:

A = 6 × .5020112 = 3.0121

They use five from the lists in step 2:

B = 5 × .2746147 = 1.3731

They use only one of the methods from step 3:

C = 1 × .2134615 = 0.2135

Their CEO delegates all training and is not directly involved:

D = 0 × .7612833 = 0

The formula is computed for AEC as follows:

Score = $-.9776179$ + A $-$ B + C $-$ D
Score = $-.9776$ + 3.0121 $-$ 1.3731
+ 0.2135 $-$ 0
Score = 0.8749

Analog's score is significantly above 0, indicating that their program has a healthy number of successful components. Analog's management training is comparable to companies in the Conference Board survey that were pleased with the results of their training and is different from unsuccessful programs at other companies.

If Analog wants to improve its score and make its program even more effective, it should concentrate on increasing factors A and C since these are given positive weights in the model. Factors B and D had a negative impact on satisfaction with management training in the study.

In general, companies can improve their chances of success dramatically just by removing the CEO from the training process (!) and also by replacing traditional forms of classroom and workshop training (see the list in step 2) with alternative training methods such as those listed in steps 1 and 3.

Reference

Ruth Gilbert Schaeffer. *Developing Strategic Leadership: A Research Report from The Conference Board.* The Conference Board, 1984. (See pages 38–45 for details of the study.)

NEMOTO'S TEN PRINCIPLES OF LEADERSHIP

Applications

- Adapting leadership style to the needs of quality-improvement programs.
- Training managers and supervisors.
- Using Japanese management techniques.

Procedures

Review the principles to see how they apply in your organization, to compare them to your style of management, or to develop directives and training material for your managers and supervisors.

Cross-Reference

Manufacturing and Operations—managing quality-control or JIT programs.

Masao Nemoto, managing director of Toyota, spearheaded many of the efforts to develop total quality control and JIT production at his company. He found that managers often had personal styles that conflicted with the goals of quality control and made it difficult for quality circles to perform. To counter this he wrote down his principles of management and distributed them to his associates whenever he took a new position. These principles were compiled by a number of managers at Toyota and are now called "The Sayings of Nemoto." Here they appear condensed from an English translation by David Lu.

INSTRUCTIONS

Use these principles, as Nemoto does, to let your company know what is expected of managers and supervisors when a company pursues quality improvement. Most quality programs, from in-house establishment of quality circles to a statistical process control program by consultants, focus on lower-level employees. This method focuses on upper-level employees. Nemoto's sayings are a useful checklist for managers who want to make sure their leadership and the leadership of their associates furthers the quality improvement program. And most of them can be generalized to other management problems and programs, providing guidance and ideas for good leadership in any context.

PRINCIPLES OF LEADERSHIP

1. *Improvement after improvement.* Managers should look continually for ways to improve the work of their employees. Advance is a gradual, incremental process. They should create an atmosphere conducive to improvements by others.

2. *Coordinate between divisions.* Managers of individual divisions, departments, or subsidiaries must share responsibility. Nemoto offers this advice to his managers:

> One of the most important functions of a division manager is to improve coordination between his own division and other divisions. If you cannot handle this task, please go to work for an American company.

A corollary of this is that upper management should not assign important tasks to only one division.

3. *Everyone speaks.* This rule guides supervisors of quality circles at Toyota, ensuring participation and learning by all members. It has also been generalized to all meetings and the annual planning process. By hearing everyone's view, upper management can create realistic plans that have the support of those

who must implement them—an essential element in quality programs.

4. *Do not scold.* An alien concept to most managers. At Toyota the policy is for superiors to avoid giving criticism and threatening punitive measures when mistakes are made. This is the only way to ensure that mistakes will be reported immediately and fully so that the root causes (in policies and processes) can be identified and amended. Assigning blame to the reporter clearly discourages reporting of mistakes and makes it harder to find the underlying cause of a mistake, but it is difficult to train managers to take this approach.

5. *Make sure others understand your work.* An emphasis on teaching and presentation skills is important because of the need for collaboration. At Toyota, managers are expected to develop their presentation skills and to teach associates about their work so that collaborations will be fuller and more effective.

6. *Send the best employees out for rotation.* Toyota has a rotation policy to train employees. There is a strong tendency for managers to keep their best employees from rotation. But the company benefits most in the long run by training its best employees.

7. *A command without a deadline is not a command.* This rule is used to ensure that managers always give a deadline or schedule for work. Employees are instructed to ignore requests that are not accompanied by a deadline. The rationale is that without a deadline, tasks are far less likely to be completed.

8. *Rehersal is an ideal occasion for training.* Managers and supervisors give numerous presentations and reports. In a QC program there are frequent progress reports. Mr. Nemoto encourages managers to focus on the *rehearsal* of reports and presentations, and to require that they be rehearsed. Rehearsal time is used to teach presentation skills and to explore problems or lack of understanding of the topic. Because it is informal, rehearsal time is better for learning.

9. *Inspection is a failure unless top management takes action.* The idea behind this is that management must prescribe specific remedies whenever a problem is

observed or reported. Delegating this task (i.e., by saying "shape up" or "do your best to solve this problem") is ineffective. So is failing to take any action once a problem is defined.

10. *Ask subordinates, "What can I do for you?"* At Toyota this is called "creating an opportunity to be heard at the top." In the first year of a quality-control program, managers hold meetings in which employees brief them about progress. Three rules guide these informal meetings:

1. Do not postpone the meetings or subordinates will think their project is not taken seriously.
2. Listen to the process, not just the results, since QCs focus in on the process.
3. Ask the presenters whether you can do anything for them. If they ask for help, be sure to act on the request.

This philosophy can be generalized. If top management is perceived as willing to help with problems, employees are more optimistic about tackling the problems and will take management's goals more seriously.

Reference

Masao Nemoto. *Total Quality Control for Management: Strategies and Tactics from Toyota and Toyoda Gosei*, ed. and trans. David Lu. Englewood Cliffs, NJ: Prentice Hall, 1987. (See Chapter 1 for a detailed discussion of these principles and their implementation.)

PETERS'S LEADERSHIP TOOLS

Applications

- Enlisting the support of an organization for a new program or strategy.
- Using the visibility of your position to lead by example.
- Overcoming problems in implementation of directives and programs, especially those that require a new philosophy for the organization.

Procedures

1. Allocate your time so as to demonstrate your commitment to the project or strategy.
2. Use promotions to signal the importance of the new program or strategy.
3. Adopt persuasive techniques in memos and meetings to emphasize your discussion of the new program or strategy.
4. Review policies and practices to ensure consistency with the new program or strategy.

Cross-Reference

Strategic Planning Decisions. (This method is useful in implementing a strategy.)

Tom Peters (author of *In Search of Excellence*) has worked with many managers who are frustrated in their efforts to make their organizations focus on a new program or goal. For example, Many CEO's who

From *Thriving on Chaos: Handbook for a Management Revolution* by Tom Peters. Copyright © 1987 by Excel, a California Limited Partnership. Used by permission of Alfred A. Knopf, Inc.

have introduced quality programs find it difficult to get their organizations to really adopt a quality-first mentality. A new strategic direction can be intangible and very difficult to achieve.

He has a novel approach to ensuring that an organization pays more than lip service to a new priority. His method involves a manager's demonstration of commitment to those who report to him or her—a form of leadership by example. It is unquestionably hard to turn a company in a new direction, in part because managers and employees tend to stick to the status quo unless something really shakes them up and convinces them that the rules have changed. While the devices Peters recommends are simple, they send a strong signal down the chain of command that gives needed emphasis to the normal memos and announcements.

Use his methods to develop an implementation plan or to diagnose problems you currently encounter in implementing new ideas or directions. This approach is also valuable as a pragmatic general model of leadership, since its emphasis is on easily controlled variables as opposed to the personality traits and elements of organizational culture emphasized in many academic models of leadership. It may provide inspiration to the manager in solving a wide range of problems of communication and leadership.

INSTRUCTIONS

1. Time Allocation.

Principle: Employees won't change their emphasis unless you change yours.

This means that a clear, visible shift in your calendar is needed to signal your new commitment to a project, and it also means that you will be giving time to communicating the goals of the new program. Peters tells senior managers that "we are our calendar." Here are specific suggestions for calling attention to a new program through your calendar:

- Schedule formal monthly reviews and informal weekly briefings.
- Attend seminars or workshops on the topic.

- Meet regularly with long-time customers to discuss the topic (especially suitable for a quality program). Circulate notes on the meetings.
- Circulate articles on the topic and make relevant books visible in your office.
- Schedule off-site sessions with managers.
- Schedule time to "poke around" and ask questions about your topic at lower levels of the organization.

Quantify time allocation. Set goals for the percent of time you spend on the program personally and the percent of your meeting time you give to it. A minimum initial target might be 15% of your total time; higher amounts will have more impact.

Example: Bob Townswend of Avis once fired his comptroller and gave 100% of his time to the job for several months in order to solve major problems with financial reporting (this is an extreme example, but it illustrates the commitment of some managers to the technique).

2. Promotion.

Principle: Promotions signal priorities.

Use openings as opportunities to recognize those who have taken the new program most seriously, even if it means passing over the "next in line." A surprise promotion sends a strong signal to the organization.

3. Persuasion.

Principle: A good story or strong symbol is more compelling than a directive or facts and figures.

Use drama to get your message across. You need to communicate your excitement about a program in order to create a sense of urgency about it throughout your organization. Specific suggestions:

- Collect good-news and bad-news stories on the topic of the program and use them in meetings and memos. Ask your managers to become story-tellers also.
- Use tangible symbols to make your point. For example, a pile of defective parts is a good prop for a discussion of quality control.

4. Consistency.

Principle: Many small issues combine to create a visible pattern signaling priorities.

Make sure *all* signals support the message of your new program. Do your questions at staff meetings focus on your key strategic concern? What about your memos and notes to staff? Do your visits reflect your priority? For example, if quality is the issue, do you make many visits to your plants and customers? If supplier partnerships are key, do you meet regularly with suppliers?

Also look at indirect signals. In an austerity program executives should not travel first class. In a quality program the air conditioning system should work and memos should not have typos. Remember that employees notice where you park, what is on the menu at the cafeteria, and whether you "hide" in your office!

Reference

Tom Peters. *Thriving on Chaos: Handbook for a Management Revolution.* Harper and Row, 1987. (See Chapter L-3—this book is full of good ideas for senior managers!)

STANFORD POWER MATRIX

Applications

- Ranking individuals, positions, or departments by the amount of decision-making power they have in an organization.

- Identifying power centers for a reorganization or organization development study.

- Deciding what an organization's functional orientation is for strategic-planning purposes (i.e., operations-oriented versus market-oriented).

- Updating or redesigning the formal organization chart to better reflect informal decision-making patterns.

- Evaluating the impact of a proposed management transfer or promotion.

Procedures

1. Identify and list the major decision areas in the organization.

2. Create a table of decision areas and decision-makers.

3. Distribute the table as a questionnaire to managers. Instruct them to rate the importance of each decision area and the influence of every other manager on that decision area.

4. Calculate decision scores for each manager by averaging influence ratings and weighting these by the importance rating for each decision.

5. Create a summary table showing which managers have the most influence over each decision and which manager has the most influence over all.

Cross-Reference

Organization and Human Resources

This method was developed by two researchers at Stanford to help them understand how decisions are made at microcomputer companies. Decision making does not always follow departmental lines, and it is often unclear, even to a company's managers, exactly how decisions are made. This method uses a short survey to rate each manager's influence over decisions. Influence in specific decision areas is also averaged to create a "power score" for each manager. The power scores can be used to compare the influence of individual managers, to find out which departments have the greatest influence in a company, to compare an organizational chart with actual distribution of power, or to find out which decision areas would be most affected by a proposed transfer or promotion.

In some cases an organization does not really want to see data about the power of individual managers. But this information is surprisingly useful when diagnosing problems, considering changes in organizational structure, or making promotion decisions. It is also useful in strategic planning, where it can be adapted to rank the importance of departments or SBUs, rather than managers, in decision making. Because the information may be controversial, CEOs should consider keeping the summary table confidential.

INSTRUCTIONS

1. Identify the key decision areas in a company. Start with the functional areas such as finance, manufacturing, and sales suggested by the organization chart and break these areas down into two or more areas if they represent multiple functions. For example, the marketing function might include advertising, new product development, and customer research. Finance might break down into external financing, funds management, and corporate ex-

penditure approvals. If this analysis is performed by a consultant or other outsider, it may be helpful to interview managers in each functional area to find out what they think the key decision areas are.

2. Turn the list of decision areas into a questionnaire by building a table with one column headed "Importance to Long-Run Health of Company." and additional columns labeled with the names or titles of managers. Head this section "Amount of Influence Manager Has on Decisions." Instructions should specify a 1 to 10 scale with 1 = unimportant/little influence and 10 = very important/very strong influence.

3. Each manager, including the CEO, completes the questionnaire independently (but not anonymously). Managers evaluate the influence of other managers, but *not* their own influence.

4. Calculate a weighted-average power score for each manager and decision area. First, multiply each influence rating by the importance rating for the relevant decision area. These are the weighted influence scores. Second, compute the mean of all weighted influence scores for each manager.

Example: Manager A gives advertising a 5 for importance and gives manager X a 6 for influence over advertising decisions. The weighted score is $5 \times 6 = 30$. X's weighted influence scores for advertising from the other managers are 28, 30, and 42. The four weighted influence scores total 130. The mean is 32.5, which is X's power score for advertising decisions.

5. Enter the mean power scores into a table with decision areas down the left and managers across the top. Sum each column and divide by the number of rows (or decision areas) to calculate the total power score for each manager.

Idea: Calculate department scores by averaging manager's scores from each department. The department scores indicate which function drives the company. For example, in a company that is technology-driven the R&D and manufacturing departments will have the highest power scores.

CHERRY COMPUTERS POWER MATRIX

Decision area	President	VP mfg	VP U.S. ops	VP europe	VP finance	VP R&D
U.S. Sales and Marketing	**8.3**	2.8	8.2	6.3	2.7	3.5
European Sales & and Marketing	4.7	2.3	7.8	**9.1**	2.5	3.2
R&D	5.8	5.6	4.5	2.5	3.7	**9.3**
Manufacturing	5.3	**9.2**	5.7	3.2	3.2	6.5
Purchasing	7.0	**8.1**	5.4	2.6	5.0	5.0
Financing	5.4	3.5	2.6	2.4	**5.5**	2.6
Total Power	**6.1**	5.3	5.7	4.4	4.5	5.0

Example

A power matrix is provided for a hypothetical computer company. The matrix shows a fairly even distribution of power—the spread between the highest and lowest total power scores is not great. In general, each manager has a strong influence over his or her functional area. However, note that the president has as strong an influence as the vice-president of U.S. operations over decisions concerning sales and marketing within the U.S. Either this vice-president is not performing up to par or the president is meddling in a favorite area. The president also has a strong influence in financal decisions, which is not unusual.

The organization has clearly made the transition to a marketing orientation; in some computer companies manufacturing and R&D managers continue to have a strong influence over sales and marketing decisions. But the matrix does indicate one possible problem: Note that the vice-president, Europe, has little input in R&D and manufacturing decision areas—the organization is probably not considering the needs of its European markets when making product-development decisions.

Reference

L.J. Bourgeois, III and Kathleen M. Eisenhardt. "Strategic Decision Processses in High Velocity Environments for Cases in the Microcomputer Industry." *Management Science* (July 1989.)

STANFORD STRESS ANALYSIS

Applications

- Identifying and reducing sources of stress.
- Helping employees or work groups identify and reduce stresses that interfere with performance.

Procedures

1. List the issues and problems that create stress.
2. Identify those that are easily avoidable.
3. Identify those that may be avoided with further effort or analysis.
4. Identify unavoidable stresses. Define responses based on whether the stresses are avoidable or not.

Cross-Reference

Organization and Human Resources.

This method is taught in Stanford University's controversial course on creativity for business managers. It is a simple device for identifying causes of stress, both personal and work related, and developing strategies to reduce them. Michael Ray and Rochelle Myers of Stanford argue that stress interferes with a manager's ability to think creatively about tough decisions. Feelings of stress are usually pushed to the back of one's mind and allowed to accumulate rather than being dealt with one by one.

Because management positions tend to be stressful, many managers will find this method helpful for identifying and responding to the stresses associated with leadership. Managers may also find this a useful leadership tool. Make it an exercise for staff or a project team to help the group overcome stresses that may interfere with effective collaboration and group performance.

INSTRUCTIONS

1. List individual issues that cause you stress. Issues range from the trivial to the complex, and both personal and work-related issues may be relevant to stress on the job. Since some issues can be very personal (i.e., sex life), the list should be considered confidential when this method is used in a group setting. Examples of issues include: being behind on project deadlines; conflict with another manager; car needs repair; secretary can't spell; daughter wants to drop out of college. Try to make this list exhaustive, including anything that causes stress or anxiety.

2. Identify avoidable stresses. Review the list you have made and mark those items that you have direct influence over. These are the sources of stress that can be eliminated by specific actions. Make a new list of only these avoidable stresses and indicate on it the type of action needed to take to eliminate each item. To reduce stress, either act on each item, schedule a time to cope with it, or delegate it to someone with specific instructions for what action should be taken and when. Although items on which action may be taken may seem less important than others, the overall level of stress can usually be reduced by eliminating them.

3. Identify stresses that might be avoidable. It is not always clear whether you have any influence over an item, or what action should be taken. This is often the case with problems involving human relationships, for example. In addition, lack of understanding of interpersonal conflicts often adds to their stressfulness. Make a third list composed only of the items from your first list that may prove avoidable with further research or thought.

These items are characterized by uncertainty or ambiguity. They generally have elements that are within your control and are thus avoidable, as well as elements that are within someone else's control or are not controlled by anyone. On this list, write next to each item the action necessary to clarify your understanding of the item and increase your control over it. For example, talk to a subordinate to find out why work in his or her department has fallen behind schedule. Find out what can be done to solve the problem.

4. List the remaining stresses—those that are unavoidable. Some of the items on the original list will fall into this category. High crime rate, illness, or entry of foreign competitors into your industry may all be beyond your direct control. Ray and Myers suggest that such issues require a new approach or philosophy; stress is reduced by accepting the unavoidable. However, many managers will prefer a proactive approach for these items as well. One action-oriented approach is to write down on the list what actions are required to upgrade an item from this list to the list of items that might be avoidable. (Similarly, items on that list may be moved to the "avoidable" list as more is learned about them.) Example: Entry of foreign competitors may be viewed as an unavoidable threat, but there may be strategies to keep additional competitors from entering the market and ways to minimize the impact of those that have already entered (erecting barriers to entry, cementing customer relationships, forming an allegiance with their strongest new competitor). Formulating effective responses to unavoidable events reduces their stressfulness.

CLASSIFICATION OF STRESSES AND RESPONSES	
Type of stress	Response
Avoidable	Act immediately
Avoidable–Unavoidable	Clarify (Observation, analysis)
Unavoidable	Change attitude; Plan response

Reference

Ray, Michael, and Myers, Rochelle, *Creativity in Business*, Doubleday, 1987. (See pages 155–6.) Excerpt from *Creativity in Business* by Michael L. Ray and Rochelle Myers. Used with permission of Doubleday, a division of Bantam Doubleday Dell Publishing Group, Inc.

VROOM-YETTON DECISION STRATEGY TREE

Applications

- Deciding how much employee involvement, if any, is appropriate for a decision.
- Improving the quality of decisions by finding the optimal decision style for each.
- Speeding decision making by reducing participative decision making to those cases in which it is really necessary.

Procedures

1. Use the checklist to categorize the decision according to the seven variables.
2. Use the decision tree to key out the appropriate decision style(s).
3. Choose a decision style from the set of appropriate styles.

Cross-Reference

General Decision-Making Tools: Organization and Human Resources.

This method takes a pragmatic approach to leadership—perhaps surprising in light of its academic origins—by assuming that decision-making strategy must adapt to the situation. It was developed by two researchers and is based on an extensive review of the research literature on decision making. It pre-

Adapted and reprinted from *Leadership and Decision-Making*, by Victor H. Vroom and Philip W. Yetton, by permission of the University of Pittsburgh Press. © 1973 by University of Pittsburgh Press.

scribes the type and extent of staff involvement in decision making given the specific character of the decision. Use it to decide whether to delegate a decision, hold a meeting to discuss the decision, or make the decision without any staff involvement. The method appears awkward at first, but it is quick and simple to use once you are familiar with it, and it can improve both the quality and the acceptability of your decisions.

Note: Research indicates that managers tend to use participative decision styles more often than necessary. The decision strategy tree will tend to reduce participation in decisions without sacrificing quality or acceptance. The result should be faster and easier decision making.

INSTRUCTIONS

1. Answer the following yes/no questions about the decision you have to make. (Once familiar with these questions, the manager can go directly to the tree to key out a decision strategy where a summary of the questions is provided. But the first-time user will benefit from this step.)

Yes No
☐   ☐   A. Is the quality of the decision important? (In other words, is the specific answer important or will any answer do as long as it is acceptable to all?)

☐   ☐   B. Does the manager have enough information and expertise to answer the question or solve the problem without help from subordinates?

☐   ☐   C. Is the problem/decision structured and unambiguous? (The alternative is a problem that is difficult to state and hard to find information about.)

☐   ☐   D. Is acceptance of this decision by subordinates essential for good implementation?

☐   ☐   E. If the manager were to make this decision alone, would it most likely be acceptable to subordinates?

☐   ☐   F. Do subordinates share the organization's goals as the goals relate to this problem?

☐   ☐   G. Will subordinates probably disagree and be in conflict over the outcome of this decision? (For example, would they probably disagree with the leader?)

2. After thinking through the answers to these questions the leader should follow the answers through the decision tree. It is a key in visual format. Each yes or no answer leads to another question until the possibilities have been narrowed down to a specific set of decision styles.

To use the decision tree, start with question A. If there is a quality requirement, follow the lower arrow, marked *yes*, to question B. If there is not a quality requirement, follow the upper arrow (marked *Yes*) from A all the way to question D. Ask question D, "Is acceptance important?" If the answer is no, follow the arrow marked *no* all the way to the preferred decision strategy, which in this case is strategy A1. Step 3 provides a table for looking up strategy A1, which is "Manager makes decision alone."

3. Choose a decision strategy from the acceptable set of styles prescribed by the decision tree. In cases where more than one decision style will give good results the tree lists the most autocratic (and therefore efficient) strategy first, and the other choices are given in parentheses. In these cases managers can choose the strategy they prefer from the acceptable set.

Note that the tree lists only alpha-numeric codes for each decision strategy. For a full description of the strategy indicated by the tree, look up the code in the following table:

Decision strategy	Description
A1	Manager makes decision alone.
A2	Manager requests information from subordinates, then makes decision alone.
C1	Manager requests information and opinions in one-on-one meetings, then makes decision alone.
C2	Manager holds a group meeting with subordinates to discuss the problem, then makes decision alone.
G2	Manager holds a group meeting with subordinates to discuss the problem, and the group makes a decision.

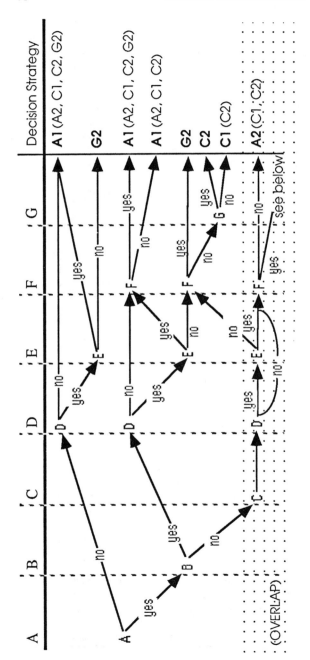

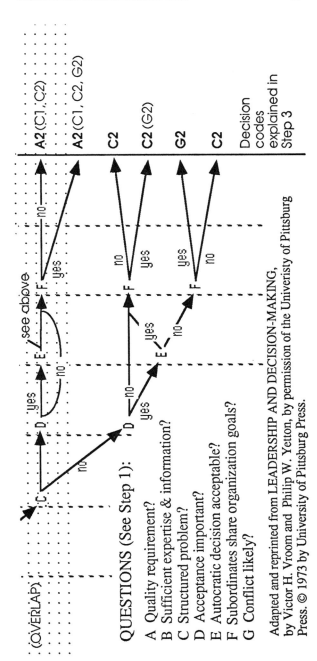

QUESTIONS (See Step 1):

A Quality requirement?
B Sufficient expertise & information?
C Structured problem?
D Acceptance important?
E Autocratic decision acceptable?
F Subordinates share organization goals?
G Conflict likely?

Adapted and reprinted from LEADERSHIP AND DECISION-MAKING,
by Victor H. Vroom and Philip W. Yetton, by permission of the Univeristy of Pittsburg
Press. © 1973 by University of Pittsburg Press.

References

Richard Steers. *Introduction to Organizational Behavior*. 2nd Ed. Scott, Foresman and Co., 1984. (See pages 343 and 340.)

Victor Vroom and Phillip Yetton. *Leadership and Decision-Making*. University of Pittsburgh Press, 1973. Adapted and reprinted from *Leadership and Decision-Making*, by Victor H. Vroom and Philip W. Yetton, by permission of the University of Pittsburgh Press. © 1973 by University of Pittsburgh Press.

PART 3

MANUFACTURING AND OPERATIONS

BURROUGHS QUALITY-ASSURANCE ANALYSIS

Applications

- Establishing tolerances for manufacturing processes.
- Calculating the probability of products exceeding established tolerances.
- Performing quality checks on only a sample of products produced when there are too many, or measurement is too costly, to permit inspection of every product.

Procedures

1. Draw a random sample of the product you want to evaluate, or of products from the machine or process you want to evaluate. Measure each item in the sample on each dimension specified.

2. Calculate the mean and standard deviation for each set of measurements.

3. Find the probability of products exceeding an established tolerance by calculating z for each sample and looking up the probability in a table of the standard normal distribution.

This method comes from Burroughs Corporation's Office Products Group, which uses it for applications like analyzing dies used to cut bank cards for the automated teller machines Burroughs produces. For example, reports from banks about cards being rejected by machines led to the discovery of dies that did not cut the credit cards to the correct dimensions. The method was used to estimate the probability of each machine producing cards that exceeded tolerances, enabling identification of machines needing repair or replacement.

Besides being used to track down a problem or do a periodic check on equipment, the method can also be used in quality checks where there are practical obstacles to checking every product produced. Instead, draw periodic samples, measure their variation from specifications, and use Burroughs' statistical analysis to estimate the total number of products that will not meet tolerances or specifications. Then use this information to decide whether to modify the production process or continue to allow production as is.

INSTRUCTIONS

1. Draw a random sample of the product being produced. Measure each product in the sample accurately to determine how it varies from specifications. In the bank card example, the height and width of cards were measured.

2. Calculate the mean and the standard deviation for each sample. In the bank card example, mean and standard deviation were calculated for samples from each individual die.

Note on calculations

Standard deviation, σ, is the square root of variance. Calculate variance according to the following formula:

Variance $(x) = \sigma^2 = \epsilon (x - \mu)^2 f(x)$

$x =$ the random variable representing the measurement

$f(x) =$ the probability function; the probability of x taking on a specific value. Calculated by identifying the percent of occurrences of that specific value in the sample.

$\mu =$ the mean

3. Assume a normal distribution for each sample with the mean and standard deviation you have calculated. Now, given that distribution, find the probability of a product exceeding the tolerance. (Tolerances should have been established previous to this analysis.)

Find this probability by calculating z for the tolerance and looking up the value of z in a table for the standard normal distribution (found in the back of any book on statistics or in the companion book to this one, *The Vest-Pocket MBA* from Prentice Hall). Calculate z according to the following formula:

$$Z = \frac{T - \mu}{\sigma}$$

T = maximum or minimum tolerance, depending on whether x is above or below the specification

μ = Mean value of measurements from the sample

Example

A sample of bank cards from one of the dies at Burroughs has a mean length of 3.367 inches and a standard deviation of .0010 inches. The minimum acceptable length is 3.365 inches. What is the probability of a card produced on the same die being less than the minimum acceptable length? The value of z was calculated as follows:

$$Z = \frac{3.365 - 3.367}{.001} = -2$$

A normal distribution table was consulted to determine, given this z, that the probability of a length of 3.365 inches or less is 2.3%. Thus 2.3% of all the cards on this machine will be too short and will probably not work correctly in automated teller machines.

Reference

Based on David Anderson, Dennis Sweeney, and Thomas Williams, *Quantitative Methods for Business*, 2nd Ed. (pp. 89–91). West Publishing Co., 1983.

CUSUM CHART

Applications

- Tracking product quality through frequent samples from the production process.
- Controlling product quality where tight conformance to specifications is needed and deviations must be detected quickly.

Procedures

1. Develop a procedure for measuring samples on a regular basis.
2. Find the difference between the measured value from a sample and the reference value or specification.
3. Maintain a running total of these differences and plot the new total on a chart each time a sample is taken. Use the slope of the line on the chart to indicate when action is needed.

The Cumulative Sum Chart, or CuSum Chart, is used like the Mean Chart (also in this section) to track and control product quality through measuring the deviation of samples from specifications. However, the CuSum Chart provides rapid warning of even the smallest deviation from a specified measurement and is best used when great accuracy is required. More frequent samples are usually used for the CuSum Chart, and individual product measurements rather than means from large samples are plotted. See the discussion of mean charts for ideas on training and JIT production that apply to the CuSum Chart as well.

INSTRUCTIONS

1. Take periodic samples and measure them carefully. If production workers are going to maintain

the CuSum Chart, provide clear instructions and training to make sure sampling and measurement are consistent and accurate.

2. The specification or reference value is then subtracted from the measured value of the first sample item, and the difference is plotted on a chart like the one illustrated. When the second sample is measured, the reference value is subtracted from it, and the remainder is added to the remainder from the first sample. The sum is plotted on the chart. A running total of the differences between each sample and the reference value is maintained.

Idea: Include three columns next to the chart. Label them "Measurement" "Measurement–Reference," and "Cumulative M–R" to make sure the calculation is done correctly.

CUSUM CHART

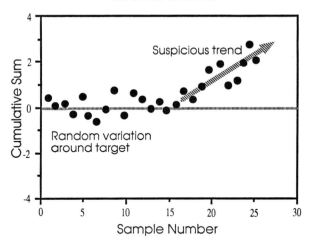

3. You will need to maintain a separate chart for each measurement that is tracked. If the inside diameter, outside diameter, and length of a part need to be controlled closely, use a separate CuSum Chart for each of these specifications.

The logic behind this chart is that as long as the average measurement of the samples is very close to the specification and varies only slightly from it by chance, the cumulative sum of the differences will be close to 0. Further, even if an occasional measurement is considerably off, the plot of the differences will have a horizontal trend if the rest of the samples are close to specifications. But if the samples start to drift away from the specification in a consistent manner, this will show quickly and clearly as a diagonal line sloping upward or downward on the chart.

The Mean Chart uses warning and action lines set by management to indicate when operators should stop production and make adjustments to bring production closer to specifications. The CuSum Chart is usually controlled through the use of templates—V-shaped cutouts in heavy paper, for example—that can be laid over the chart to see whether the trend line is steep enough to warrant action.

ECONOMIES OF SCOPE PROCESS CHART

Applications

- Identifying appropriate manufacturing process configurations based on production quantities per part and variety of parts to be produced.
- Developing manufacturing strategies in light of new computer-aided design and manufacturing equipment.
- Designing flexible production systems using computer-controlled manufacturing equipment or robotics.

Procedures

1. Identify relevant business strategies and objectives. Modify strategies if necessary to reflect manufacturing options and constraints.
2. Use the process chart to identify the process or processes most appropriate for the volume and flexibility requirements implied by the business strategy.

Cross-Reference

Strategic Planning Decisions—integrating the capabilities of modern software-based production equipment and the product scope it makes possible into competitive strategy decisions.

This tool was developed as an aid for managers of manufacturing companies. It is intended to help identify which modern production technologies to use in any given circumstance and also to aid in managers' strategic planning and competitive positioning.

Many manufacturers are facing increased competition, either within their traditional markets or from abroad, and are looking to new computer-based production systems and equipment to help reduce costs and make their companies more competitive. The inventors of this method, two professors studying the new manufacturing technologies, find that new technologies can have an impact on far more than costs. In fact, their most important impact is on the scope of products that can be produced:

> A computer-controlled machine does not care whether it works in succession on a dozen units of the same design or in random sequence on a dozen different product designs—within, of course, a family of design limits.
>
> -Joel Goldhar and Mariann Jelinek
> in *Harvard Business Review*

Furthermore, the machine will make the product as efficiently the first time around as the millionth, providing the product is designed for efficient production and the machine is properly programmed. This means that traditional ideas about economies of scale may not apply.

While greater scope is possible with new machinery, not every manufacturer is in a position to take advantage of the opportunities presented, nor is every manufacturer ready to handle the added design and control responsibilities. And the risks of investing in the wrong equipment are high since the cost of new computer-aided manufacturing systems can be astronomical. Senior management needs to be closely involved in the decision, which, through the use of this method, can be looked at from a strategic (rather than technical) perspective.

INSTRUCTIONS

1. Analyze production processes and opportunities from a strategic perspective. This involves looking at the assumptions that currently guide manufacturing decisions and modifying them if necessary to reflect new process technologies.

ASSUMPTIONS AND OBJECTIVES UNDERLYING PRODUCTION STRATEGIES

Traditional	CAD/CAM environment
Economy of scale	Economy of scope
Experience curve	Shorter product life cycles
Task specialization	Multimission companies
Work as a social activity	Unmanned systems
Separable variable costs	Joint costs
Standardization	Variety
Centralization	Decentralization
Large plants	Multiple small plants
Balanced lines	Flexibility
Smooth flows	Surge and turnaround ability
Standard product design	Many custom products
Low rate of change	Innovation and responsiveness
Inventory used as buffer	Production tied to demand
Batch systems	Flow systems

CAD = Computer-aided design
CAM = Computer-aided manufacture

(Adapted from Goldhar & Jelinek, *Harvard Business Review*, Nov-Dec 1983, p. 143. Copyright ©1983 by the president and fellows of Harvard College; all rights reserved.)

Bringing new production technologies into the traditional manufacturing environment does not take full advantage of their capabilities and probably will not be cost-effective. As the contrasting assumptions and goals make clear, the underlying economics of the new technologies are dramatically different and imply a different, and often contrasting, set of assumptions and goals for management to pursue.

The new technologies can be used to gain competitive advantage through:

- Producing more and more individualized products for more narrowly defined segments,
- Producing rapidly in response to demand,
- Exercising greater control over conformance to specifications (an important aspect of quality),
- Speeding the product-development cycle

Strategies to take advantage of these capabilities include shortening distribution channels, using more focused marketing and distribution, building leadership through frequent product innovations/introductions, and employing consultative selling backed by custom manufacturing. Business strategy should drive the adoption of new technologies, and senior management should examine the implications of new technologies to see where competitive advantage can be gained before moving on to technical evaluations of new systems or plants.

2. Use the process chart to identify the process configuration that is most appropriate for the volume and flexibility requirements of your business strategy. The chart indicates which types of manufacturing systems make the most sense for planned production quantity and production variety—the variety of parts or products to be produced by the system. Contrast the prescriptions of this chart with those of Process Selection Factor Analysis (also in this section) for a "second opinion."

Process configurations indicated on the chart are defined as follows:

Independent

Basic tools whose design is independent of the product design. Can be used for many different products, but generally only perform a small portion of the total manufacturing task. Example: Stand-alone machining tools.

Programmable

Programmable, computer-controlled tools that can handle a wide range of product designs. Example: Computer-controlled machining equipment.

ECONOMIES OF SCOPE
PROCESS SELECTION CHART

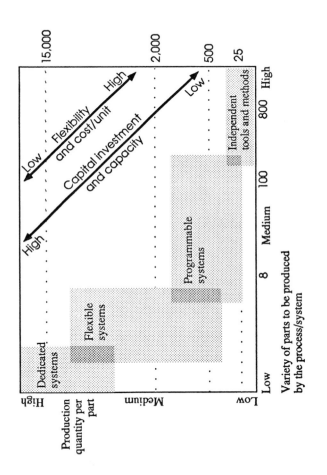

Flexible

Production-line oriented, but able to handle a variety of products within a basic design configuration. Example: Production line that can make more than one model of automobile.

Dedicated

Manufacturing equipment that is specific to a single product. Example: Single-model production line for automobiles.

Note that although the chart's main axes are "Production Quantity" and "Variety of Parts," it also indicates ranges in capital investment, flexibility, capacity, and cost per unit that are associated with each of these process configurations.

Reference

Joel D. Goldhar and Mariann Jelinek. "Plan for Economies of Scope." *Harvard Business Review* (November–December 1983): 141–148.

GARVIN'S EIGHT DIMENSIONS OF QUALITY

Applications

- Measuring product or service quality.
- Comparing the quality of competing products or services.
- Developing a quality-based competitive strategy.

Procedures

1. Identify your product's strengths and weaknesses on each of the eight dimensions of quality.
2. Select specific dimensions on which to compete (may require collaboration with marketing and other departments).
3. Assign responsibility for targeted dimensions. Make sure each department's quality goals are consistent with an overall quality strategy.

Cross-Reference

Marketing Decisions—use the eight dimensions of quality in attribute or trade-off market research to identify which dimensions are most important to consumers.

David Garvin of Harvard Business School, author of *Managing Quality*, developed this approach to quality control because he sees a need for U.S. companies to "define the quality niches in which to compete" in order to meet the challenge of high-quality imports. The key concept is that quality is usually multidimensional from the customer's perspective. A company can choose to excel on certain dimensions of quality based on what customers value most, what the company's strengths are, and what opportunities exist from a competitive perspective. A quality program focusing on selected dimensions can be far more cost-effective and strategic than a broad emphasis on quality.

INSTRUCTIONS

1. The first and key step in Garvin's method is to describe and measure your product or service's quality on each of the following dimensions:

1. The first and key step in Garvin's method is to describe and measure your product or service's quality on each of the following dimensions:

1. *Performance* (primary operating characteristics).
   Examples:

TV	Sound and picture clarity; reception
Banks	Speed and accuracy of check cashing

2. *Features* (supplemental characteristics; bells and whistles).
   Examples:

Airlines	Free drinks
Software	Portability

3. *Reliability* (probability of failure).
   Examples:

Automobiles	Number of breakdowns per year
Investment analyst	Percent of accurate predictions

4. *Conformance* (consistency with specifications).
   Examples:

Manufacturing	Variance from specified measurement
Publishing	Number of typos per book

5. *Durability* (expected product life).
   Examples:

Light bulb	Average time until filament burns out

| Software | Time until obsolescence |

6. *Serviceability* (ease, speed, cost, and pleasantness of repair or correction).
   Examples:

| Farm equipment | How short down-time is during harvesting |
| Credit cards | How cooperative and easy to reach customer service is |

7. *Aesthetics* (how pleasing the product experience is—look, feel, sound, or taste).
   Examples:

| Freeze-dried coffee | How close taste and smell are to fresh-brewed |
| Home construction | How clean and organized the site is; how neat and professional the crew is |

8. *Perceived quality* (indirect evidence about the other dimensions of quality; especially important when direct measures are unavailable).
   Examples:

| Appliances | Maytag's advertised reputation for durability |
| Food | The misconception that granola bars are good for you |

How does your product compare to that of competitors or to customer expectations on each dimension? Where are its greatest strengths and weaknesses? The answers to these questions are obvious in some markets. In others, collaboration with the marketing department may be required to find the answers.

2. After analyzing your product or service on these eight dimensions, compare its ranking with its competition and with information on customer desires, if available from the marketing department. Develop a quality strategy, for example, to specialize

on several dimensions on which competitors are weak and customer interest is strong. Pursuing all eight dimensions at once is usually inappropriate and unrealistic (unless the product is priced very high).

In many cases, manufacturing is not expected to develop product strategy. But manufacturing is often held accountable for product quality and asked to produce higher-quality products. In this situation, manufacturing can use the quality analysis to identify current quality problems and require more specific strategic goals from the marketing department. When multiple departments cannot cooperate effectively to define a multidimensional quality strategy, the involvement of the CEO is necessary.

Caution: Occasionally there is a trade-off in which improvement in one dimension would cause deterioration in another.

3. Once a quality strategy has been agreed on and certain dimensions targeted, assign responsibility within the company for each targeted dimension. This ensures that every department is aware of its specific impact on product quality and will not look solely to manufacturing or production for quality improvements. Every department's quality targets should be consistent with the overall quality strategy.

By breaking quality into eight separate dimensions, management can better define quality goals and can better develop strategies for achieving them. Not all dimensions of quality are controlled at the design and production stages—for example, marketing is responsible for perceived quality and customer service is partly responsible for serviceability. However, the most important decisions concerning quality are usually made at the production level. Typically the emphasis is on conformance in a quality-control program, but reliability, durability, and other dimensions can also be controlled at this level. Production and product development can collaborate to influence most of the other dimensions as well.

Reference

David A. Garvin. "Competing on the Eight Dimensions of Quality." *Harvard Business Review* (November–December 1987): 101–9.

ISHIKAWA CAUSE-EFFECT DIAGRAM

Applications

- Making improvements in product quality through identification and improvement of contributing factors.
- Giving employees responsibility for identifying factors contributing to quality problems and a vehicle for suggesting changes.
- Creating informal causal models for analyzing any complex process.

Procedures

1. Target a specific effect. Select a group of people, including production workers and engineers, marketing staff, or any others with the necessary expertise.
2. Establish specific goals for the impact of the method on the effect (i.e. $x\%$ reduction in rejects in six months).
3. Draw a cause-effect diagram and have the group brainstorm to fill in potential causes.
4. Analyze and prioritize causes. Have the group make recommendations for eliminating the most significant causes of quality problems.

Cross-Reference

Product Development and Innovation

In QC one cannot simply present a goal and shout "work hard, work hard."

- Kaoru Ishikawa

This method was developed by Kaoru Ishikawa, the father of Japanese quality control, as an aid in analyzing a process and identifying the factors that need to be controlled in order to improve the quality of the process. It is used by a group of engineers, production workers, or other experts to analyze the factors that affect the quality of a product or process. Sometimes the group that does the analysis is the QC circle, but it can also be used by an ad hoc committee if your manufacturing facilities do not use QC circles.

INSTRUCTIONS

Start by identifying the effect to be analyzed. An *effect* in this context means the quality characteristics of interest. Characteristics can be defined very narrowly—conformance with a set of engineering specifications—or they may be defined more broadly to include the *perceived* quality of a product or service. Define the effect clearly and make sure it can be measured accurately.

Bring together a group of people with relevant expertise and a diversity of backgrounds. Make sure they are familiar with or receive instruction in basic brainstorming techniques. Draw a cause-effect diagram of "fishbone" design, with a central line and arrow to the right pointing to the effect and branches joining the line from above and below. These branches will be filled in with various causes, by the group and subbranches may be added to break down causes into subcauses.

Brainstorming or other idea-generating processes can be used to help the group generate a laundry list of possible causes. Causes are any processes or factors that have an influence on the effect—the quality characteristics. For example, design, raw materials, machines, and operators are obvious causes for the quality characteristics of a manufactured product. But "design" by itself does not tell the group anything that is likely to result in action to improve quality. Further thought will therefore be needed. Breaking design into number of parts, accuracy of specifications, and so forth will allow the group to pinpoint certain design causes of importance.

The Five P's: If the group has a hard time generating causes, start with the Five P's—product, plant, process, program, and people.

ISHIKAWA DIAGRAM

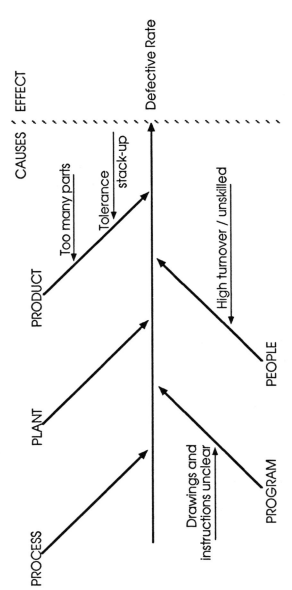

From *What Is Total Quality Control?* The Japanese Way. By Kaoru Ishikawa, Translated by David J. Lu © 1985. Reprinted by permission of the publisher, Prentice-Hall, Inc., Englewood Cliffes, NJ.

After building a multicause model, the group needs to verify the assumptions concerning causality through conventional forms of analysis and research. Gather data, examples, or observations and review this evidence to improve or verify the cause-effect model.

The final and most important stage of model building is identifying the *most important* causes. An infinite number of causal factors probably exist, but only a few account for most of the variation in quality. Focus on those that seem most important, and thus hold the most promise for quality improvement. Identify several and develop ideas for altering them so as to improve quality.

For example, if engineering's designs seem to be a major contributor to product problems because the designs are difficult to assemble, work on a set of criteria for engineering to follow in improving its designs. Reduce the number of parts through re-design. Observe the impact of this change on quality and pursue the engineering cause as long as significant improvements can be gained. Then move on to other causes. The diagram can provide guidance for the group through a series of efforts to improve quality, and it can be redrawn as new factors take priority or new information is gathered.

A basis for quality goals

The Ishikawa Cause-Effect Diagram can provide a foundation for quality-improvement efforts in any process as it gives employees a way to break down quality, which is too broad to manage directly, into a number of well-defined and manageable causal factors. It can be combined with a quantitative goal for quality improvement. For example, management can say that reject rates must drop by 50% by the end of the year and create a special QC group to accomplish this goal. The group can be trained in the use of the diagram and given the support needed to tackle major causes of rejects. As Kaoru Ishikawa explains, "In QC one cannot simply present a goal and shout 'work hard, work hard.' One must understand the meaning of process control, take hold of the process, which is a collection of cause factors, and build within that process ways of making better products, establishing better goals, and achieving effects."

Reference

Kaoru Ishikawa. *What Is Total Quality Control? The Japanese Way*, Trans. David J. Lu. Englewood Cliffs, NJ: Prentice Hall, © 1985. (See especially pages 63–64 and 202-204.)

JOURNEYS-BETWEEN CHART

Applications

- Measuring the efficiency of a facility or process.
- Redesigning a manufacturing process to reduce the time wasted on moving materials between departments.
- Making quick design changes in response to the changing requirements of a batch or to-order facility.
- Applying principles of efficient manufacturing to administrative and operational processes in an organization.

Procedures

1. Construct a travel chart.
2. Observe movement of material for a sample period and enter number of movements between each pair of points on the chart.
3. Analyze by summing directional movements and enter sums in a second chart. *Options*: Diagram direction and number of movements. Weight movements by the time needed for each movement and calculate a weighted total.

Cross-Reference

Organization and Human Resources

The origin of this method is unclear as it is used in various forms by many manufacturing companies. It is a simple, manual tool for planning optimal layout of production equipment and functions. It helps the manager or engineer minimize movement of loads between nonadjacent departments and reduce the overall time wasted in material movement. Alternative approaches involving complex computerized optimization programs are often not worth the time and effort and are harder to adapt to a process's unique (and changing) requirements and constraints. This method is a practical tool for the manager who needs a usable evaluation of the current setup in a hurry.

Idea: The Journeys-Between Chart is also useful for improving the efficiency of data processing, clerical, order fulfillment, parts warehousing, and many other processes in a company where transfers of material take significant time and energy. Upper management can stimulate these departments to adopt the more rigorous approaches of manufacturing by requesting a chart from the process managers. Operational-efficiency goals can then be defined by upper management using a chart-based statistic such as percent decrease in nonadjacent material movements. The chart might even be adaptable to knowledge-based functions in accounting, marketing, finance, and engineering departments by counting the number of verbal and written communications (instead of materials movements) between individuals or groups.

INSTRUCTIONS

1. Construct a travel chart by listing each separate department or process. Create a table with the full list across the top (with the label "To") and again down the side (with the label "From").

2. Fill in the chart by counting the number of separate loads, no matter what they are, that move between any two points. Enter this total in the appropriate cell of the chart. Do this count for a fixed period of time—ten minutes, an hour, or a day—whatever provides a good sample of work-flow patterns for the process under investigation. You may need several observers or several observation periods if the process is complex or the facility large.

3. Analyze the data by combining "to" and "from" movements between each point or department. Some users fill in a copy of the table by entering the summed amounts above the diagonal. But it might be more useful to create a list of pairs of origins/

JOURNEYS BETWEEN CHART

A. Number of Directional Journeys Between Each Station Pair

Station:

From \ To	A	B	C	D
A		25	10	6
B	4		8	100
C	10	50		35
D	14	1	30	

Station:

JOURNEYS BETWEEN CHART

B. Total Journeys Between Each Station Pair

Station:

	A	B	C	D
A		$\cancel{25}$ ^{29} $4 + 25 = 29$	20	20
B			58	101
C				65
D				

④

destinations and numbers of movements in a spreadsheet program in order to be able to sort the pairs and focus on those with the most movements.

4. Enter the totals onto a map or diagram of the facility to see whether the highest numbers of movements are between adjacent points or between distant points. For a more rigorous analysis, determine the distance or average travel time between each point and multiply this by the number of journeys. Sum the weighted measures for an estimate of total time required for material movement. This statistic can be used to set efficiency goals, to evaluate alternative process-configurations, and even to create competition between different plants producing the same product.

MEAN CHART

Applications

- Tracking product quality through periodic samples from the production process.
- Training production workers and equipment operators to track product quality and take action when necessary to prevent defectives or significant deviations from specifications.

Procedures

1. Establish a sampling procedure and train production workers in accurate sampling and measurement procedures.
2. Create a mean chart indicating target mean and including warning and action lines. Train production workers to plot sample means.
3. Establish procedures for action by production workers when the mean crosses an action line.

Cross-Reference

Organization and Human Resources.

The Mean Chart is most commonly used in just-in-time manufacturing, but it can also be used by workers for rapid identification of quality problems, whether or not a facility adopts JIT methods. It is one of the best tools for building worker responsibility for production quality, as it gives workers responsibility for ongoing measurement and analysis of the product. Companies which are adopting JIT methods will find this a good starting point for worker training. (The importance of training is stressed by Stephen Mangelsen, CFO of Raytek, which implemented JIT in 1986. See "Reference.")

The mean chart method can be implemented rapidly and, since its procedures rely on the concept of worker responsibility for quality control, it teaches the concept of workers responsibility more effectively than any amount of talking or writing about it can. (Note: The CuSum chart, also in this section, can be used when tighter conformance is required.)

INSTRUCTIONS

1. Start by establishing a sampling procedure for the product or part in question. Specify the size of the sample and the frequency between samples. Let the rate and nature of problems guide this selection—if the equipment needs frequent adjustment, for example, a sample should be taken every hour or less. Samples of 30 or more usually give the best results, but smaller samples may be better if measurement is slow or if production quantities are low. If workers are going to do the sampling, develop standards for sampling and measurement that can be taught clearly. Try teaching these standards to a few workers to make sure the standards meet this important criterion.

2. Next, create a mean chart for tracking the means of the samples (the average of sample measurements). The chart consists of a piece of graph paper with the measurement scale on the vertical axis. Each sample mean is plotted in succession along the horizontal axis over time. Draw a dark horizontal line in the middle of the chart indicating the specification. Establish an upper and lower warning line to indicate when the mean is deviating far enough from the specification to warrant special attention. (You might want to specify procedures such as notification of supervisor and more frequent sampling when a warning line is reached.) Beyond the warning lines, add an upper and lower action line. These lines represent deviations from the specification that are too great to permit continued production.

3. Procedures for workers to follow should be established for when an action line is crossed. The first action should probably be to stop production. Then the workers could be directed to try adjust-

MEAN CHART

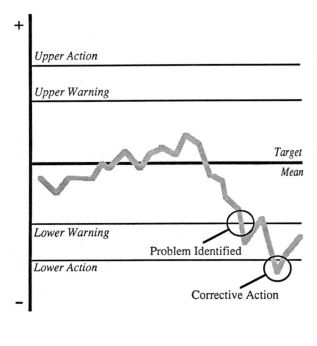

Sample means over time

ments to the equipment, measure the results, and either resume production or call a supervisor or engineer, depending on whether the new sample is within the warning lines.

Where should the warning and action lines be placed? If there are specified limits for the product, these can be used as the action lines, and warning lines can be placed slightly within these limits. Otherwise, the conventional mean chart sets warning limits at values that will be exceeded by chance only 1 in 40 times; 1 in 1,000 for action limits. These limits are intended to correspond to two and three standard deviations from the mean, and the limits may be defined as:

Warning limits = Mean +/− 1.96 × standard error of the mean

Action limits = Mean +/− 3.09 × standard error of the mean

$$\left(\text{Standard error} = \sqrt{\frac{\sigma}{n}}\;\right)$$

Reference

Steven B. Kaufman. "For Rayteck, Inc., just-in-time inventory control isn't a foreign concept—it's an operational imperative." *CFO* 3(7), July 1987, pages 32-38.

OSCAR MAYER CLAIMS ANALYSIS

We can tell you how many jar lids have become
loose on a certain type of pickle.
— James Baker, Oscar Mayer

Applications

- Improving customer service by making claims
  settlements faster and more accurate.
- Reducing the cost of claims analysis.
- Increasing the accuracy and usefulness of claims
  data for use by manufacturing, distribution,
  marketing, and other functions.

Procedures

1. Centralize claims reporting.
2. Act on claims immediately if possible, giving
   claims representatives the necessary authority
   to do so.
3. If a claim is filed, identify the necessary action
   at time of filing.
4. Settle all claims daily unless investigation is
   needed. Provide daily, prioritized lists of unset-
   tled claims to the plants responsible for them.
5. Analyze claims by customer, freight carrier, and
   product. Alert the appropriate department of
   any relevant trends or problems. Support inquiries by various departments.

Cross-Reference

Marketing Decisions

Oscar Mayer's claims analysis was inefficient.
Problems were not identified quickly, and departments did not collaborate effectively. Claims prob-

lems had a negative effect on customers, and the organization was not as good at identifying and correcting causes as desired. To overcome these problems, the distribution, marketing, and MIS departments developed an improved method of claims handling. The new method makes extensive use of computers for both claims reporting and analysis, but the real innovation is the method's basic principles and procedures. These are applicable to many claims systems, both computerized and manual. At Oscar Mayer the new method led to improvements in customer service, reductions in the cost of claims handling, and a dramatic increase in the accuracy of claims handling and claims data.

INSTRUCTIONS

The claims analysis method was developed in five modules corresponding to the numbered instructions below. Each module was implemented independently, from 1 through 5, so that each could be field-tested before the entire system was linked together.

1. *Central reporting.* Claims, which originate from customers, truck drivers, plants and salespeople, are phoned into a central location. (At one time Oscar Mayer processed claims at nine independent locations.)

2. *Immediate action.* If possible, the problem is handled immediately and no claim is filed.

Note: At most companies this means giving claims representatives more authority and training so that they can actually solve problems. If the claim cannot be solved right away it is accurately coded by cause. Oscar Mayer went from a 9-code classification of cause to one that gives more than 100 options as well as a half-dozen common standards—hence the excitement about pickle jar lids.

3. *Action orientation.* At time of filing, the claim is categorized according to what type of action is needed. For example, the claim should indicate whether investigation is necessary. Note that this also

requires expertise and knowledge on the part of the claims representative.

4. *Daily disposition and follow-up*. Claims are resolved daily. At the end of each day the claims department charges or credits the relevant customer statements. The majority of claims can therefore result in a charge or credit to the appropriate customer within a day, which is a dramatic improvement over most claims systems. (Claims is the slowest customer service at many companies. At Oscar Mayer, it may be the fastest.)

Follow-up is ensured for those claims that cannot be resolved at the end of the day, usually because investigation is needed. The originating plant is notified so that it can pursue an investigation. The fate of these open claims is monitored centrally, and each plant is given a prioritized list of its open claims every day.

5. *Analysis*. Historical data is readily available when claims are reported to a central location, which facilitates analysis by distribution, sales, manufacturing, production, and other functions that (should) take an interest in reducing claims. Oscar Mayer analyzes claims by customer, by freight carrier, and product. Any trends or problem areas are reported to plants, the marketing department, or the distribution department as appropriate.

Implementation

The understanding and cooperation of employees are needed for rapid, accurate, and full reporting of claims. Oscar Mayer held training sessions for their own sales and plant employees and also the employees of their freight carriers in order to introduce the new claims method.

Idea: Training for employees of major customers might also be beneficial and a good way to introduce the new method and its benefits.

Potential Problem: The database will not be complete unless those claims that are resolved immediately and not filed are recorded and added to the records of claims filed.

Reference

Jack Farrell. "A Lesson in Claims Management." *Traffic Management* (December 1986): 54–57.

PRICE WATERHOUSE JIT FACTORY WALK-THROUGH

Applications

- Using Japanese just-in-time concepts to identify opportunities for productivity improvements in manufacturing facilities.
- Evaluating JIT programs.
- Training employees or suppliers in JIT concepts.

Procedures

1. Walk through the facility examining quality-assurance and control systems. Identify non-conformance with JIT standards by answering the questions provided.

2. Evaluate internal transportation systems, looking for inefficiencies and wasted energy.

3. Evaluate the work-flow system with an emphasis on batch size. Identify opportunities to reduce batch size and make work flow more smoothly and rapidly.

4. Look at worker activity next. Identify opportunities to standardize work, balance workloads, and reduce idle time and set-up times by going through the checklist provided.

This method fills the need for a quick, nonquantitative way to analyze any manufacturing facility from a just-in-time perspective. It is an easy way to look at facilities from a new perspective and come up with incremental improvements without going through the cost and pain of a full-blown just-in-time program. It gets managers out on the floor as observers, which by itself can lead to useful ideas, and also provides specific guidelines about where to look for possible improvements. It is a good first step for any company considering JIT, as it will give a quick indication of the amount of room for improvement if JIT were to be applied. It is also useful as a quick assessment of existing JIT programs.

Price Waterhouse markets Kawasaki Heavy Industries' just-in-time production system in the U.S., and as a result the firm has considerable experience in evaluating the efficiency of manufacturing facilities from a JIT perspective. They use a formal visual inspection of facilities to identify areas where JIT methods can have the most impact. Their walk-through facility tour can also be used by managers to perform a quick, practical analysis of their own operations. Price Waterhouse takes a video camera along on their facility tour, taping examples of inefficiency and waste as they go. This is a simple and persuasive way to record problems or opportunities and is especially recommended if the proposed changes must be presented to a manager or board that is unfamiliar with the facility and JIT methods.

Another way to use this method is as a way to study a facility from a functional perspective. Many managers are unfamiliar with the details of their firms' production processes, making it difficult for them to plan efficiency or JIT programs. According to Richard Walleigh of Arthur Young & Co., "I haven't walked into a company yet and found a production manager who could accurately describe his production process." Use the walk-through as an excuse to get out on the floor for an extended period of time and focus on the details of the production process (see the Raytek case in "References").

Idea: If your firm already uses JIT management, use the walk-through as a way to teach the principles of JIT as part of employee training, supplier training, and management training.

INSTRUCTIONS

Allow at least a half day for the walk-through. Rather than taking a conventional tour, plan to zigzag across the floor many times as you take a tour of each of the four different systems described below. Look at each system in turn, identifying problems and opportunities by answering the designated questions.

1. Quality assurance and control.

Are less than 100% of products visually inspected on the production line? Does conformance measurement of products occur at each stage? Is it possible for defectives to move beyond the origination point before discovery? Any negative answers are inconsistent with JIT principles and suggest aspects to look at in order to improve productivity at your facility.

2. Internal Transportation.

Follow the movement of parts and work in progress through the plant, looking at distances traveled and at how material is transported. Consider changes in equipment layout that would reduce the longer distances or eliminate cumbersome or expensive transportation methods (such as forklifts).

3. Batch size.

Look at inventories between steps in fabrication and between fabrication and assembly. If inventories are large between certain steps, look at the operating parameters in these steps to determine why. A lack of synchronization between steps or overly complex batch processes (as opposed to the one-piece flow of JIT production) can probably be found by looking at the processes and talking with workers or supervisors. A final factor to look at is the production lead time. If it is long, identify the stages which take the most time and look at these more closely for the same kinds of problems.

4. Worker activity.

Observe individual workers and look for any of the following:

- Lack of standardization;
- Inefficient or difficult-to-access parts (look especially at location, the way parts are packaged

within their containers, and how easy it is to change to a new container);

- Location and types of tools;
- Idle time between tasks or, for machine operators, during the machine cycle;
- Imbalance between the workloads of different workers or jobs;
- Lengthy equipment set-up time.

By going onto the floor and looking at these specific items, a manager can easily identify several inefficiencies that, when addressed, will contribute to the performance of the facility. The method is consistent with an incremental approach to facility improvement and does not require full-blown commitment to remodeling and job modification. Management might find that a walk-through once a month generates enough good ideas to keep them busy with implementation and to provide continual incremental improvements in performance. Even in a facility that has been the subject of a systematic JIT plan this method may produce a list of problems or ideas. Plants that are supposed to be operating under JIT systems can be evaluated using this method to see whether they have overcome all the common problems observed by the Price Waterhouse consultants.

Reference

Mark R. Jamrog. 'Just-in-Time' Manufacturing: Just in Time for U.S. Manufacturers." *Price Waterhouse Review #1,* (1988). (Especially pages 27–28.)

Steven B. Kaufman. "For Raytek, Inc. just-in-time inventory control isn't a foreign concept—it's an operational imperative." *CFO* 3(7) (July 1987): 31-38.

PROCESS-SELECTION FACTOR ANALYSIS

Applications

- Analyzing manufacturing process requirements for products.
- Evaluating process needs based on one or a number of factors.
- Providing quick estimates of manufacturing requirements for proposed products or production runs.
- Identifying relevant criteria for analyzing and costing products or services from a production perspective.

Procedures

1. Use the 11-factor model to analyze products and identify factors of importance to manufacturing process or production cost.
2. Use the process selection chart to select a production process that is indicated by factor rankings.
3. Prepare a factor graph to look at or present differences among products on 2 key factors.

Cross-Reference

Strategic Planning Decisions and Marketing Decisions—useful in cost and resource analyses when evaluating new product or market opportunities.

This is a good tool for planning as it allows rapid analysis of the impact of many factors and requirements on the selection of an efficient production process. Use it to help model the requirements of a proposed product. It may also be useful as a basis for process selection decisions when costing a custom order or responding to inquiries from R&D. Another use is as a general model of production requirements when considering diversification into new markets or distribution channels and when analyzing unfamiliar markets and industries.

INSTRUCTIONS

1. Evaluate the product, order, or production run under consideration according to the following characteristics:

No.	Evaluation factor	Range of options (limits)
1	Range of product or service	Highly diverse/ Standard
2	Customer order size	One-off/Large
3	Repetitiveness of operation	Low/High
4	Product flexibility	High/Very low
5	Make-to-stock	No/Yes
6	Dominant performance criteria	Service/Price
7	Orientation	Capability/Product
8	Number of setups	Many/Very few
9	Process flexibility	Very flexible/ Inflexible
10	Process time	Long/Short
11	Cost of capital investment	Low/High

One option is to create a scale and rate the product according to where it falls between the limits for each factor. This will be most useful when analyzing a large number of products.

Idea: A questionnaire listing the factors and their ranges can be prepared and given to experts in appropriate industries or markets to rank each product if in-house knowledge is insufficient.

Each of these factors can have an impact on the production requirements of a product. In some cases only a few of these factors will be important.

Example: If you typically produce products with a similar profile on these factors but are asked to produce something new, a comparison of the new and old products often reveals differences on only one or two factors. Perhaps the old products required few setups but the new will require many, and the new may also have a stronger orientation toward capability as opposed to product. It is important to identify exactly how the new product differs by using this factor analysis. Then you can focus on what impact specific factors might have on the production requirements of that new product.

A visual display can be used to contrast the "factor profiles" of two or more products. Use a numerical scale for each factor (1 to 5 is easy), as previously described. Then plot a bar chart showing the rating of each product on each factor. You will need to attach text to the chart describing the factors and their limits, as in "1", since there is too much information to present clearly on the chart itself.

You can mark the bar chart to indicate factors on which a significant difference is observed (arrows are used on this example to indicate differences on factors 1, 2 and 11).

2. Evaluate factors to select the appropriate manufacturing process. One of the strengths of this method is that it ranks each factor on a spectrum which is directly relevant to the spectrum of production processes. At one end of the spectrum, unique or custom production is indicated. In the middle, batch processes are best. And at the other end, continuous processes make the most sense.

The bar chart shown includes a process characteristic scale. The list of factors and their limits in "1" follows a standard format in which the first limit corresponds to custom production and the second to continuous processes. As long as the factors are presented in this same format, any graphic display such as the bar chart will show characteristics suited to continuous production on the right, and characteristics making the product suited to custom produc-

EVALUATION FACTOR CHART

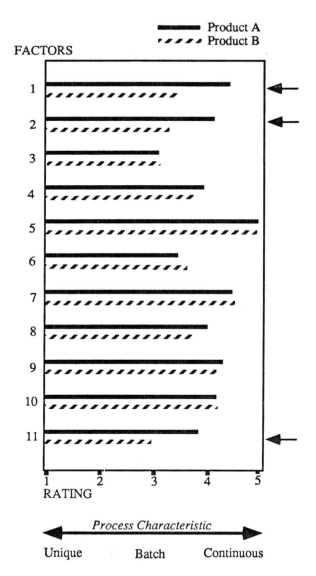

FACTORS

Legend:
- ▬▬▬ Product A
- ╱╱╱╱ Product B

RATING axis: 1 2 3 4 5

Process Characteristic
Unique — Batch — Continuous

From *Manufacturing Strategy* by T.J. Hill, © 1985. Used by permission of Macmillan, London and Basingstoke.

tion to the left. The middle corresponds to batch processes.

The following table illustrates this relationship for each factor:

Factor	Process Characteristic		
	Unique activity	Batch	Continuous
Range of product or service	Highly diverse .... Standard		
Customer order size	One-off .... Large		
Repetitiveness of operation	Low .... High		
Product flexibility	High .... Very low		
Make-to-stock	No .... Yes		
Dominant performance criteria	Service .... Price		
Orientation	Capability .... Product		
Number of set-ups	Many .... Very few		
Process flexibility	Very flexible .... Inflexible		
Process time	Long .... Short		
Cost of capital investment	Low .... High		

If production facilities and processes are considered a given, as in short-term cost analysis, it may be more useful to look at the costs associated with each factor than to look at each factor's impact on the selection of production process characteristics. Unfortunately, there are no general models for the impact of variations from a standard factor profile on manufacturing cost—every manufacturer will have unique cost structures. However, it is a good bet that larger deviations from the current factor profile will cost more in the short run and make a new product more difficult to produce in the existing facilities and processes. A review of cost structures and previous experiences may permit manufacturing management to establish quantitative models of costs for each factor.

3. A helpful device in analyzing the influence of key factors or presenting the results of analysis is the factor graph. Prepare a graph showing one factor on the vertical axis and another on the horizontal. Map different products on the two factors. See the example, in which customer order size and cost of capital investment form the two axes of the graph. These factors were picked because the products from the bar chart example (step 2) differed significantly on them.

FACTOR/PROCESS GRAPH
(PRODUCTS A & B)

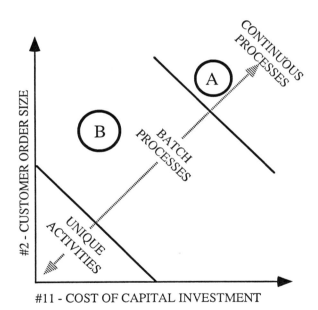

References:

Hill, T.J. *Manufacturing Strategy—The Strategic Management of the Manufacturing Function.* London:

Macmillan, 1985. (Hill developed the factor list and process selection chart in this book.)

Amrik Sokal and Keith Howard. " Effective Operations Management." *Management Decision* 26(2), 1988. (A general discussion of Hill's methods and their application.)

TAGUCHI CONFORMANCE GRAPH

Applications

- Analyzing the conformance of parts to their specifications.
- Identifying and preventing deviations that are likely to result in tolerance stack-up.
- Training employees in the principles of statistical process control in manufacturing, logistics, and other settings.

Procedures

1. Sample parts from the manufacturing line—either parts you are producing for later assembly or parts you have purchased for assembly.

2. Measure the parts on a specified dimension(s). Create a frequency table indicating the number of parts of each size observed.

3. Plot the distribution on a graph or bar chart that indicates the target specification. If the distribution is not centered on the target, take action to move it closer.

This method comes from the Japanese statistician Genichi Taguchi, who emphasizes analysis of the distribution of variations from specifications. His research indicates that it is better to produce parts whose distribution is centered on the target specification than parts whose distribution is not centered on the target, even if the latter distribution is tighter. This is due in large part to the problem of tolerance stack-up. If one part is at the upper end of its specified limits and the other at the lower, the *combined* variation from specifications may prevent the two parts from fitting together properly. Taguchi's approach to quality conformance is to make sure the distribution of each part is such that the number of cases of tolerance stack-up is minimized and is therefore especially useful in cases where multiple parts are being made for assembly into products. It can be applied to parts produced in your facilities or to the incoming parts provided by suppliers.

Note: Similar types of analysis are used by a number of U.S. consulting firms under the name *statistical process control*.

INSTRUCTIONS

Draw a large sample of parts from the production line (or from those supplied by vendors)—at least 30 and preferably more. Measure them. A separate graph should be used for each of the specified measurements if there is more than one.

Analyze the distribution of measurements; count the number of parts with like measurements and create a table, as in the following example for a sample of 70 parts.

Length (millimeters)	Number
4.10	1
4.11	1
4.12	3
4.13	5
4.14	11
4.15	21
4.16	14
4.17	6
4.18	4
4.19	3
4.20	1

Plot this data on a graph with the horizontal axis for the measurements and the vertical axis for frequency. Draw a vertical line to represent the target specification. If tolerances or specification limits have been set, add these as vertical lines.

In the example, the data from the table is plotted on a bar chart and the target is indicated. The sample is not centered on its target, and the graph therefore indicates a potential problem that should be addressed before further production. The graph also shows that an action limit is exceeded, which is a further indication of trouble. But according to Taguchi's theory, this is less important than the fact that the center of the distribution is off target.

TAGUCHI CONFORMANCE GRAPH

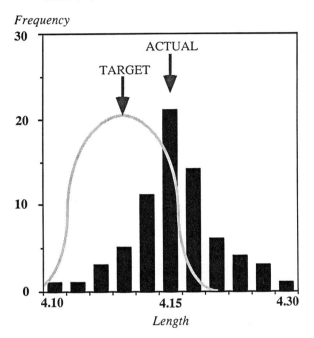

Reference

Sullivan, L.P. "Reducing Variability: A New Approach to Quality." *Quality Progress*, (July 1984).

TOYOTA PROBLEM-REPORTING PROCEDURE

Applications

- Improving the quality of products and production processes.
- Reducing the impact of production-line problems on customers and downstream processes.
- Eliminating obstacles to rapid reporting and solving of problems.

Procedures

1. Train managers and workers in Toyota's principles of problem solving.
2. Establish the problem-reporting procedures (in which production is stopped first and cause identified last).

Cross-Reference

Organization and Human Resources

Toyota's method focuses on how defectives are reported and the cause investigated. The approach is simple and thus easy to implement. It adds value by encouraging immediate reporting of problems and preventing cover-ups. Note that implementation can require a significant change in labor-management relations—time and attention should be allocated to make the transition. The method may not be applicable where relations are strained and discipline emphasized.

INSTRUCTIONS

1. Establish basic principles of problem solving within your organization by training both workers and managers in these principles:

   1. No disciplinary action for reporting a problem, even if it means shutting down the production line or halting distribution of products for a false alarm or mistake by the person reporting the problem.

   2. Prevent use of defective parts or delivery of imperfect products before seeking the cause of a problem. This principle runs against the grain at many plants because it may cause delays in starting up the production line or delivering products, but it minimizes the negative impact that a problem will have on product quality.

   3. Every worker in a process or on a line has authority to stop the work flow. This allows work to be stopped as soon as a problem is noticed, rather than waiting for a supervisor to make the decision, and so prevents continuation of a defect.

   4. Solve problems at the lowest possible level. This requires all employees to take responsibility for problem solving, instead of bumping problems up the hierarchy unless absolutely necessary. It therefore speeds problem solving.

   Note that the method is premised on acceptance of these principles and cannot be implemented without first adopting the principles.

2. Establish the following basic procedures for reporting any problem that could affect product quality.

Reporting Procedures

1. Stop production

2. Make first report (to *all* people who may need to be involved in correction—reports that problem exists; does not identify cause).

3. Stop delivery (of any defective parts or products).

4. Investigate (to identify cause(s) and correct them).

Discussion and example

These simple procedures and the principles on which they are based have helped Toyota and other Japanese companies produce high-quality products with low defect rates. But are they applicable outside of Japan? Recent cases suggest that application is possible, but not always easy.

The method is now used at the Nummi plant, a GM/Toyota joint venture in Fremont, California. For example, all workers have cords at their stations they can use to ring a bell and turn on a light when they fall behind or encounter a problem. Team members and group leaders (Nummi uses the Quality Circle concept) immediately begin to work on the problem, and if the team cannot solve it in a minute the line is stopped. The union agreement includes an article giving workers the right to stop the production line without being subject to discipline. The method appears to work well at Nummi, and the plant has developed a reputation for low defect rates.

At Nummi the principle of solving problems at the lowest possible level is even applied to labor relations. For example, the *New York Times* reports that "…if a worker calls a union representative, the union official is likely to arrive with a member of the company's labor relations staff. The three will try to work out the problems on the spot, eliminating the need for a grievance."

References

Masao Nemoto. *Total Quality Control for Management: Strategies and Techniques from Toyota and Toyoda Gosei.* ed. and trans. David Lu. Englewood Cliffs, NJ:

PART 4

MARKETING DECISIONS

BERRY'S PRINCIPLES OF SERVICE MARKETING

Applications

- Adapting marketing strategy to the unique needs of services.
- Identifying which strategies are useful for which types of services.
- Developing marketing advantages for products by differentiating them on the basis of associated services.

Procedures

1. Identify the characteristics of the service or services marketed by your organization.
2. Use the matrix or review the material in "Instructions" to identify one or more of the four marketing strategies.

Cross-Reference

Strategic Planning Decisions.

Leonard Berry, professor of marketing at Texas A&M, developed a list of strategies for marketing services that is useful both for identifying the marketing issues of importance for a particular service and for diagnosing problems with any service marketing strategy. It also may be of interest to the product marketer wishing to focus on services such as maintenance and training that are associated with the product purchase.

Reprinted by permission from *Business* Magazine. "Services Marketing Is Different," by Leonard L. Berry, May-June 1981. Copyright 1981 by the College of Business Administration, Georgia State University, Atlanta.

INSTRUCTIONS

1. Berry's four strategies for service marketing are based on the premise that services differ from products to the extent that they are intangible (physically or mentally), simultaneously produced and consumed, and not standardized or uniform. The extent to which a strategy is applicable depends on the characteristics of the service. To use his model for developing service marketing strategies, first identify the characteristics of the service you wish to market. Characteristics are defined as follows:

Intangible

Many services are intangible in the sense that they cannot be touched. They can be consumed but not possessed. Sometimes services are intangible in the sense that they are difficult to define or grasp mentally. Services vary in their intangibility. *Note*: Many products have intangible elements such as warrantees and service.

Simultaneous purchase and consumption

Unlike products, services are often produced and consumed at the same time. The provider is often involved one-on-one with the customer in performing the service. How the service is provided becomes an important and hard-to-control variable in these cases.

Example: Bank tellers produce a service that is consumed simultaneously. Automated teller machines reduce the variability in performance of this service, but also limit the options for customization (see next item).

Less standardized and uniform

If people play a large role in providing the service, it will tend to vary. If the service is provided primarily by machines (e.g., telephone service), it may be more standardized. However, in general services are harder to standardize than products.

2. Next, use the matrix to identify which service marketing strategies are applicable to your service given its characteristics. The following discussion describes the strategies.

Note: The matrix indicates the strategies that are most likely to be applicable given the service characteristic. But in some cases other strategies may apply—review *all* the strategies to look for ideas that may help you develop or refine your marketing plans.

1. *Internal Marketing.* Where there is high contact between customer and provider, the company benefits from focusing its marketing effort on its own employees. The goal: To have employees who are enthusiastic and knowledgeable about their jobs and the company's services. Internal marketing means treating employees like customers and their jobs like products to be designed and marketed to meet their needs. The employee is viewed as a link in the distribution channel.

2. *Customizing service.* This strategy takes advantage of simultaneous production and consumption. If the provider is already producing the service for customers one at a time, the additional costs of tailoring to the customer's needs are relatively low. However, detailed information about customers must be collected to implement this strategy.

3. *Managing the evidence.* Potential customers must evaluate evidence or clues about service quality when the service is too intangible to evaluate easily. Evidence may include the environment in which the service is provided, the appearance of the service providers, and the price (higher price might suggest higher quality). Through advertising or distribution a firm may link its intangible services with a well-regarded tangible product or product distributor, using the product reputation as evidence of service quality.

4. *Making services tangible.* A tangible symbol or representation of an intangible service can help make the service seem tangible—the credit card and the rock in the "own a piece of the rock" campaign perform this function. Creating a distinct physical environment for the service also makes it more tangible—the bricks and mortar strategy of banks is a traditional example.

The intangibility of many services makes it impossible to inventory them and make it hard to cope with fluctuations in demand. Strategies that synchronize supply and demand or reshape either can address this issue.

Services which are intangible because they are difficult to grasp mentally are especially suited to this strategy.

Example:

The rental car companies have pursued several strategies to make services more tangible. Ads focus on cars—the tangible aspect of the service. Cards are given to customers. Two less-tangible aspects of service—preparing the rental agreement and settling the bill—are subject to delays since the services cannot be inventoried as a product could be. Car rental companies have been working to mechanize returns for some time, and in 1989 National Car Rental System introduced the industry to a system that allows regular customers to bypass the rental counter. They also manage the evidence aggressively: Employees wear uniforms and cars are kept clean to suggest they are in good condition. But rental car companies could benefit further from improvements in the physical environment of rental counters, shuttle vans, parking lots and payment counters, and they could also make maintenance facilities more visible to customers.

Service is customized to the extent that different sizes and prices of cars are available. Corporate price programs are also offered, and frequent users are offered special conveniences (e.g., Hertz's No. 1 Gold Service). But this strategy has not been emphasized

CHARACTERISTICS/STRATEGIES MATRIX

Service Characteristic	Internal marketing	Strategy Customizing service	Managing evidence	Making tangible
Intangible	✓		✓	✓
Simultaneous Production/Consumption		✓		
Nonstandard		✓	✓	

and many opportunities exist for the car rental companies in this area.

Some internal marketing is used to improve the performance of service providers (Avis's "We try harder" campaign was directed internally as well as externally), but this strategy is also under utilized.

Idea: Many service companies have different services that vary in their extent of intangibility, simulteneous production/consumption, and uniformity. These companies usually do not group their services on the basis of these variables; but grouping this way is a natural as far as strategy goes.

Example: A bank should have one strategic plan for teller services (including ATM's) and other face-to-face services since these have in common simultaneous production/consumption and opportunities for customization. Loan, credit line, insurance, and similar products are unified by their long-term nature (not produced and consumed at once) and by lack of tangibility. They can be addressed by another plan. Bank statements and reports of various kinds are another natural service group, having in common nonsimultaneous production/consumption, tangibility, and greater uniformity.

References

Leonard L. Berry. "Services Marketing Is Different." *Business* (May–June 1980).

Johnie L. Roberts. "Car Rental Companies Move to Eliminate Dreaded Bottleneck: The Rental Counter." *The Wall Street Journal* (January 24, 1989).

BIBEAULT'S TURNAROUND STAGES

Applications

- Adapting marketing strategies to the needs of financially troubled companies.
- Selecting a marketing strategy that is consistent with an organization's turnaround stage.
- Evaluating product lines and marketing tactics during turnaround.
- Strengthening the case for cutting unprofitable segments from the product portfolio.

Procedures

1. Determine which of the five turnaround stages best fits your organization.
2. Use the decision table to identify marketing strategies that are consistent with the organization's current turnaround stage.
3. Review existing product lines and marketing programs to see where they deviate from the model's prescriptions and make whatever changes are necessary.

Cross-Reference

Strategic Planning Decisions

Donald Bibeault's experiences as a turnaround manager for Pacific States Steel and other troubled companies, combined with his research for a Ph.D., provided the basis for this matrix of marketing strategies by turnaround stage. Use it to focus the marketing effort on priority issues for a troubled company and to identify unnecessary or counter productive marketing expenditures.

Marketing can play a significant role in turning around a troubled company or profit center, but marketing strategy in a turnaround is quite different from that in a normal case and is highly sensitive to the turnaround context. For these reasons it is difficult to develop effective and appropriate marketing strategies in a turnaround situation without a context-specific analysis such as can be performed with this method. (Turnaround marketing differs from the norm in one other important respect: The CEO is typically more involved than usual. For CEO's without extensive marketing experience this method provides a useful framework for a venture into the nuts and bolts of marketing strategy.)

INSTRUCTIONS

1. Identify the turnaround stage the organization is currently in based on Bibeault's five-stage model of the turnaround life cycle. In this model, the organization enters stage 1, management change, when it first recognizes that there is a serious problem. (*Note:* While firms often bring in a new manager, this stage does not always involve management change.) The organization moves on to the evaluation stage then to taking emergency action, stabilizing, and, if the turnaround is successful, returning to growth. The following table describes characteristics of each stage to help you identify which one applies:

Stage	Characteristics
Management Change	Problems acknowledged and new leadership selected to solve them.
Evaluation	New leadership identifies problems and losers, develops turnaround plans.
Emergency	Cash-flow problems are solved through surgery if necessary, to ensure survival in the short term.

Stage	Characteristics
Stabilization	Management focuses on building profits, improving operating efficiency, and repositioning for growth.
Return to Growth	Internal and external development is undertaken to create revenue growth and build the strength of the organization.

2. Develop a marketing plan based on the indicated strategy for your company's current stage. The Strategy Table identifies strategies for market share, price, promotion, and product-line decisions.

3. Modify current marketing programs to reflect the decision strategies indicated. When a company gets into trouble it takes abnormal, sometimes extreme, measures to get back on track. Traditional approaches to price and promotion are usually inappropriate during turnaround, and product lines generally need heavy pruning. The Bibeault model helps management identify needed changes in marketing strategy and strengthens resolve to make marketing contribute to the turnaround effort. One of the most controversial issues when companies are in the emergency stage is what to do about traditional lines of business that no longer make a positive contribution. Often a company has defined itself as serving a particular segment for so long that management and the board have trouble seeing it differently. But in general, experience indicates a company cannot try to salvage its losers during the emergency stage. In the early 1980s International Harvester sold profitable segments first in order to retain its focus on truck manufacturing, but it was unable to turn this loser around quickly enough to avoid reorganization. Goodrich, however, went through a successful turnaround in the mid-1980s after realizing that its traditional focus on tires was no longer viable.

Decision	Emergency	Stabilization	Return to growth
Focus	Cash	Profits	Revenues
Market Share	Low priority	Build in high-return segments	Build in all segments
Price	Raise	Stabilize. Maintain increased margins	Lower
Promotion	None	Use cautiously where requisite	Use to build share
Product Line	Cut low and negative contributors. Add only sure winners	Emphasize high-profit products. Add selectively and limit commitment to new products	Add new products and lines

Example:

In early 1989 Salomon Inc. was still struggling through a painful turnaround that began when the market it dominated—U.S. government and corporate bonds—declined dramatically in 1987. Pretax earnings for the securities segment of Salomon's business fell 67%, from $787 million in 1986 to $261 million in 1987, then recovered partially to reach $486 million in 1978. (Securities contributed 99% of total pretax earnings in 1986.)

When the Bibeault model is applied to Salomon's case, it appears that turnaround marketing strategy violated several of the model's prescriptions, perhaps explaining why the turnaround has taken longer than desired. During the emergency stage the product line was not cut as rapidly or deeply as results indicated was necessary. Government and corporate bonds were unprofitable, and Salomon may have been overly hesitant in cutting staff in these segments because its chairman and CEO, John Gutfreund, stayed at the helm during the crisis rather than bring in a new turnaround manager. This hesitancy to "cut low and negative contributors," as the model prescribes, may have prolonged the emergency stage.

A second conclusion from the model is that Salomon probably tried to add too many new products during the emergency stage. Efforts included investment banking, mergers and acquisitions, arbitrage in bonds, foreign-currency trading, and Japanese government-bond trading. Some of these (especially Japanese bonds) proved to be sure winners, but Salomon probably spread its efforts too thin and backed too many risky ventures for a company in the emergency stage.

In 1988 the firm struggled into the stabilization stage, mostly on the strength of earnings from its oil trading and refining subsidiary Philbro Energy. The Bibeault model indicates that Salomon should now build market share in high-return segments such as investment banking and energy, but should continue to limit the product line in order to focus on winners and to be able to commit sufficient resources to each new product. In investment banking and merchant banking in general, Salomon must fight with well-established competitors for share. This effort will require a high level of commitment, which means that efforts to gain share in other major segments cannot be pursued simultaneously. Once a significant share of this segment has been built and the firm has returned to profitability overall, it will enter the return-to-growth stage and will be able to pursue aggressive share strategies in all segments, including trading.

References

Donald B. Bibeault. *Corporate Turnaround: How Managers Turn Losers Into Winners.* New York: McGraw Hill, 1982.

Steve Swartz and Mathew Winkler. "Salomon Claims Its Turnaround Strategy Is Paying Off." The *Wall Street Journal* (February 8, 1989): A9.

COMBUSTION ENGINEERING'S COMPETITOR ANALYSIS

Applications

- Anticipating major moves by an important competitor.
- Using internal expertise and information sources to perform competitor analysis.
- Shortening the time required for competitor analysis and reducing staff needs in the area.

Procedures

1. Assemble managers and ask them to collect relevant experience and information. *Optional*: Appoint a mediator.
2. In a follow-up meeting, review the information gathered and do a relative strengths/weaknesses analysis.
3. In the same meeting, do a comparative cost analysis by breaking down costs, ranking the competitor as higher or lower on each cost, and then quantifying the difference.
4. In the meeting, examine past performance and current performance measures to analyze the competitor's motivation.
5. To conclude the meeting, combine these analyses to create a total picture of the competitor. Identify likely competitive moves.

Resources

Two meetings of the management team are required, the second lasting several hours minimum. Individual managers will need a week or two between meetings to gather information and material, and may want to commit staff time to the project as well.

Cross-Reference

Strategic Planning Decisions

Most U.S. companies now gather competitor information. But in many cases they find that filling files with newspaper clippings and sales material does not give them insight into future competitor actions. A common solution is to hire additional staff to specialize in competitor analysis; but this is an expensive approach, and it can take years for staff to learn as much about an industry as managers already know. Combustion Engineering's method uses management expertise and input to identify competitor strategies and predict competitor moves. It can be performed by existing staff and management.

The method focuses on the logic behind competitor behavior, which often seems irrational at first glance. The most logical future moves are easily identified once the underlying logic is understood. CE's method is easy to implement because it uses the most readily available sources of competitor information—those found within one's own organization.

Note: CE analyzes one competitor at a time and uses a management team in the research stage. (Most companies delegate research to staff and prepare a report covering all competitors at once.) Use CE's method when you need to focus on a major competitor, but not for routine background research on the whole field of competitors.

INSTRUCTIONS

1. Select the competitor for analysis and hold a meeting attended by all managers who might have access to information about that competitor, including the CEO or general manager and the marketing, sales, manufacturing, and financial managers. (*Idea*: Even the personnel manager might be helpful by identifying and debriefing new hires that have come from competitors.)

Broad representation provides access to the many internal sources of information collected by your organization in the form of documents, observations, and personal experiences. Have everyone present discuss the sources of information available to them and agree to collect recent information, either in person or by delegating the work to their staff. *Recommendation*: John Rhode, a vice president at Combustion Engineering, recommends using a facilitator—someone not involved in the competitor analysis—to lead the meeting.

2. Hold a second meeting to review and discuss the information gathered by the managers. (Each manager should present his or her information to the group.) Using this information, the group performs a relative strengths/weaknesses analysis. This requires the group to list any areas that meet two criteria:

• The competitor is distinctly stronger or weaker than your company

• The area has the potential to affect customer behavior

Unless an area qualifies on both criteria, it should not be discussed or analyzed. Managers do not always agree on which areas to include; a moderator can be helpful if conflict arises.

3. Next, the team does a comparative cost analysis. This is a three-step process:

• Prepare a simple breakdown of the costs incurred in bringing your product or service to market (e.g., labor, material, manufacturing, distribution, sales, overhead).

• Rank the competitor's cost for each factor on the following scale:
    significantly higher
    slightly higher
    slightly lower
    significantly lower

Idea: If consensus is a problem use the Nominal Group Technique described in "General Decision-Making Tools."

• Quantify the overall cost difference by first translating the judgmental rankings into plausible percentage differences (e.g., 10% higher,

5% higher, 5% lower, 10% lower). This should also be decided by a consensus. Second, weight each cost factor by its relative contribution to *your* total product or service costs and sum to estimate the competitor's total costs.

4. Next CE analyzes their competitor's motivation by determining how the competitor measures success and what its objectives and strategies are. Surprisingly, considerable information is usually available on this topic, and can be gathered from press clippings describing awards and promotions; annual reports; hiring, review and promotion policies as described by former employees; press releases; executives' speeches, investment analyst's reports; your sales force (which usually knows the competitor's sales force); and the opinions of mutual clients or suppliers. Motivation is closely tied to measurement systems. For example, the competitor that wants to build its share of a particular market is pretty likely to measure success in terms of market share, revenue growth, or new accounts, but will probably not hold salespeople accountable for the profitability of the new business. The competitor that wants to "harvest" its investment in your industry will usually measure success in terms of profits or ROI.
Motivation may also be indicated by recent competitive moves.

5. The final step is to create a total picture of the competitor by combining information on its relative strengths and weaknesses, relative cost structure, goals, and strategies. Even with imperfect information, the analysis generates a clear enough picture to allow identification of likely competitive moves.

Example: A competitor emerges from the analysis stronger in direct sales, with a cost advantage in labor, and focused on growing from a regional to a national firm. Conclusion: The competitor may try to assemble a direct sales effort nationwide, positioning itself on the basis of low price.

The phantom competitor

Like most competitor analysis, CE's method focuses on existing customers. But what if an outsider enters the market with a new approach and blows everyone out of the water? CE uses another analytical tool to anticipate moves by nonconventional competitors.

To use this method, work with the management group assembled for the competitor analysis described above. Ask the group to look at the market as an objective third party would and to design an imaginary company that would penetrate the market very successfully. Then compare this phantom competitor with yourself and your competitors to see if any of the traditional competitors in your market could adopt the phantom's approach with reasonable ease. Also compare the phantom with other companies that could be tempted to enter your market to see if any of them could easily adopt the phantom's strategy.

When CE's phantom analysis reveals a strategy that traditional competitors might easily adopt, CE adopts it as a preemptive move. When analysis indicates an outsider could enter the market successfully, CE tries to create additional barriers to entry, or it forms an alliance with an outsider company in order to pursue the phantom strategy itself.

Warning: CE's defensive strategy assumes that opportunities will eventually be exploited by another company if CE does not exploit them first. However, it takes a strong position in the marketplace to make this preemptive strategy work. A weaker competitor might use the analysis to decide when to withdraw from a market and pursue other markets with fewer competitive threats (see Trout & Reis Marketing Warfare Strategies in this section for more ideas on competitive strategy).

Reference

"Calculating Competitor Action: Combustion Engineering's Strategy." *Management Briefing: Marketing* (October–November 1988). The Conference Board.

CRAVENS MARKETING STRATEGY MATRIX

Applications

- Identifying feasible strategic options given a specific market context.
- Evaluating marketing plans and proposals to see if their underlying strategies are realistic given the marketing situation.

Procedures

1. Select one of the five generic strategic situations that best describes the marketing context for your business and product.
2. Use the matrix to identify applicable strategies and tactics or to see whether a strategy is appropriate for the given situation.

Cross-Reference

Use to bring a marketing perspective to Strategic Planning Decisions.

This is a prescriptive tool that links marketing strategy to market context. The position of the firm in its market has significant implications for strategy, and the marketing strategy matrix can be used to identify these implications and make sure the strategy reflects them. The marketing manager can use this tool for generating strategy or for reviewing strategies proposed by staff or operational managers. The CEO may find this tool useful in checking the

From *Business Horizons*, September-October 1988. Copyright 1988 by the Foundation for the school of Business at Indiana University. Used with permission.

internal consistency of marketing plans and proposals, as it can be used to compare the context and the strategy as defined in a marketing plan. The prescriptions of the matrix are based on a compilation of many studies of marketing strategy, and while not 100% valid in every situation, they can be expected to be valid in most circumstances. Deviations from the prescriptions of the matrix should be justified by an explanation of how the situation differs from the norm.

INSTRUCTIONS

1. Identify the context by selecting one of the five possible strategic situations. Choose the one that best describes the current situation for your product and your company's position in the product market. Strategic situations:

Market development

Early entry or technical leadership makes a company a pioneer in its market (e.g., Cetus in biotechnology).

Market domination

The leader in an established market. Holds an advantageous and influential position (e.g., IBM in computers).

Differentiated advantage

A firm (not necessarily the leader) has a sustainable advantage such as low cost or patent protection (e.g., Apollo in computer workstations).

Market selectivity

Characterized by differentiated buyer wants (many segments) and many small firms addressing these wants. Local service businesses such as restaurants are good examples (segmentation based on price, menu, and location).

STRATEGIC SITUATIONS

STRATEGY OPTIONS	Market development	Market domination	Differential advantage	Market selectivity	No advantage
New-Product Development	Yes	Yes. Develop product portfolio	Consider	Yes	No
Segmentation and Targeted Marketing	Yes. Top priority markets first	Yes. Target many segments	Yes. Make sure focus is right	Yes. Make sure focus is right	Yes. Narrow focus
Product positioning through research and marketing	Establish marketing mix first	Cover multiple positions	Position to highlight advantage	Only if current position is ineffective	May not be cost-effective
Sales and Marketing Productivity Improvement	Delay	Yes	Yes	Yes	Consider
Acquisition of Merger	Questionable	Consider	Consider	No. Evaluate acquisition threats	Yes
Harvest or Divest	No	No	Questionable	Consider	Yes

No advantage

The other situations all imply a strategic advantage or at least the potential to create one. Sometimes there is no immediate or obvious basis for creating an advantage (e.g., International Harvester, early 1980s).

2. Refer to the matrix to see which generic strategies are appropriate for the given strategic situation. The matrix also provides advice on tactics to pursue for certain of the strategies (when tactics are dependent on the strategic situation). The generic strategies in the matrix are

1. New-product development
2. Segmentation and targeted marketing
3. Product positioning through research and marketing
4. Sales and marketing productivity improvement
5. Acquisition or merger
6. Harvest or divest

Reference

Cravens, David W. "Gaining Strategic Marketing Advantage." *Business Horizons* (September–October 1988), pp. 44-54. (Published by the Indiana University Graduate School of Business.)

EATON MARKETING COMMUNICATIONS AUDIT

Applications

- Managing a decentralized marketing communications function, as in a multidivision company.
- Increasing the consistency and quality of marketing communications.
- Encouraging cross-selling and cooperation between separate units of a company.

Procedures

1. Create a task force of communications managers.
2. The task force defines key issues (with executive input if desired).
3. Assign subcommittees of the task force responsibility to investigate each issue and propose solutions to problems.
4. Present recommendations to senior management for approval or modification.
5. Ensure follow-up and compliance with recommendations by creating a group of communications directors drawn from divisional communications managers.

Cross-Reference

Sales Management Decisions—useful in coordinating sales communications.

It is unusual to find a company doing a structured, organizationwide analysis of its marketing communications. Generally, marketing communications follow marketing and PR strategies in a loose manner, with decision making in the hands of many different managers, units, and outside agencies. A periodical analysis and reorganization can increase the organization's control over the form, style, and content of communications; bring communications into closer alignment with corporate objectives; and increase the efficiency of the marketing communications function. Many companies can benefit from an audit of marketing communications, and those who choose to perform one will find Eaton's approach straightforward, adaptable, and a useful standard on which to base their own procedures.

At Eaton, management was frustrated by the disorganization and lack of coordination in marketing communications. Automotive components, industrial, truck components, defense electronics, and other groups tended to pursue their own communications strategies, sometimes placing their ads in the same publications without realizing it or checking for consistency of appearance. Their was no cross-selling between divisions, and many opportunities for cooperation were missed. A large number of advertising agencies were employed with little coordination by different decision makers throughout the organization.

Eaton did not want to solve these problems simply by centralizing the marketing communications function. This would have reduced both Eaton's ability to meet the different needs of its units and the creativity of marketing communications. Furthermore, Eaton had *decentralized* a few years earlier to cut costs, and there was some concern that centralization would lead to cost increases. The Marketing Communications Audit was developed to provide control over the function without losing the benefits of decentralization.

INSTRUCTIONS

1. Appoint a task force of communication managers or advertising directors, including managers from multiple divisions or units as well as managers from the corporate office. Eaton's task force consisted of 11 people, 8 from divisions. It is a good idea to have the majority of the task force be from divisions.

2. The task force outlines the main issues. These may be problems of coordination, trade shows, use and selection of advertising agencies, and many other topics (see the list of Eaton's subcommittees under step 3 for the issues of concern in their audit).

3. Divide the task force into subcommittees, assigning each subcommittee one or more of the specific issues. Here are the issues Eaton defined for subcommittee study:

- Marketing communications planning
- Visual continuity and quality
- Specialty promotional items
- Corporate advertising
- Product advertising and placement
- Product publicity
- Trade-shows inquiry management
- Agency selection
- Oversight and coordination
- Professional selection and development

Subcommittees gather the information and ideas necessary to evaluate current performance in each area and develop proposals to improve performance. Resources within the company are consulted first, then outside experts are consulted if necessary. At Eaton, this step took approximately one year. Subcommittees devoted considerable time to their issues, studying how Eaton currently handled each issue, identifying problems and complaints, and finding options for improvement.

4. Each subcommittee develops recommendations, and the task force prepares a summary report identifying problems and recommending changes. Recommendations are made to senior management (and should not be evaluated by anyone with a vested interest in the current marketing communications function!). Recommendations that are approved are then implemented by the task force with the support of senior management. At Eaton, recommendations included a significant reduction in the number of ad agencies employed and the creation of a review procedure to make ads more uniform and effective.

5. Follow-up of some kind is needed to make sure recommendations are implemented and, in some cases, to improve the management of the marketing communications function. Eaton's solution was to create a group of four directors of communication, drawn from the divisions' communications managers, and give them oversight responsibility. The directors can monitor compliance with recommendations, reporting any problems directly to senior management.

Reference

Business Marketing (January 1989): 36.

ERNST & WHINNEY CUSTOMER-SERVICE PRINCIPLES

Applications

- Improving customer service by making it more effective and customer-oriented.
- Diagnosing problems with customer-service programs and measures.

Procedures

Use the checklist as a basis for an evaluation or audit of the customer-service function at your company, or establish strategies and guidelines for customer service based on it.

Cross-Reference

Strategic Planning Decisions—may be useful in developing strategic and marketing plans.

This checklist was developed by Gene Tyndall, a partner at Ernst & Whinney, in response to problems with the customer-service function at client companies. At many companies there is a lack of coordination among departments and a lack of a clear, customer-oriented vision when it comes to managing customer service. Use this list to measure how effectively your firm manages customer service and identify areas in need of improvement. Why not do a "customer service audit"? An audit is especially useful when problems and complaints have forced management to take a careful look at customer service, as it provides definition to an open-ended, company-wide issue.

Reprinted from *Marketing News*, published by the American Marketing Association. Gene R. Tyndall, "Seven Principles Help Achieve Successful Customer Service." September 26, 1988, vol. 22, No. 20.

THE CHECKLIST

Effective customer-service policies and activities have these characteristics:

1. *Linked to business strategy.* The company's approach to customer service should flow from its strategy, and a commitment to customer service is an important element of most strategies.

2. *Tailored to customer needs.* Assessment of customer needs and expectations should be a routine element of customer-service management. Often companies focus their resources on less-important aspects of customer service while overlooking aspects of more importance to customers.

3. *Uses customer-oriented measures of customer service.* How do customers evaluate and measure customer service? If the organization does not use the same approach, performance measurement is meaningless or at best misleading.

4. *Predictable and consistent.* Can customers rely on your organization's service? Consistency is important. Measurements of customer-service quality should consider distributions as well as means.

5. *Applied selectively.* Some customers are more important than others at most organizations. Multiple standards or a range of acceptable performance gives the company the ability to focus its resources on the most valuable customers. Also, customers may fall into groups based on differences in their needs—there can be different standards for each group.

6. *Designed to balance cost and benefit.* Customer-service programs should aim for an optimal balance between increased sales or profits and increased costs. Investments in customer service should be directed toward areas offering the greatest returns to the company.

7. *Constantly revised and renewed.* Customers evaluate a company's customer service relative to its competitors, so a program that is excellent today may be inferior tomorrow. Other factors

can also affect customer needs and perceptions, so to manage customer service well a company must continually evaluate needs and make innovations to meet their needs.

Reference

Tyndall, Gene R. "Seven Principles Help Achieve Successful Customer Service." *Marketing News* (September 26, 1988): 20. (Publication of the American Marketing Association.)

OGILVY'S SIXTEEN TIPS FOR TV ADS

Applications

- Reviewing proposals for TV advertising to make your commercials more effective and cost-effective.
- Identifying flaws in an unsuccessful advertising campaign.
- Providing specific instructions and feedback to ad agencies.

Procedures

Use the 16 tips as a checklist for reviewing ads or specifying new ad campaigns.

...I suspect that there is a negative correlation between the money spent on producing commercials and their power to sell products.
                              - David Ogilvy

Executives often have input into advertising decisions and tend to take special interest in TV advertising because of its cost and visibility. Various traditional methods for reviewing TV commercials—such as asking one's spouse or children for their opinion—are frowned upon by advertising agencies. Some agencies try to discourage any input by the client's management. But with advertising budgets in the millions and many bad commercials on the air, executives need to take a close look at advertising regardless of the agency's preferences.

David Ogilvy of Ogilvy and Mather has developed a list of tips for television advertisers that serves as a good checklist of errors to avoid, as well as a source of ideas and suggestions to make ads more effective and cheaper to produce. Review this list for ideas or use it as a screen when reviewing proposals and story boards from your agency. (I have edited and revised most material in this book with a heavy hand, but in this case I am reproducing the tips verbatim as Ogilvy's comments are both brief and entertaining.)

Ogilvy's sixteen tips

1. *Brand Identification.* Research has demonstrated that a shocking percentage of viewers remember your commercial, but forget the name of your product. All too often they attribute your commercial to a competing brand.

Many copywriters think it crass to belabor the name of the product. However, for the benefit of those who are more interested in selling than entertaining, here are two ways to register your brand name:

- Use the name within the first ten seconds. I have seen a brilliant commercial which repeated the brand name 20 times in 340 seconds without irritating anyone.

- Play games with the name. Spell it. Veterans will remember Alex Templeton, the blind pianist, spelling out the name C–R–E–S–T–A– B–L–A–N–K–A– to the accompaniment of pizzicato strings.

  When you advertise a new product, you have to teach people its name on television.

2. *Show the package.* Commercials which end by showing the package are more effective in changing brand preference than commercials which don't.

3. *Food in motion.* In commercials for food, the more appetizing you make it look, the more you sell. It has been found that *food in motion* looks particularly appetizing. Show chocolate sauce in the act of being poured over your ice cream, or syrup over your pancakes.

4. *Close-ups.* It is a good thing to use close-ups when your product is the hero of the commercial. The closer you get on the candy bar, the more you make people's mouths water.

5. *Open with fire.* You have only 30 seconds. If you grab attention in the first frame with a visual suprise, you stand a better chance of holding the viewer.

People screen out a lot of commercials because they open with something *dull.* You know that great things are about to happen, but the viewer doesn't.

She will *never* know; she has gone to the bathroom. When you advertise fire extinguishers, open with the fire.

6. *When you have nothing to say, sing it.* There have been some successful commercials which sang the sales pitch, but jingles are below average in changing brand preference.

Never use a jingle without trying it on people who have not read your script. If they cannot decipher the words, don't put your jingle on the air.

If you went into a store and asked a salesman to show you a refrigerator, how would you react if he started singing at you? Yet some clients feel short-changed if you don't give them a jingle.

Many people use music as background—emotional shorthand. Research shows that this is neither a positive nor a negative factor. It does no harm and it does no measurable good. Do great preachers allow organists to play background music under their sermons? Do advertising agencies play background music under their pitch to prospective clients?

7. *Sound effects.* While music does not add to the selling power of commercials, sound effects—such as sausages sizzling in a frying pan—can make a positive difference.

A commercial for Maxwell House was constructed around the sound of coffee percolating. It worked well enough to run for five years.

8. *Voice-over on camera?* Research shows that it is more difficult to hold your audience if you use voice-over. It is better to have the actors talk *on camera.* A manufacturer made two commercials, identical in every respect except that one used voice-over and the other used on-camera voice. When he tested them, the voice-on-camera version sold more of his product.

9. *Supers.* It pays to reinforce your promise by setting it in type and superimposing it over the video, while your soundtrack speaks the words.

But make sure that the words in your supers are *exactly the same as your spoken words.* Any divergence confuses the viewer.

Many people in agencies resist the use of supers. If you tell them that they increase sales, as they do, the stupid buggers turn a deaf ear.

10. *Avoid visual banality.* If you want the viewer to pay attention to your commercial, *show her something she has never seen before.* You won't have much success if you show her sunsets and happy families at the dinner table.

The average American family has seen the television turned on for six hours a day, and is exposed to 30,000 commericals a year. Most of them slide off the memory like water off a duck's back. For this reason you should give your commercials a touch of singularity, a visual burr that will stick in the viewer's mind. One such burr was the herd of bulls thundering towards the camera, with the superimposed title "Merrill Lynch is bullish on America."

11. *Changes of scene.* Hal Riney uses a great many scenes without confusing people, but I can't, and I bet you can't either. On the *average*, commercials with a plethora of scenes are below average in changing brand preference.

12. *Mnemonics.* This unpronounceable word is used to describe a visual device repeated over a long period. It can increase brand identification, and remind people of your promise. Example: the car driving through the paper barrier in Shell commercials.

13. *Show the product in use.* It pays to show the product being used, and, if possible, the end result of using it. Show how your diapers (nappies) keep the baby dry. In a commercial for motor oil, show how the pistons look after 50,000 miles.

14. *Everything is possible on TV.* The technicians can produce anything you want. *The only limit is your imagination.*

15. *Miscomprehension.* In 1979 Professor Jacoby of Purdue University studied the "miscomprehension" of 25 typical television commercials. He found that *all* of them were miscomprehended, some by as many as 40 percent of viewers, none by fewer than 19 percent.

If you want to avoid your television commercials being misunderstood, you had better make them *crystal clear.* I cannot understand more than half the commercials I see.

16. *The great scandal.* Television programs cost

about $4 a second to produce, but commercials cost $2,000 a second. Which is $60,000 for a 30-second commercial.

This obscene extravagance is largely the fault of the agencies. Says Hooper White, "Production dollars are typed into the commercial by the copywriter and drawn into the commercial by the art director." Miner Raymond of Procter & Gamble tells the story of an art director who objected to a table on the set. The client pointed out that it was covered by a cloth and thus invisible. "But *I* would know what's under the cloth," said the art director, "and it just wouldn't be right." So another table was found and the delay cost the client $5,000.

The easiest way to reduce the cost of a commercial is to cut actors out of the storyboard. Every actor you cut will save you between $350 and $10,000, depending on how long you run the commercial.

Copywriters specify that a commercial should be shot in Bali when it could equally well be shot in a studio for half the price. They insert expensive animation into live-action commercials. They insist that original music be composed for background purposes, as if there were nothing suitable in the whole repertoire of existing music. Worst of all, they use expensive celebrities when an unknown actor would sell more of the product.

I have no research to prove it, but I suspect that there is a negative correlation between the money spent on producing commercials and their power to sell products. My partner Al Eicoff was asked by a client to remake a $15,000 commercial for $100,000. Sales went *down*.

There you have it. Ample ammunition for the client-agency wars and good advice for anyone who is reviewing or developing TV commercials. If you find this advice helpful, I recommend the referenced book as well.

Reference

Ogilvy, David. *Ogilvy on Advertising* (pp. 110-13): New York: Vintage Books, 1985.

OTTESEN'S MARKET MAP

Applications

- Translating awareness and usage data into a visual display as an aid to developing marketing strategies and plans.

- Comparing competing products or a portfolio of products on the basis of consumer awareness and usage.

- Presenting survey research data to senior management.

Procedures

1. Obtain data on consumer awareness and usage of the product(s) in question (perform market research if necessary).

2. Create a market map for each product or brand by plotting trial and usage percentages on the vertical axis of a graph and awareness on the horizontal axis.

3. Use the market maps to develop marketing strategies and plans and to present survey statistics in a visual format for marketing plans and proposals.

Idea: Senior managers may want to request that the marketing department present all awareness/usage data from surveys in a standardized market map format to make interpretation easier.

Most market research surveys collect information on consumer awareness of a product, consumer usage of the product, and similar statistics on the product's competitors. Studies often break consumer behavior into unaided and aided awareness, trial, usage, and preference, and sometimes into even more detailed categories.

This information is useful in developing marketing strategies and tactics. For example, if a product has a low awareness figure (say only 15% of the market knows it exists), then the strategy should be to build awareness, probably through educational advertising and promotion. But when a company performs multiple surveys on many products, often using multiple research firms, a large, confusing collection of awareness and usage statistics is created. Management can find it difficult to sift through the reports and compare statistics to evaluate the appropriateness of a proposed strategy or tactic. The market map provides a simple, visual summary of these statistics, making it easier for management to utilize survey data for strategy development and oversight.

The only problem with the market map is that it contains so much information that it takes a little study to get used to the format. Once you are familiar with it, however, you should find it a simple and useful aid to marketing decisions.

INSTRUCTIONS

1. You need good data on awareness, trial, and usage of the brands you want to map. In general, larger companies' marketing departments already collect this information at least annually, but some industrial companies and smaller firms will not have current statistics. In this case, seriously consider hiring a research firm to perform a basic benchmark study. As long as you tell them to confine their research to the statistics needed, it should not prove too expensive. A survey should include the following:

- Unaided awareness (asks consumers to name brands/products/companies in the market)
- Aided awareness (asks if they have heard of specific brands)
- Trial (asks if they have tried the brand recently)
- Usage (asks if they have used the product regularly)
- Preference (asks if they prefer the product over competitors)

Sometimes studies break consumer behavior down into many more categories, depending on the model of consumer behavior and product adoption that the company and its research firm decide is most appropriate.

You must study a random sample of the potential users of your product, of course, in order to produce legitimate results. A telephone survey will give better results than a mail survey in most cases because the response rate will be much higher; thus the chances of respondents providing a fair representation of the original sample is higher. In addition, the name of your company and product should not be associated with the survey—the main reason why these surveys are usually performed by an independent research firm.

2. Create a market map for your product. Ottesen's market map simplifies survey results slightly by breaking consumers into the following categories:

1. Those who are aware of the product (versus those who aren't);
2. Those who have tried the product and prefer it;
3. Those who have tried the product, but have no strong preference—they are indifferent;
4. Those who have tried the product and do not currently use it—they have in essence rejected it.

Review your data to identify the percentage of consumers falling into each of these categories.

Note: These categories may or may not correspond to the data you have to work with. But simple logic should be sufficient to translate any study into Ottesen's categories. For example, the consumers who report trial of a product but do not report current, regular use or preference for it make up the group of rejectors—even if the survey did not specifically ask consumers whether they "rejected the product."

Next, create a graph with both axes ranging from 0 to 100%. Label the horizontal axis "Awareness" and draw a vertical line from it to represent the percentage of consumers who are aware of the product.

OTTESEN'S MARKET MAP

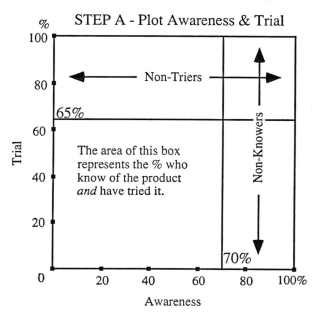

STEP A - Plot Awareness & Trial

The area of this box represents the % who know of the product *and* have tried it.

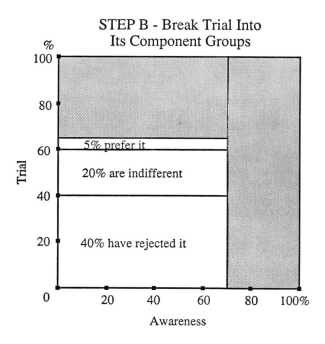

STEP B - Break Trial Into Its Component Groups

5% prefer it

20% are indifferent

40% have rejected it

Label the vertical axis "Trial" and draw a horizontal line representing the percentage of consumers who have tried the product (including those who have rejected it, are indifferent to it, and prefer it). Now divide the resulting box with additional horizontal lines to break down the group of triers into their three constituent groups. (Use the scale of the vertical axis to keep these areas in proportion to the rest of the graph.)

The illustration shows two steps in the creation of a market map—the first shows awareness and trial, and the second breaks down trial into its components.

3. Interpret the map. Use the map to identify and illustrate the key challenges and issues facing a product. (Prepare a time series of maps, and maps for a product's competitors in order to illustrate trends and competitive issues.)

Example:

The illustrations are for a product that has a 70% rate of awareness and 65% trial. This suggests that the company has done a good job of converting awareness to trial and does not need to focus on this in future marketing. But building awareness is good strategy, and marketing communications should adopt this as an objective.

When the triers on the map are broken into those who prefer, are indifferent to, or have rejected the product, other objectives are indicated as well. Only 25% of the respondents in the survey were users, and only 5% preferred the product. These statistics point to a need to encourage usage among those who try the brands, perhaps through promotional incentives to increase the trial period. The statistics may also indicate a lack of product strength. Advertising should be used to emphasize product benefits, and the product should be compared with its competition to see whether the low preference rate reflects a product weakness or simply a competitive market.

References

Otto Ottesen. "The response function." *Current Theories in Scandinavian Mass Communications Research*, ed. Mie Beg, Grenaa, Denmark: G.M.T., 1977.

Philip Kotler. *Marketing Management: Analysis, Planning, and Control*, 5th ed. (pp. 614–15). Englewood Cliffs, NJ: Prentice Hall, 1984.

ROGERS'S DIFFUSION OF INNOVATION FORECASTING

Applications

- Projecting adoption and use of a novel product or service.
- Structuring analysis of consumer attitudes for surveys of high-tech markets and potential markets.

Procedures

1. Develop a model of the evolution of consumer attitude toward your new product or service.
2. Test the model through focus-group research and usage surveys.
3. Use the model to project sales and map the product life cycle.

Cross-Reference

Product Development and Innovation.

High-tech companies frequently prepare revenue projections for products that do not yet exist. This is a difficult task, and the projections often prove wrong. Techniques from consumer-product research are not directly applicable to the problem, but market research can be used to improve projections if it is integrated into Rogers's model of adoption of innovation.

The model identifies a series of stages through which any consumer must go in the adoption process, then makes some assumptions about the rate at which different consumers go through this process. Use the model to help forecast adoption of any innovative new product, process, or service. It is helpful when deciding whether to fund an R&D project and also in setting marketing budgets and revenue projections for new products.

Some years ago I had the job of preparing revenue projections for the R&D proposals of a biotechnology company. Every day we would wrestle with the projections for another proposed product or process, and usually it came down to making our best guess. I trust executives will not be deceived by impressive graphs and tables—most market projections for new innovations are based on someone's best guess. Here is a method that helps refine the guesswork, at least ensuring that it will be in the ballpark in most cases. Insist on projections that address the rate and process of adoption if you want greater accuracy in new-product projections.

INSTRUCTIONS

1. Build a model of the adoption process.

The boiler-plate model hypothesizes that adopters must move through five stages:

1. *Awareness.* Has heard of it, but does not know much about it.

2. *Interest.* Thinks it might be good; looking for more information.

3. *Evaluation.* Considering the information to see whether it is worth pursuing.

4. *Trial.* Experiments with it to see whether it will work out.

5. *Adoption.* Likes it and decides to use it regularly.

This model is generally applicable, even to the diffusion of new ideas, but for some products additional stages may be necessary. For example, trial can be a lengthy, multistep process for a major new process-technology.

After defining the stages, identify the obstacles to adoption that are likely to arise at each stage. Start by thinking about the innovation and the target market and try to hypothesize what the obstacles will be. For example, if a new banking service requires access to a personal computer and modem, then acquisition of this equipment will be an obstacle in the movement from interest to evaluation.

Now form one more set of hypotheses—these concerning the rate at which people in the target market will move through the adoption process. Are there many obstacles? Then the rate will be slow. Are the majority of consumers in this market innovators and eager to adopt any hot new product? Then the average rate will be fast, and a high percentage will adopt the innovation early. Are some resistant to changes in the way they work and thus unlikely to adopt innovations that might change their work? Then they will lag well behind the early innovators.

The theory holds that consumers fall into multiple groups based on how fast they move through the stages of adoption and that the distribution of adoption rates over time is statisically normal (a standard bell shape). Use this normal distribution as a boilerplate model of the rate at which different consumers will adopt the innovation and alter it based on any extenuating circumstances:

ADOPTION RATES AND GROUPS

Group	Percent of population	Formal definition
Innovators	2.5	$X - 2\sigma$
Early Majority	34.0	X to $X - \sigma$
Late Majority	34.0‘	X to $X + \sigma$
Laggards	16.0	$X + \sigma$

X = Average time of adoption of the innovation
σ = Standard deviation of the distribution of adoption over time

2. Test the model through primary research.

If the projection is important, it is worthwhile to go the extra mile and test your hypotheses concerning the adoption cycle and the rate of adoption (the latter includes estimates of the average time of adoption and the distribution of consumers around this mean).

Qualitative methods, such as focus groups, are generally most useful at the early stages of product development. Gather potential adopters, describe the innovation, and ask them what obstacles they see in adopting it. Ask them how long it would take them to adopt it. Show them your hypothetical models and see what they think. While people do not always predict their own behavior with accuracy, they probably can predict it better than you can, so their feedback should be helpful.

The easiest and best way to do focus-group research is to hire a firm or individual specializing in recruiting the members and facilitating the meetings. When amateurs try this as a money-saving measure, the focus groups rarely go well. If you do not want to spend $10 to 30,000 on professional focus-group research, the best alternative is to conduct in-depth, one-on-one interviews.

Primary or secondary research should also be directed toward identifying and profiling consumers based on the speed with which they adopt innovations. Who are the innovators and how do you reach them? Are they really only 2.5% of the population? (If this is true, then scale down the first year's revenue projections!) Who is the early majority and how is it reached?

3. Use the model as an aid to revenue projections.

Steps 1 and 2 produce a fairly detailed model of the adoption process and provide a basic understanding of the demographics of adoption. Use the adoption process model to anticipate how long, on average, it will take the consumer to move through each stage. Use the demographic information to project how many will move through the adoption cycle at any specific time ahead of or behind the average.

Lay these projections over the typical data on projected market share. (It is important to project what the potential market is and what percent of it your marketing will capture, just as you would in a standard revenue projection.)

Example

You project a market of 100,000 consumers next year and expect that with a conventional product your firm's marketing effort could capture 20% of them as customers. Since you are introducing an innovation, your analysis also indicates that the average adoption time will be three years and that the "innovators," 2.5%, will be the only ones to adopt it in the first year. A conservative projection would therefore be 2.5% of the 20% share figure, or only 500 consumers who will adopt your innovation in the first year.

References

Everett M. Rogers. *Diffusion of Innovations.* New York: Free Press, 1962.

Philip Kotler. *Marketing Management: Analysis, Planning and Control.* 5th Ed., Englewood Cliffs, NJ: Prentice Hall, 1984.

STRATEGIC PLANNING INSTITUTE QUALITY ANALYSIS

Applications

- Ranking the product line of a business unit and its competitors on the basis of overall quality.
- Measuring quality for use in business-unit value maps.
- Developing quality-based positioning strategies for business units and product lines.

Procedures

1. Select a team of managers and staff to identify key product attributes affecting customer purchase decisions for a product line.
2. Weight each attribute by its importance to the purchase decisions of customers.
3. Rate each business unit's product line (yours and your competitors') by its relative quality on each attribute.
4. Verify managers' perceptions with market research if possible.
5. Multiply importance scores by quality scores and sum to create an overall quality score for each product line.
6. *Optional.* Rank business units on the basis of relative price, then plot quality and price on a value map.

Cross-Reference

Strategic Planning Decision.

The Strategic Planning Institute, a nonprofit consulting group that maintains the PIMS (profit impact of market strategy) database started at Harvard Business School, uses a simple method to assess product quality. Quality is an important variable in the PIMS database of companies, and because it is not measured and reported like financial statistics, the institute has had to develop its own method of measuring it.

The measurement of quality is of growing concern in many industries as the strategic implications of quality position are better understood. The PIMS database has been used to show that companies with higher quality products tend to be more profitable and hold more market share, for example. The Strategic Planning Institute emphasizes the concept of *value* in strategic planning and market positioning, drawing a value map for an entire business unit or portfolio using the method for measuring quality outlined in the following instructions. This is similar in concept to the James River Cost/Performance Matrix (in the product development and innovation section of this book) but can be applied more broadly, making it more suitable to development of broad marketing strategies.

INSTRUCTIONS

Before using this method it is important to define the business unit for study. As in a number of the methods in the section on strategic planning (Boston Consulting Group Matrix, GE Matrix), the unit of analysis must be a discrete business from a *marketing* perspective, not necessarily from the organization's accounting and reporting perspectives.

If, in the discussions associated with steps 1 and 2, it becomes apparent that there is more than one major segment of the market with important differences in attitudes and buying habits, then it is necessary to perform a separate analysis for each segment.

1. Managers and staff from various departments are selected for their knowledge of the business and their ability to bring multiple viewpoints to the table. They are asked to identify product or service attributes, aside from price, that have an impact on customer purchase decisions. If they have difficulty achieving consensus on this list, try using the Nominal Group Technique (in "General Decision-Making Tools").

Note: Sometimes an industry overlooks an attribute, only to have an upstart come in and steal share by emphasizing this overlooked attribute. So it is important to cast a broad net in this inquiry, looking at the product positioning and advertising of competitors as well as your own.

2. The management group assigns importance weights to each attribute. These weights reflect the importance of each attribute in customer decisions. Use decimal ratings that sum to 1 or percents that sum to 100%. (For ideas on how to do this, see step 3B in the GE Matrix in "Strategic Planning Decisions.")

3. Next, the managers rate the business unit's product line, and the product lines of all the major competitors on each of these attributes. Use a numerical scale (I prefer a 1 to 10 scale with 1 equaling bad and 10 equaling excellent).

One way to do this is to draw up a list of the attributes, adding a 1 to 10 scale to the right of each. Then duplicate this list for each competitor and hand the lists out for rating by each manager. Collect the scores, average them, and if there was an unacceptable amount of variation in the answers, discuss the ratings and repeat the process.

4. Verify managers' perceptions. If possible, refer to existing market research studies or perform survey research to verify the list of attributes and the ranking of each competitor's product line by attribute. Existing studies are more likely to include attribute analysis by product than for entire product lines, but this information ought to show some correspondence with the product line ranking by management.

Note: When management views are tested against customer perception, it is not uncommon to find that management overestimates the quality of its product line relative to competitors and *overestimates* the importance of attributes on which its products are strongest.

5. Create an overall measure of the quality of each business unit's product line. This is a simple mechanical process—multiply the importance weights from

step 2 by the quality ratings from step 3 to establish the quality score (between 1 and 10) for each business unit.

6. *Optional.* Use the quality measure to create a quality/price map of the market. To do this you will have to create an overall rating of price position as well as product-line quality for each business unit. Ask managers to rank overall price position on a 1 to 10 scale, with 1 = very low and 10 = very high. Or,

STRATEGIC PLANNING INSTITUTE VALUE MAP
With Average Performances from the PIMS Database

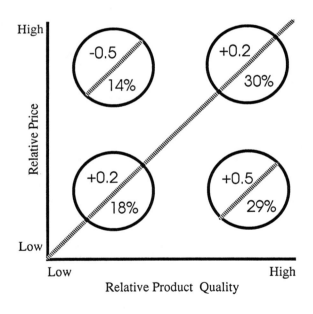

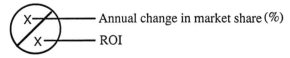

Annual change in market share (%)

ROI

for a more lengthy but more accurate method, rank each product in the line versus the competition and average the individual product rankings for each product line.

Plot each business unit on a graph with relative price on the vertical axis and relative quality on the horizontal axis. A diagonal line sloping upward from the origin represents combinations of price and quality that are of equal value. Businesses above this line are offering lower value (higher price for the quality) while firms below the line offer higher value by pricing lower for the quality offered.

It is interesting to note that the PIMS database, summarizing the performance of hundreds of businesses over time, supports the theory that firms benefit from a strong quality position. The illustration of the value map includes summary statistics from PIMS showing market share and ROI benefits.

References

Bradley T. Gale, *How Advertising Affects Profitability and Growth for Consumer Businesses.* Cambridge, MA: The Strategic Planning Institute, 1987.

Luchs, Robert. "Successful Businesses Compete on Quality, Not Costs." *Long Range Planning* 19(1), (1986): 12–17.

"Study Product Quality/Profit Relationship so Firms Can Leapfrog over Foreign Competitors." *Marketing News* (January 21, 1983). (Interview with Bradley Gale of Harvard Business School and the Strategic Planning Institute.)

TECHNOLOGY MARKETING'S MISSING-PIECE ANALYSIS

Applications

- Identifying key weaknesses in competitors to plan competitive strategy and anticipate competitor moves.
- Organizing and presenting competitor information and market research for use in planning marketing strategy.

Procedures

1. Rate each competitor's strength on the six dimensions:—product, manufacturing, sales and marketing, finance, management, and corporate culture.
2. Create a competitive-strengths matrix to display each competitor's scores on each dimension and highlight the weakest dimensions.

Missing-piece analysis translates the wealth of competitor intelligence now collected at many firms into specific, action-oriented information by focusing on finding each competitor's greatest weakness. The technique was developed by F. Michael Hruby of Technology Marketing Group and founder of the Society for Competitor Intelligence Professionals.

Missing-piece analysis involves a strengths/weaknesses analysis of each competitor on six competitive dimensions. The goals are (1) to identify weaknesses on each dimension and (2) to see whether any one weakness stands out as a major vulnerability. Usually

Adapted from *Marketing News*, published by the American Marketing Association. F. Michael Hruby. Missing Piece Analysis targets the Competitor's weakness. January 2, 1989, pages 10–12.

companies have a key weakness that can be exploited—the "missing piece" of missing-piece analysis.

INSTRUCTIONS

1. Rate the competitor in each of the six areas using the following scale:

> 5 excellent/superior
> 4 very strong/competitive
> 3 adequate/average
> 2 weak/uncompetitive
> 1 very weak

The six areas are:

1. *Product.* How strong the competitor's product and/or product line is relative to yours from the consumer's perspective.

2. *Manufacturing.* How the competitor stands relative to you in capabilities, costs, and capacity.

3. *Sales and marketing.* How well the competitor sells its product: effectiveness of positioning, sales force, strategies, advertising, and so on.

4. *Finance.* How strong the competitor's financial resources and performance are relative to the requirement for launching a strong competitive strategy.

5. *Management.* How effective, aggressive, and qualified the competitor's management is based on past performance or recent changes.

6. *Corporate culture.* Whether values and history make the competitor likely to enter or try to dominate your markets, or to develop new products for them.

Repeat the analysis for every competitor of interest.

2. Enter scores in a competitive-strengths matrix, as in the illustration. This is a table listing competitors down the right side and competitive dimensions across the top; scores are entered in the appropriate cells. Highlight the worst score for each competitor— this is their weakest point and should be watched. It

is important to strategy to anticipate which competitors will try to enter a new market and whether and how to attack a competitor or respond to a challenge in existing markets.

COMPETITIVE-STRENGTHS MATRIX

Competitor	Competitive dimensions					
	1	2	3	4	5	6
A	5	3	4	**2**	4	3
B	4	4	3	**2**	3	4
C	**1**	3	3	5	2	3
D	4	5	4	4	5	4

Competitors A and B are weak on the fourth competitive dimension, finance. They do not have the strength to launch major advertising campaigns in support of a new product. A product launched to attack their positions will probably succeed if you are willing to spend a lot of money on advertising. Company C's product is not as good as yours, so your strategy could also include an effort to gain share from C by emphasizing product differences in your marketing communications. However, efforts to gain share from competitor D are less likely to succeed since it is strong on all dimensions. The matrix also provides clues to a competitor's future behavior. Competitor D, with an aggressive and competent management team and a strong product, is likely to make a strong move—perhaps establishing a cost position since it is also strong in manufacturing. Competitor C, with a poor product but financial strength, might be expected to launch a new product soon. But they may delay—their management score is very low. Competitors A and B also are unlikely to introduce major new brands in the near future due to financial weakness.

Reference

F. Michael Hruby. "Missing Piece Analysis Targets the Competitor's Weakness." *Marketing News* (January 2, 1989): 10–12 (Published by the American Marketing Association.)

TEMPLE, BARKER & SLOANE CROSS-SELLING FACTORS

Applications

- Evaluating a proposed cross-selling strategy (new product or service for an existing sales or distribution channel).
- Diagnosing problems with new-product or service introductions.
- Developing an agenda for new-product market planning.

Procedures

1. Determine whether the new product (or service) has a strong or weak strategic fit with the products currently sold through the distribution channel by looking at the six factors that make up the strategic dimension.

2. Evaluate the support structures available for the new product by looking for any one of the four factors making up the support dimension.

3. Evaluate the management practices to make sure that none of the four factors on this dimension are missing.

Cross-Reference

Sales Management Decisions

Narrowing margins in the financial services industry have pushed companies to add new products in an effort to keep sales channels profitable. Deregulation has also encouraged expansion of product lines into new areas; but cross-selling of financial services has proven difficult and many new products and services have failed. The experience of the financial services industry suggests that a cautious strategic approach to cross-selling is necessary.

William Sherden, who heads Temple, Barker & Sloane's Financial Services Industry Group, has developed a qualitative 14-factor model for evaluating proposed cross-selling programs based on his observations of success and failure in the financial industry. It organizes relevant factors along three dimensions: strategic fit, support structures, and management practices. Cross-selling proposals are evaluated on each of these dimensions to identify problems and estimate the chances of success. The model also provides insight into the type of cross-selling strategy to use. Although developed for financial services companies, it is general in nature and can be applied by any company. It is especially useful for service companies, which often encounter problems in introducing a new service through an existing distribution channel.

INSTRUCTIONS

1. Strategic fit.

To evaluate a proposed cross-sell, first determine whether it has a strong or weak strategic fit with the products currently sold through the distribution channel. Evaluate strategic fit based on the six factors that contribute to it:

Factor	Description
Customer Match	New product is for existing customers.
Point of Need	The distribution channel can deliver the new product when and where needed.
Preference for Shopping	Customers will prefer buying the new product through the existing channel (versus shopping around).

Factor	Description
Value Added	Additional value is brought to the customer by selling the new product through the existing distribution channel.
Sales and Service Match	The new product's requirements for sales and service are similar to current products' requirements.
Credibility	Customers are loyal to the distribution channel, and new product introductions will be considered credible as a result.

2. Support structures.

Next, evaluate the support structures available for the new product. Any one of four factors contributing to support can determine whether the new product is supported well enough to succeed:

Factor	Description
Product Bundling	The new product is so similar to old products that it scores high on all strategic fit factors and can be bundled with them. No special support needed.
Full-Service Distributors	The new product is similar to existing products, and distributors can therefore take responsibility for all aspects of sales and service.

Factor	Description
Team-Selling	The new product is too dissimilar to existing products for distributors to take full responsibility, but a sales support structure exists to team-sell with the distributors.
Referral Systems	When a new product is too different to support it through bundling, distributors, or team-selling, a dedicated division can be used to sell it. The existing channel is used only to generate prospects and refer them to the separate sales organization.

3. Management practices.

Evaluate the management practices that provide the context for the product introduction. Management practice is the third essential dimension for successful cross-selling. Management can create an atmosphere and policies conducive to cross-sales by focusing on these four factors. If any of the factors are missing, problems can be expected.

Factor	Description
Single-Product Focus	Adding only one product at a time to a channel makes it easier for the organization and customers to absorb the change.
Reward Systems	Incentives must be altered to encourage sales of the new product.

Factor	Description
Marketing	Marketing systems must support the cross-selling through training and collateral, and information systems for the distributor or salesperson.
Organizational Harmony	Policies and reward systems should be designed to reduce conflict and turf wars, and the home office must avoid becoming too secluded to be able to support distributors effectively.

Review each of the factor tables point by point and develop an overall evaluation for the cross-selling plan on each of the three dimensions. A weakness on any dimension—strategy, support, or management—should be addressed before the plan is implemented. A strength of this model is that the factors are quite specific, so it generates an evaluation based on specific and action-oriented weaknesses.

Reference

William S. Sherden. "Practical Strategies for Cross-Selling." *The Bankers Magazine*, (January–February 1989): 12–17. (Warren, Gorham & Lamont, Boston.) Copyright Warren, Gorham & Lamont Inc., 210 South Street, Boston, MA 02111. All rights reserved.

TROUT & REIS MARKETING WARFARE STRATEGIES

Applications

- Analyzing strategic options in competitive markets.
- Developing marketing strategies that reflect your competitive position in the marketplace.
- Reviewing marketing plans and projections to see if they make realistic assumptions about competitors.
- Evaluating the significance of competitors' moves and developing responses.

Procedures

1. Determine what position a product is in based on its share and other measures of competitive strength.
2. Apply the appropriate marketing warfare principles to develop a marketing strategy consistent with competitive position or to review current strategy for consistency.

Cross-Reference

Strategic Planning Decisions

Al Reis and Jack Trout applied principles of warfare to marketing strategy to provide insight into the increasingly competitive consumer markets of their firm's advertising clients. Urging a retreat from marketing's traditional focus on customer needs, they preach a doctrine of competitor orientation in their book and workshops. But even if you are not ready to embrace this doctrine whole-heartedly, the four marketing strategies they identify and the associated principles are a useful aid to decisions concerning marketing strategy.

INSTRUCTIONS

1. Analyze your company's position in the marketplace. The most important variable in this analysis is market share, but other statistics relating to "share of mind," such as awareness and geographic coverage, should also be considered to determine whether your company (or an individual product) is a leader, a strong #2 or #3, a weak contender for a leadership position (i.e., #3 or #4), or a small-fry in the marketplace.

2. Your position in the market—leader, contender, or guerilla—determines what types of marketing warfare you can pursue.

The principles of the four types of marketing warfare strategies are as follows:

Defensive

1. Only the leader can play defense.
2. The best defensive strategy is to attack yourself, not your enemy.
3. Always block strong competitive moves.

Comments: Leaders should never ignore challenges, but neither should they wait for a challenge before introducing new products and services. A moving target is harder to hit.

Caution: A company should not claim leadership lightly or it will not have the strength to implement a true defensive strategy.

IBM is clearly a market leader. But Consolidated Freightways, one of three leading less-than-truckload trucking companies in the U.S., proclaims itself "miles ahead" beneath its logo. However, this does not give it the dominance of an IBM; its management must not be seduced by the advertising claim into pursuing a defensive strategy.

Competitive Strategy

Position	Defensive	Offensive	Flanking	Guerilla
Leader	X		X	
Strong Contender		X	X	
Weak Contender			X	
Small Fry				X

Offensive

1. Focus primarily on the strength of the leader's position.
2. Find a weakness in the leader and attack it.
3. Launch as narrow and focused an attack as possible.

Comments: Challengers act like leaders when they act independently. Do not adopt the goal of increasing your share by $x\%$. On the offensive, your goal must be to *decrease* the leader's market share or increase yours relative to theirs. The best way to do this is to be strongest where the leader is weakest. Since the leader is stronger, an offensive strategy must focus narrowly on key weaknesses.

Flanking

1. Move into an uncontested area.
2. Surprise is important in a flanking move.
3. Pursuit is as important as the initial attack; reinforce successful flanking moves.

Comments: Flanking strategies require innovation—development of new products or markets. Many great flanking moves involve resegmenting the market by introducing lower-or higher-priced products, smaller or larger products, or products and services with some other distinguishing character. Recognizing a trend early and tailoring a product to it is a good way to attack through flanking, but surprise is obviously important. As soon as the flanking move is proved successful (even in a test market) it may be copied by competitors. Therefore speed or stealth is essential.

Caution: Flanking usually involves a new product or market segment, making it a high-risk, high-reward strategy.

Guerilla marketing

1. Find a market segment that is small enough for you to defend.

2. Don't let success tempt you to act like the leader.

3. Be prepared to retreat—and to enter new niche markets quickly.

Comments: This is the strategy for most of the players in any market—companies that are too small to take on the leaders directly but are able to become big fish in ponds that are small enough and far enough from home for the leaders to ignore. (In contrast, a flanking move targets a segment that is important to the leader.) The guerrilla marketer must establish dominance over the leader in a small niche market. If the leader moves into this market and gains superior share, it is time to find another market.

Caution: Trout and Reis warn that guerillas seldom succeed when they try to expand from their local markets and launch flanking attacks against the leader because they do not have the resources to compete "in the open." They call this the "line extension trap." They also warn against becoming staff-heavy and formal like the market leaders since guerillas need to concentrate their people in the field and to make decisions quickly.

Reference

Al Ries and Jack Trout. *Marketing Warfare*. New York: McGraw-Hill, 1986.

PART 5

Organization and Human Resources

ALBRECHT'S ORGANIZATIONAL POLITICS ANALYSIS

Applications

- Identifying major political elements of an organization's culture and management style.
- Analyzing the role of politics in organizational decision making.

Procedures

The method breaks politics down into five types of activities. Look for each type of activity in the organization and identify participants.

Politics plays a role in the decisions of most organizations and helps determine which managers have the most influence. Sometimes politics interfere with effective management, but in many cases the overall impact is neutral or even positive. The senior manager who assesses the role of politics in the organization can benefit from a better understanding of the actions and advice of managers. Political activity can also be assessed to see whether it is "out of control," interfering with the business of the organization or denying certain managers access to needed resources. If an assessment of politics is necessary, this is one of the few methods available. It is a qualitative tool that relies on the judgment and observations of the evaluator, so it is best used by someone familiar with the organization. Its focus is on the politics at the top of an organization, since this is where politics can have the strongest influence.

INSTRUCTIONS

The method is based on a model of organizational politics that breaks down political actions into five general categories. Each category represents a range of possible political activities. When an organization is analyzed category by category, a clear and detailed picture of political relationships emerges. The five categories are defined as follows:

1. *Inner-circle relationships.* Status of "inner circle" upper managers in relation to the chief executive. Friendliness of relationships among inner-circle managers. Amount of collaboration. Existence of special groups or an out-group or ostracized member.

2. *Axis of influence.* Any links from middle management on up to the executive office or near it that provide a certain manager or area with more influence than others (sometimes based on friendship interests).

3. *Informal power centers.* People or departments that carry an unusual amount of weight in the organization. Can be due to special expertise, control over limited resources, or a real or perceived special relationship with senior management.

4. *Polarizing elements.* Feuds or long-standing disputes between managers or between a manager and his or her subordinates. Any competitive or negative interpersonal relationships that bring an emotional element into interactions and lead to disagreements.

5. *Informal coalitions.* Groups of managers that tend to take sides in disputes or discussions.

Use the preceding list to identify any of these political elements within the organization. Together they form a political landscape that, when understood and mapped, helps explain the behavior of managers.

Idea: If you want to look at the role of politics in multiple organizations (such as the subsidiaries or departments of a company), you can attach rating scales to the above list and pass it out to organization members to find out how they assess the strength of each of the possible political elements on the overall direction of management decisions in their organization. Add a sixth rating scale for an overall assessment of the influence of politics.

If politics has an undue influence on management actions and decisions, as is the case when a bitter feud divides executives, it is sometimes necessary to move people in order to deemphasize a political element.

Reference

Karl Albrecht. *Organization Development: A Total Systems Approach to Positive Change in Any Business Organization* (pp. 86–88). Englewood Cliffs, NJ: Prentice Hall, © 1983.

ALLERGAN INTERNATIONAL'S HR PLANNING

Applications

- Creating competitive advantage for an organization through strategic management of human resources.
- Integrating corporate objectives into the management of the human resources function.
- Building human resources and increasing the returns on human resources.

Procedures

1. Human-resource management participates in and studies corporate strategic plans.
2. Human resources' key issues are identified based on corporate strategies and objectives.
3. Specific objectives are identified after studying the issues.
4. Strategies are set for human resources.
5. Specific programs and actions are defined.
6. A plan is prepared and submitted to senior management for feedback and approval.

Cross Reference

Strategic Planning Decisions

This multistep planning model was developed by the director of human resources of Allergan Pharmaceuticals' International Division in collaboration with the Business Strategy Institute. It was developed in response to rapid (20%) annual growth and associated changes in organizational structure. The organization's staffing needs were changing, and the jobs of current staff and managers were evolving. A method was needed to identify and address key human-resources issues and to build the contributions of human resources to the organization's strategic objectives.

The human-resources function is moving toward a more active role in many corporations, whether due to the demands of growth, international competition, or increasing need for skilled labor and management. This method is applicable to many businesses, and any that are not happy with their current human-resources planning should take a close look at it.

INSTRUCTIONS

1. Participation in corporate strategy.

Human resources (HR) is integrated into the corporate strategic planning process in two ways. First, HR management should participate in the development of corporate strategy by presenting an assessment of HR and identifying important HR issues for the corporate plan. Second, HR managers should study the corporate plan to identify its implications for management and planning within human resources. The corporate plan is the foundation of the HR planning effort.

2. Definition of HR issues.

Issue analysis is used to develop a list of key issues and to select one or a few to focus on in the plan. The primary source for issues is the corporate plan. Changes brought about by diversification, entry into new markets or geographic areas, new manufacturing technologies, new distribution channels, and so forth all have implications for staffing, performance evaluation, culture, and organization. Here are examples of key issues selected by Allergan:

- Future mix of managers (percent inside versus outside)
- Reward and compensation needed to attract future managers
- Values and beliefs to be fostered

3. Identify HR objectives.

Performance objectives are defined for HR. These follow from the issues—if an important issue is how to meet anticipated sales staffing needs, analysis of the problem might lead to the objective of developing new sales-compensation policies to attract more and more technically sophisticated sales personnel. Objectives should be defined as clearly and specifically as possible.

4. Set HR strategy.

Strategies to accomplish the objectives are developed for the human-resources function and for any specific component functions if necessary. This is the stage at which management has to decide how to pursue objectives, identifying specific strategies that will contribute to each objective. Increasing the technical training of current salespeople is a strategy that might contribute to the objective of increasing the technical sophistication of the sales force.

5. Set programs and actions.

Programs are developed in two categories—those addressing existing problems and those addressing problems or needs that are anticipated due to organizational changes and strategies. Action plans should be associated with each program, specifying how and when the programs will be accomplished and who will be responsible for them. The programs should follow directly from the strategies. For example, a program of three-day intensive-training seminars for salespeople follows from the strategy of increasing the technical sophistication of the sales force. The action plan for this program should include who will do the training, where, how many times, and so forth. Budgets can be developed at this stage as well.

6. Review and approval.

The objectives, strategies, and programs are put into written form and submitted to senior management for review. If certain programs do not fully meet strategic needs, feedback can be incorporated and the plan modified at this stage.

These procedures are not unlike those used in some companies for corporate planning, but it is unusual to find them applied within the human-resources function. The authors of this method offer the following advice to human resources executives who are not accustomed to the strategic-planning process:

> The strategy can be fully implemented only if it is methodically and patiently put together and if the HR executives are fully committed to using the strategic plan to direct departmental activities.
>
> - R. Kent Nethery and Y.N. Chang

Reference

R. Kent Nethery and Y.N. Chang. "Developing Human Resource Strategy." *Handbook of Business Strategy: 1986/1987 Yearbook*, ed. William D. Guth (pp. 24–1 to 24–8). Warren, Gorham & Lamont, 1986.

GRAPHIC PERFORMANCE-RATING SCALE

Applications

- Rating of performance in quantitive terms on standardized evaluation criteria.
- Overcoming supervisor bias/inconsistency in existing rating scales.
- Bringing qualitative information into a performance-rating system.

Procedures

1. Establish standard rating scales for evaluators to use in your organization.
2. Establish a standard distribution for evaluators' ratings and procedures to allow occasional deviation from the standard distribution.
3. Integrate critical-incident analysis into the evaluation.

This rating method is in use in many organizations in one form or another because it brings a measure of objectiveness and standardization to performance evaluation without increasing the time or difficulty of the task. It also provides a simple vehicle for senior management to set performance criteria throughout the organization

Note: This method has two important flaws, and this presentation of the method includes strategies to overcome them. The first flaw is lack of consistency between different supervisors. Some tend to rate higher or lower than others while some stick to the middle of the rating scale, making company wide comparisons of scores unfair. The second is a lack of qualitative and personalized evaluation. The use of any standard scale does not allow room for either qualitative feedback or recognition of unusual performance, and it does not provide detailed feedback to employees. But a rating system can be designed that addresses these concerns while maintaining the standardization and simplicity of graphic rating scales.

INSTRUCTIONS

1. Establish standardized rating scales. Select general descriptors of performance, emphasizing aspects of performance that are important to your organization or a class of jobs within it. Typical descriptors include quantity and quality of work, initiative, reliability, cooperativeness, and knowledge of the job. Define each in a short sentence or two to make sure all evaluators interpret them similarly (e.g., define *reliability* as dependability, conscientiousness, thoroughness, accuracy, and conformance with the organization's schedules and customs for work performance, breaks, and arrival and departure times).

Prepare a form listing these performance variables and their definitions down the left side, and providing a five-point scale (often composed of separate squares to be checked) across the right side. Label the scale as follows:

> outstanding
> good
> satisfactory
> fair
> unsatisfactory

2. Assign a distribution to the categories that each evaluator should follow under normal circumstances. For example:

outstanding	10%
good	20%
satisfactory	40%
fair	25%
unsatisfactory	5%

By requiring each supervisor to match or approximate this distribution, evaluator bias is minimized. However, in some cases differences in distribution would be justified by an exceptional number of good or bad performers, or simply because small numbers keep a department from achieving anything like a statistically normal distribution. So evaluators must also be permitted to make exceptions to the standard distribution.

To accommodate this requirement, ask each evaluator to summarize his or her evaluations in a standard format that includes a distribution and a justification of any deviation from the required distribution. If management observes that certain evaluators routinely vary from the norm without compelling justification, their appraisals can be revised.

3. Add a "critical-incident" evaluation to the evaluation form (or integrate another personalized evaluation technique).

The object of this step is to provide a vehicle for recognition of noteworthy individual performance that falls through the cracks of the standard evaluation categories. The critical-incident approach involves maintenance of a weekly or monthly log on each employee. Supervisors enter notes on incidents leading to exceptional performance (whether bad or good) in this log. To make sure the discipline of maintaining the log is kept up, require supervisors to enter *something* every period for each employee, even if it is simply a note that no critical incidents were observed. At evaluation time, the critical incidents are summarized in a written report and/or reviewed face-to-face with the employee.

Add a separate item, "Critical Incidents," to the standardized graphic rating scale to summarize the critical incident log. Use the following five-point scale:

> exceptionally positive
> positive
> neutral/none
> negative
> exceptionally negative

Then the written summary of the critical incidents can be attached to provide detailed feedback on performance.

Reference

A. H. Locker and K. S. Teel. "Performance Appraisal: A Survey of Current Practices." *Personnel Journal* (May 1977). (Discusses use of graphic rating scales and other techniques.)

HERZBERG JOB ENRICHMENT MODEL

Applications

- Improving employee performance by increasing satisfaction and motivation.
- Making work more interesting and challenging for employees through changes in the nature of the job they perform.
- Increasing productivity and reducing problems such as turnover and absenteeism in "problem" jobs.
- Obtaining long-term increases in employee motivation (versus the short-term effects of monetary incentives).

Procedures

1. Select a specific job in which employees are performing below desired levels and are difficult to motivate.
2. Identify accurate and meaningful measures of the quality of these employees' work to facilitate analysis of the impact of the methodology.
3. List job characteristics that could be changed to increase motivation, concentrating on "motivator" rather than "hygiene" factors. (Motivator factors are aspects of the work which facilitate employee growth.)
4. Develop a list of possible changes in job content and structure, referring to the job characteristics list developed in step 3 and Herzberg's principles of vertical job loading.
5. Select the changes that are easiest to implement and most likely to motivate according to Herzberg's theory.

6. Measure performance to identify the impact of job changes.

Cross-Reference

This method is related to Doyle's Sales-Force Motivation Model in "Sales Management Decisions."

Most employee motivation efforts focus on factors such as salary, work conditions, and supervisor relations. But these are *not* strong motivators according to Frederick Herzberg's model.

His theoretical approach is difficult to understand without a brief grounding in the theory. Studies by Herzberg and others have identified factors related to work experiences and divided these into "hygiene" versus "motivator" factors. Hygiene factors are related to the fulfillment of physical needs, such as the need for food or housing. Salary is a hygiene factor since it provides money for satisfying physical needs. Motivator factors, in contrast, are related to the fulfillment of needs for *psychological* growth through achievement, recognition, interesting work, responsibility, and advancement. Motivator factors are typically intrinsic to the job and for this reason are sometimes called job content factors. Hygiene factors constitute the environment for the job.

In the Herzberg model satisfaction is equated with motivation and dissatisfaction with lack of motivation. Herzberg has found that hygiene factors can be powerful dissatisfiers, but rarely are powerful satisfiers. In other words, factors such as salary and supervision must meet expectations to avoid dissatisfaction and reduced motivation, but raising them beyond expectations does not lead to equally strong increases in satisfaction and motivation. Motivator factors, on the other hand, are much more likely to be associated with satisfaction and do not lead to dissatisfaction very frequently.

These findings led Herzberg to focus on job content factors, developing an approach to motivation that "enriches" the job content to provide more opportunities for psychological growth.

Note: This does not equate directly with the concept of giving people more responsibilities or higher targets as a motivating factor. Unless the right job content factors are emphasized, changing the job content will not build motivation.

INSTRUCTIONS

1. Select a job for an enrichment program. In many companies there is more than one job that has frustrated managers' previous efforts to overcome productivity and quality problems, improve employee attitudes, and reduce turnover and absenteeism. One of these problem jobs will make a good test case for the Herzberg method, especially if efforts to cure the problem have become costly. (Avoid jobs in which the nature of the work cannot be altered without extensive changes to expensive machinery, however.)

2. Identify useful measures of work quality for the group you wish to motivate. It is essential to start measuring their productivity before job content is modified in order to make before-and-after comparisons possible. Many staff and manufacturing jobs lend themselves to direct measures of both the quantity and quality of work. Other jobs are harder to measure directly, but surveys of the workers and/or the consumers of their work can be used for sales, management, and other jobs that are hard to measure directly. Turnover, absenteeism, complaints, and similar statistics from the personnel department are also useful for before-and-after comparisons.

Note: A measurement tool of some kind is advisable since Herzberg's method is still considered experimental and most managers will want hard evidence that it works on a pilot group in their company before they apply it broadly.

3. Identify job characteristics that are likely to create motivation. This is a two-step process. First, in cooperation with the supervisors or managers who are most familiar with the job in question (and perhaps several employees as well), create a detailed

list of the important factors affecting the employees in this job. (Herzberg's research approach is to ask employees what events lead to satisfaction or dissatisfaction on the job, then group these events into general categories to define a list of factors. But in most cases the user will not need to do an employee survey.)

After asking hundreds of people what on-the-job events led to satisfaction or dissatisfaction, Herzberg has identified 16 categories of job factors. He reports that 1,753 different events fall into one of these categories, so the list should encompass all the factors you identify as well. (The list follows.)

Second, match your list of job factors to the list to see which of the factors you identified are likely to be strong motivators. The list is ranked based on how likely factors are to determine extreme satisfaction for employees.

Very High Impact:	Achievement
	Recognition
High Impact:	The work itself
	Responsibility
Medium Impact:	Advancement
	Growth
	Salary
Low Impact:	Company policy and administration
	Supervision
	Relationship with supervisor
	Work conditions
	Relationship with peers
	Personal life
	Relationship with subordinates
	Status
	Security

The items at the top of the list are the motivator or job content factors; many managers will be surprised to see them ranked higher than salary, relationship with supervisor, status, and other factors that are traditionally emphasized in a motivation program.

Note: Reference to this list will help focus attention away from traditional factors and toward these motivators.

4. Develop a list of possible changes in job content and structure, regardless of quality or acceptability. (Apply the rules of brainstorming if you do this with a group of managers. Do not include employees in this step.) Drop changes that are based on factors having a low impact on motivation according to the list above. Try to make each item on the list specific; rather than listing "more responsibility," say what specific responsibilities will be given to employees.

Example: Make employees responsible for measuring conformance of their own work to quality standards and for rejecting poor-quality pieces. Herzberg's principles of horizontal job loading can be used to screen ideas or as an additional source of ideas about how to change the nature of the job to make it more motivating.

PRINCIPLES OF VERTICAL JOB LOADING

Principle	Motivators involved
A. Removing some controls while retaining accountability	Responsibility and personal achievement
B. Increasing the accountability of individuals for own work	Responsibility and recognition
C. Giving a person a complete natural unit of work (module, division, area, and so on)	Responsibility, achievement, and recognition
D. Granting additional authority to employees in their activity; job freedom	Responsibility, achievement, and recognition
E. Making periodic reports directly available to the workers themselves rather than to supervisors	Internal recognition

| F. Introducing new and more difficult tasks not previously handled | Growth and learning |
| G. Assigning individuals specific or sepcialized tasks, enabling them to become experts | Responsibility, growth, and advancement |

(From Harvard Business Review, Sept.–Oct. 1987, p. 114 Copyright © 1987 by the President and Fellows of Harvard College; all rights reserved.)

Warning: Supervisors may find this step difficult because many of the proposals will involve taking responsibility from the supervisor and giving it to the employee. Strategies to gain supervisor acceptance include asking them to commit to the ideas only if performance measures show they work and discussing how their jobs can be enriched using the extra time previously devoted to checking and error correction.

5. Select job changes from the list, emphasizing those that rely on job content factors and rank as high motivators; also screen them for practicality and ease of application. Apply the ideas as job changes, introducing only one per week so as to make it possible to orient and train employees to each change. (A program introducing changes for each of the seven principles of vertical job loading would need two months for the application and training phase.)

Note: Herzberg advises dividing the employees into two groups and keeping one as a control to make the measurement of impact more rigorous. If two or more groups of employees do the same job at separate locations, this is easy to do. Otherwise, it may not be practical to keep a control group isolated from the group whose jobs are changed.

6. Track performance and attitude measures to see whether the job changes improve employee performance. Expect performance to fall off initially as employees learn their new jobs. If the program is a

success, however, measures should show a clear improvement within a few weeks of the last changes. If improvements are not clear-cut, examine the job changes to make sure they represent vertical rather than horizontal loading (discussed under "Avoid Horizontal Loading").

Idea: Measure return on investment. Since Herzberg introduced his theory it has become fashionable to estimate ROI for employee training programs, and there is no reason why ROI cannot be estimated for a job enrichment program as well. The investment is largely in the form of up-front management time needed, plus the costs of training and any short-term declines in productivity resulting from job changes. The return is easily measured in a manufacturing setting using the long-term increases in productivity, plus estimates of the impact of any quality improvements and reduced turnover. In jobs which produce intangibles, returns may be harder to quantify.

Avoid horizontal loading

Job changes which challenge employees to grow in their jobs are defined as vertical loading. Changes which add to the employee's work *without* providing more opportunity for psychological growth are called horizontal loading. Job enrichment programs which impose horizontal loading will not be nearly as successful. Examples of horizontal loading: increasing production quotas, adding routine tasks, rotating assignments without making them more meaningful, taking away difficult aspects of the job, and requiring employees to perform the simple tasks more efficiently.

Examples:

Herzberg describes a successful application of the theory to employees who correspond with stockholders for a large corporation. A "shareholder service index" was created which included measures of letter quality such as accuracy and speed. The index dropped from 50 to below 30 in the first two months, but jumped up to 90 before leveling off over the next four months.

Du Pont is currently experimenting on a large scale with alternative compensation plans, including one based on profit sharing. This plan makes 6% of compensation dependent on achieving set profit levels, and also allows employees to make up to 12% if profit targets are exceeded. 82% of employees have a favorable opinion of this plan, but only 46% of managers at Du Pont think results are better so far (42% think results are the same and 12% think results are worse). Du Pont's plans focus on hygiene factors and leave it to the employees to devise ways of improving their performance. Herzberg's theory suggests that the Du Pont experiment will *not* be a smashing success since it does not utilize the strongest motivators. It will be interesting to see what the outcome of Du Pont's experiment is.

References

Laurie Hays. "All Eyes on Du Pont's Incentive-Pay Plan." The *Wall Street Journal* (December 5, 1988). (Statistics from the employee surveys were provided by the Hay Group.)

Frederick Herzberg. "One More Time: How Do You Motivate Employees?" *Harvard Business Review* (September–October 1987): 109–120. (This is a reprint of the original HBR article presenting Herzberg's method, and it also includes some interesting new material from Herzberg. For example, if you like visual models of theories, see page 119 for Herzberg's motivation wheel.)

IBM PROCESS QUALITY MANAGEMENT

Applications

- Helping a project team define its mission, build consensus, and develop a specific plan of action.
- Focusing attention on the tasks that are most important to accomplishing a company's or a task force's mission.
- Bringing structure and momentum to a group facing a difficult mission, lack of consensus, or disagreement over priorities and direction.

Procedures

1. Put together a project team and appoint a discussion leader.
2. Assemble the team for a two-day meeting.
3. Write a mission statement.
4. Brainstorm a list of success factors.
5. Prepare a formal list of critical success factors.
6. Identify the business process(es) necessary for each critical success factor and assign responsibility for each.
7. Fill out a project chart and priority graph.
8. Follow the progress of team members.

Cross-Reference

Product Development and Innovation (writing an R&D plan) and Manufacturing and Operations (introducing new equipment or methodologies).

IBM developed PQM to solve a problem experienced by both IBM's managers and many of its customers: How to get a group to agree on goals and accomplish a complex project effectively. Today the method is used by many IBM customers to coordinate and focus group projects. The cornerstone of the method is a two-day session in which all team members participate in defining the task and delegating responsibility.

INSTRUCTIONS

1. Build a team. The team should consist of up to 12 people essential to the project. The team might be a board of directors, a group of vice-presidents, a division manager and his or her top managers, or others depending on the project. The team's leader should select its members and also appoint a discussion leader, a neutral person whose interests do not depend on the outcome of the group's work.

2. Assemble for a two-day meeting. Every member and the discussion leader must attend, but nonessential participants or observers are *not* permitted. It is best to meet away from the office to avoid interruptions.

3. Write a mission statement. Write a clear, concise statement of the team's mission that everyone agrees with. This can be difficult when the team has an open-ended assignment like "Develop a strategic plan for our European operations." It is simpler but still requires discussion when the task is more concrete, as in "Introduce JIT inventory control at all plants."

Note: The team leader must try hard not to dominate the proceedings—let the discussion leader lead!

4. Brainstorm for ten minutes. Members list all the factors that may affect the group's ability to accomplish its mission. The discussion leader writes down one-word descriptions of all factors mentioned. Everyone is expected to contribute and no criticism or argument is allowed.

5. Identify critical success factors. These are the *specific* tasks the team has to accomplish to succeed in its mission. The brainstorming list is a helpful reference in this stage. The discussion leader writes each factor down, usually in the form "We need to…" or "We must…."

PROJECT CHART
Mission: Introduce JIT Inventory Control

CSF's

#	Business Process
P1	Measure delivery performance by suppliers
P2	Recognize/reward workers for contributions to QC
P3	Negotiate with suppliers
P4	Reduce number of parts in new products
P5	Train supervisors in JIT procedures
P6	Redesign production line
P7	Move parts inventory to production floor
P8	Eliminate excessive inventory buildups
P9	Select suppliers for pilot JIT program
P10	Measure attitudes and skills of workforce
P11	Eliminate defective parts

There are four requirements for the list of critical success factors (CSF's):

1. Each team member agrees on each item.
2. Each item is truly necessary to the team mission.

Rapid access to parts	Supplier cooperation	Products engineered for JIT assembly	Supportive workforce	Worker knowledge of JIT procedures	Supervisor knowledge of JIT procedures	COUNT	QUALITY
✔	✔					2	B
			✔	✔		2	D
✔	✔	✔				3	B
✔	✔	✔	✔			4	D
				✔	✔	2	C
✔		✔	✔			3	A
✔						1	E
✔	✔					2	C
✔	✔					2	B
			✔	✔	✔	3	E
	✔	✔	✔			3	D

3. Together the factors are sufficient to accomplish the mission.

4. Each item on the list must stand alone— no "and" constructions allowed.

6. Identify the business processes for each CSF. For each CSF, make a list of the work necessary and sufficient to accomplish it. Work descriptions should be specific and action-oriented (i.e., "Survey cus-

tomers to find out what product features need improvement"). Assign each work description (called a *business process* in PQM) to a member of the team, but do not give anyone more than four.

7. Fill out a project chart and a priority graph. Rank the business processes by importance to the project's success using a project chart (see example). First, decide which business processes are most important to each critical success factor. Make sure at this point that identified processes are both necessary and sufficient for each CSF. Second, count the number of processes essential to each factor. Third, evaluate each business process to see how well the organization currently performs it using a scale of:

       A = excellent
       B = good
       C = fair
       D = bad
       E = not currently performed

PRIORITY GRAPH
← QUALITY

COUNT	E	D	C	B	A
5					
4		P4	*1st Priority*	*2nd Priority*	
3	P10			P3	P6
2		P2	P5 / P8	P1 / P9	
1	P7			3rd Priority	

Now you have ranked each process by its importance and by how well it is currently performed in your organization. Plot the business processes on the priority graph, which has priority and quality as its axes.

As in the exhibit, divide the priority graph into zones. Where you draw the priority zones is up to the group, but in general top priority is assigned to the processes that affect many CSF's and are not currently performed well. *Caution*: If you make your top priority zone too big, too many processes will be prioritized and none will be done quickly!

8. Follow-up. The team leaves the PQM session with business processes assigned and ranked by priority. Follow-up by the leader should focus on whether team members are improving the assigned business processes and whether changes in the company or its environment necessitate another PQM session to modify the mission, the critical success factors, or the business processes list.

Reference

Maurice Hardaker and Bryan K. Ward. "How to Make a Team Work." *Harvard Business Review* (November–December 1987): 112–120.

MBO PERFORMANCE RATING

Applications

- Rating the performance of employees on the basis of work objectives unique to each employee or group of employees.
- Using periodic performance appraisals as a vehicle for focusing employee attention on new organizational objectives and adapting employee behavior to better achieve organizational objectives.
- Using periodic performance review as a vehicle for identifying and focusing on an employee's weak spots.

Procedures

1. Manager and employee (or employee group) collaborate to identify specific objectives for the employee(s). Training goals or strategic goals may be used as input to this process.
2. Methods of measuring performance relative to objectives are developed.
3. At the end of a given time period employee performance is compared to objectives in order to evaluate performance, identify training needs, assess the success of organizational strategies, or develop objectives for the next period.

This method was originally seen as an alternative to judgmental, and often inaccurate, reviews of employee performance by supervisors. It takes the personal issues out of performance appraisal and can be quantified, therefore reducing the apparent subjectivity of the appraisal. But it requires a lot of time and attention from both management and employees, so its use is rarely justified for these reasons alone.

It can, however, be of real value if integrated into the strategic-planning efforts and training program of an organization. The objective-setting process is an excellent opportunity for thinking about how to do a job better or how to adapt performance to reflect new organizational strategies, and the measurement of performance versus objectives can be used to identify training and support needs as well as for appraisal of individual performance. If the method is used to translate the objectives against which the organization's overall performance is measured into objectives against which the performance of individual employees is measured, employees will be more committed to achieving their objectives and they will all be "pulling in the right direction."

INSTRUCTIONS

1. Employees and their supervisor work together to establish a list of objectives for the employees. This list should be specific and action-oriented; don't include items that are beyond the control of the employee. The shorter the list, the more attention each item will receive. Try to keep the number of items to under ten.

If the main purpose is to customize evaluation and objective setting to each employee's unique needs, do the objective setting one-on-one. If the main purpose is to identify the key objectives for a particular type of job, then work with a group of employees.

Ideas: A senior manager can sit in on the objective-setting meeting to orient the supervisor and employees to the organization's objectives, for example, by explaining a new plan or mission. Then the supervisor and employees can focus on identifying job objectives that will contribute to the organization's objectives.

Note: It can be helpful to prioritize objectives or to single one key objective out for attention in each period or on a monthly basis.

After objectives are set, a number of options are open to management. A second meeting can be held to evaluate support and supervision and identify any needs in this area that could help employees achieve objectives. Or, if this is a sensitive subject, employees can be polled anonymously.

Example: A new organizational strategy is to pursue long-term contracts with large industrial companies. A sales manager explains this to salespeople, and they adopt several objectives as a result:

- Five sales calls on large industrial companies per week.
- One new long-term contract with a large industrial per month.
- Ten leads on large industrials per week.

These new objectives will compete with other objectives such as number of sales calls on small industrials per week, and some negotiation may be necessary to establish a consistent and realistic list of objectives. It may also be necessary to set some support objectives for the supervisor, like developing a database on industrial companies and some training on negotiating long-term contracts.

2. If the objectives are going to be used in performance appraisal, figure out how you are going to measure performance on each objective at the beginning of the period. In most cases this just means making sure the relevant number is collected; in the preceding example, salespeople will have to report number of sales calls and the number will have to be broken down by type of account. If you are concerned about falsification, establish checks and balances at the beginning of the period. For example, require detailed notes on each sales call on a large industrial. Create a form to be filled out and filed.

What about nonquantitative objectives? One of the risks of this method is that objectives will be selected because they are easily measured. But other objectives, such as adopting a more consultative sales approach, may be equally valuable. Think of ways to evaluate these objectives, creating rating scales to help translate qualitative judgment into hard numbers.

3. At the end of a given time period employee performance is compared to objectives in order to evaluate performance, identify training needs, assess

the success of organizational strategies, or develop the objectives for the next period.

For performance appraisal, accomplishments can be compared to objectives and the variance (percent difference) can be calculated. Appraisals should note achieved objectives (equaling 100%) and exceeded objectives (greater than 100%), and also note any shortfalls (less than 100%). Rewards can be tied to the variance on specific objectives or the average variance.

References

William Glueck. *Personnel: A Diagnostic Approach.* Dallas, TX: Business Publications 1979.

H. Tossi, J. R. Rizzo, and S. Carroll. "Setting Goals in Management by Objectives." *California Management Review* 12(4) (1970): 70–78.

ORGANIZATIONAL CLIMATE ANALYSIS

Applications

- Assessing the overall climate of an organization.
- Setting targets for specific factors affecting climate and measuring the gaps between the ideal and existing climate on each of these factors.
- Defining organizational climate in specific terms for planning, analysis, and management purposes.

Procedures

1. Rate the organization on each of the six climate factors. (A survey or census of members can be used.)
2. Define target or ideal ratings for each factor.
3. Identify the gap between target and actual ratings and adjust policies, management style, and/or job descriptions as necessary to reduce the gap.

Cross-Reference

Strategic Planning Decisions

Organizational climate is a slippery concept—often referred to but seldom managed. This simple method breaks climate into six factors that are more specific and easier to manage. Use it to analyze climate and identify specific problems and strengths, or to set goals that can be achieved through planning and management.

These factors are sometimes used to construct organization climate questionnaires for formal, quantitative analysis of an organization's climate. Questionnaire design and administration is discussed as an option, although my preference is to stick with an informal, qualitative approach whenever possible.

Note: A big advantage of this method is that it is *not* normative—managers can use it to define the ideal organizational climate as they see fit, and then work to move climate in the defined direction.

INSTRUCTIONS

An organization can be defined as a company or some smaller social or work unit, such as a plant, department, or work group.

1. Analyze an organization's climate by scoring the organization on the following factors (use a 1 = low to 5 = high scale):

1. **Organizational support.** How much interest the organization takes in the lives and goals of employees, including their professional advancement. How good care the organization takes of its members. How clearly the organization recognizes its dependence on its members.

2. **Member quality.** How well informed, skilled, and helpful the members are. (Definition should also include any specific qualities important to the work of the organization in question.)

3. **Openness.** How open members of the organization are about their personal goals, shortcomings, and opinions, and how willing they are to discuss their own and other people's goals and shortcomings.

4. **Supervisory style.** How "people-oriented" the management is, how strong the sense of direction and sharing of goals is, how well supervisors balance competing demands, or other definitions of style. This factor should be defined to reflect goals and demands of the specific organization and the optimal supervisory style given those goals and demands.
Note: The Albrecht & Assoc. Leadership Matrix in the leadership skills and methods section is helpful for defining supervisory style.

5. *Member conflict.* How much conflict there is among members; whether there are exclusive groups; how competitive members are; how frequently members complain.

6. *Member autonomy.* How much initiative is given to the members of the organization. How open the organization is to ideas and changes proposed by members. How authoritarian the organization is. How much control there is over the activities of members.

Rewrite these definitions as necessary to make them fully applicable to your organization. Then use the list of factors and their definitions to rate each factor on the 1 to 5 scale.

Management's perspective on the organization is probably going to differ from the employee's perspective, so it is helpful to ask a small group of employees to rate climate using this list of factors. Have them discuss each factor as a group but write down their ratings independently and anonymously, which ensures that they understand how each factor applies to the organization while preserving the independence of their judgments. Compare these ratings with the ratings by management to identify any misconceptions or differences of opinion. Then management can revise its ratings if necessary to reflect any changes in opinion.

2. Establish ideal ratings for each factor. Using the customized factor definitions, management decides what rating is optimal for the organization and its mission. (A recent strategic plan or mission statement is a useful input at this stage.) For example, an organization's management decides that some member autonomy is good, but does not want complete autonomy and does not want autonomy to increase rapidly. A rating of 5 would therefore be as bad as a rating of 1, and a target of 3 would probably be ideal.

3. Compare actual to target ratings. Subtract the actual rating from the ideal rating. The difference is a measure of the gap that needs to be addressed through management policies and tactics. For example, say that the target rating for member autonomy is 3. The general consensus is that it currently rates a

1. This gap can be closed by giving members slightly more responsibility and control over their own work.

Organization climate surveys

A questionnaire can be built to measure organization climate by developing a list of (three to six) statements about the organization based on each factor. For example, "This department expects employees to take their own initiative" is a statement based on the definition of member autonomy. The questionnaire is completed by rating each statement according to how well it describes the organization on a "1 = not at all" to "5 = very well" scale. The questionnaire can be completed anonymously by all members of a small or medium-sized organization, or by a random sample (100 or more) in a larger organization. There is really no need to survey 20,000 people, as General Electric did in a study of employee attitudes (see the *Business Week* article in the references) unless you want to give employees a sense of participation.

Average the ratings for each question. Sum the average ratings for all questions relating to each of the six factors. Then divide each factor's total by the number of questions relating to the factor. The average ratings will be between 1 and 5 and can be used in place of the ratings from step 1.

References

"A Productive Way to Prevent Employee Gripes." *Business Week* (October 16, 1978): 168–71.

Richard M. Steers. *Introduction to Organizational Behavior*, 2nd ed. Glenview, IL: Scott, Foresman and Company, 1984. (The construction and use of organization climate questionnaires is described on pages 246–47.)

PEPSICO EMPLOYEE BENEFITS ANALYSIS

Applications

- Taking the guesswork out of developing a flexible package of benefits.
- Identifying employee attitudes toward benefit plans.
- Providing detailed information on both the needs and the demographics of benefit planning without raising expectations any more than absolutely necessary.
- Finding out what trade-offs employees prefer if rising costs force changes or cuts in the benefit package.

Procedures

1. Develop a written questionnaire for employees that includes questions about demographics, attitudes, preferences, and satisfaction level with the current plan.
2. Survey a random sample of the workforce.
3. Analyze the results.
4. Repeat the survey every few years or after major changes in the workforce or the benefits package.

Pepsi applies market research techniques to assess employee attitudes toward benefits. In fact, Pepsi hires a market research firm to do the survey, although other companies might prefer to keep the project in house. (Perhaps the marketing department could lend staff or provide advice.) Appropriate to a company that prides itself on being marketing-oriented, Pepsi's method views employees as customers of the benefit plan.

This method can reveal unexpected attitudes toward an employee benefits plan and can reveal segments of the workforce whose needs are not well met by the existing plan.

INSTRUCTIONS

1. Develop the questionnaire. Include background questions on demographics (age, sex, family status, health history, etc.) and also ask about preferences for different types of benefits. Find out if there are any complaints about the current benefits program by talking informally with employees in different parts of the company. Identify issues of current concern to employees and ask about these in the questionnaire as well. In some cases complaints will already have been voiced by disgruntled employees. Use the questionnaire to discover how widespread the dissatisfaction is—the survey may prove that complaints are not shared by the majority.

2. Survey a sample of the workforce using the written questionnaire developed in step 1. Use as small a sample as possible to reduce the visibility of the study and to keep costs low. The objective is to sample opinion without building expectations for change. Be sure to select a random sample of the workforce; 100 is probably a good minimum but a larger sample will be needed if you plan to cross-tabulate various questions in your analysis. Tell employees they are part of a select sample; this improved response rates at Pepsi.

3. Analyze the results. If you use a consultant, the consultant may be inclined to provide a detailed statistical analysis. But David Scherb, director of employee benefits at PepsiCo, believes that "your own interpretation of results is as valid as the consultant's." A simple questionnaire and small sample make the results more amenable to qualitative analysis, but it is still a good idea to make sure differences you highlight in your analysis do test as statistically significant.

Use the results as input in designing or modifying benefits plans. A clearer understanding of employee attitudes and preferences can lead to more economical plans because benefits can be tailored more closely to employee needs. It can also reveal unexpected problems with benefits plans. For example, PepsiCo discovered an inverse relationship between satisfaction with their benefits and salary level. This lead them to focus on the needs of middle managers.

Idea: Also use the results in designing employee communications: A survey can reveal misconceptions or lack of knowledge about plans.

4. Repeat the survey using a new random sample every year or two (or more frequently if you have introduced significant changes to the benefits plan). Repeat the core questions from the original survey to provide consistent "benchmark" measures of demographics, needs, attitudes, and satisfaction. Include new questions to address current issues.

Bad News: Wendy Gray, The Conference Board's benefits specialist, recommends using PepsiCo's method when you need to reduce employee benefits but do not know what kinds of cuts would be least objectionable. In this case, include trade-off questions in the survey such as, "If cost sharing goes up, would you rather have higher deductibles or larger payroll deductions?"

Reference

Management Briefing: Human Resources (January 1989). The Conference Board.

TRAVELER'S INSURANCE JOB ENRICHMENT

Applications

- Improving performance of employees in dull or routine jobs.
- Evaluating jobs to measure how motivating they are to employees.
- Identifying the key problems with a current job design and improving it.

Procedures

1. Evaluate the job by measuring each of the five core job dimensions: skill variety, task identity, task significance, autonomy, and feedback.
2. Modify the job to raise the score on the weakest dimensions.

Cross-Reference

Manufacturing and Operations—production-line job redesign.

Traveler's Insurance used this technique to redesign the work of keypunch operators, resulting in significant improvements in productivity, accuracy, absenteeism, and attitude. Traveler's method is an application of the Job Characteristics Model, first proposed in 1976 and the subject of considerable academic research since. The method is most likely to produce good results when applied to jobs like keypunch operation, which are routine and clearly allow room for improved performance.

INSTRUCTIONS

The Job Characteristics Model is explained succinctly, if not clearly, by one of its originators:

> The model postulates that internal rewards are obtained by an individual when he *learns* (knowledge of results) that he *personally* (experienced responsibility) has performed well on a task that he *cares about* (experienced meaningfulness).
> - J. R. Hackman, "Work Design," p. 129

The parentheses identify the three psychological states that the model assumes motivate an employee to do good (or bad) work:

- Experienced meaningfulness of the work—is it important and valuable?
- Experienced responsibility for work outcomes—is the employee accountable?
- Knowledge of results—is there feedback concerning performance?

Five core job dimensions are identified in the model. The first three influence experienced meaningfulness of the work:

- The variety of skills required,
- The degree to which the job involves completing an entire, identifiable piece of work;
- The significance, or impact, of the job on others.

The fourth dimension, *autonomy* (the amount of discretion and independence), influences experienced responsibility. The fifth, *feedback concerning performance*, influences knowledge of results. The end result of all this is a formula for evaluating a job. It uses measures of the five core job dimensions to estimate the motivation potential of any job or proposed job redesign. If the motivating potential score (MPS) is near zero for an existing job, redesigning it to increase the score should improve performance.

$$\text{Motivating Potential Score} = \frac{\text{Skill Variety} + \text{Task Identity} + \text{Task Significance}}{3} \times \text{Autonomy} \times \text{Feedback}$$

1. The first step is to measure each component of the formula to calculate the MPS. While complex primary research can be used, in general it is fairly easy to make a qualitative assessment of the job through observation and discussions with a few employees and supervisors. Rank each of the five core job dimensions on a scale such as 1, very low, through 5, very high. If you use this scale the highest MPS possible is 135. Alternatively, you can use the formula as a conceptual aid but not bother with the quantitative analysis.

Example:

At Traveler's Insurance, the keypunch operator job was assessed as follows.

Skill variety	None.
Task identity	Low. Work was grouped in batches, but did not represent whole, identifiable jobs.
Task significance	Low. Keypunchers worked in isolation from other departments and the customer, so the importance of their work was not apparent.
Autonomy	Low. Were not even allowed to correct information that was obviously wrong.
Feedback	None. After they finished a batch they never saw or heard of it again.

If these assessments were given numbers on the 1 to 5 scale, they would probably receive 1, 2, 2, 2, and 1 for a total Motivating Potential Score of 6.7. No wonder the performance was poor.

2. The next step is to redesign the job so as to maximize the Motivating Potential Score. Do this by picking the core job dimensions that scored lowest. (At Traveler's all of them needed attention but in many other cases only one or two are low.) If you have difficulty thinking of ways to redesign the job, here are some principles that are based on the same model:

- Give employees work in natural work units to help them see how it fits into the bigger picture.
- Combine tasks to increase skill variety and task identity.
- Establish client relationships to increase feedback, autonomy, and skill variety.
- Reduce the gap between action and control (this is called vertical loading) to increase autonomy.

Example:

The keypunch operator job at Traveler's was redesigned as follows:

1. The work was grouped into natural work units by assigning operators responsibility for specific accounts.
2. Some of the planning and controlling tasks were taken away from supervisors and integrated into the keypunching job.
3. Keypunch operators were given channels of communication with clients. For example, they now contact clients directly to investigate possible errors.
4. The direct contact with clients increased feedback, which was further increased by returning incorrect cards to the original operator for correction. Error rates and productivity were tracked on computer and reported to operators (not supervisors) weekly.
5. Vertical loading was increased by giving keypunch operators authority to correct obvious errors and to plan their own work schedules.

At Traveler's a control group was established for comparison—no job changes were made in this group. Productivity increased 8% in the control group during a trial period while it increased 40% in the group whose jobs were redesigned. Absenteeism increased 29% in the control group but decreased 24% in the group whose jobs were redesigned. Reduced error rates and improved attitudes toward work were also measured in the group whose jobs were redesigned.

References

J.R. Hackman, G. Oldham, R. Janson, and K. Purdy. "A New Strategy for Job Enrichment." *California Management Review* 17 (1975): 57–71.

J. R. Hackman. "Work Design." In J. R. Hackman and J. L. Suttle, eds., *Improving Life at Work.* (pp. 96–162). Santa Monica, CA: Goodyear, 1976.

TRW ONE-IN-FIVE METHOD

Applications

- Assessing employee attitudes toward work and the workplace.
- Exploring attitude or productivity problems.
- Providing more accurate and in-depth information about employee attitudes than a standard survey can.

Procedures

1. Identify issues of concern to employees.
2. Survey employees using a standard rating scale or your own questionnaire.
3. Present the survey to senior management and identify noteworthy or ambiguous results.
4. Interview 20% of respondents in small groups to explore questions in depth.
5. Rank themes from interview on the basis of frequency and intensity. Present to management.
6. *Optional*: Repeat every six months to a year.

Cross-Reference

Manufacturing and Operations—useful where very high quality standards must be maintained (as in airplane manufacture), making employee morale especially important.

TRW, Inc., performs routine analysis of employee attitudes in order to assess the social climate of the

From the book, *Organizational Development* by Karl Albrecht © 1983. Used by permission of the publisher, Prentice-Hall, Inc. Englewood Cliffs, NJ.

workplace. The method combines a job attitude survey of all employees in a division followed by in-depth personal interviews with at least a fifth of the employees surveyed. This approach combines the simplicity and replicability of a quantitative survey with the greater insight possible in qualitative research, and the use of the two methods makes it easier to validate the findings.

INSTRUCTIONS

1. Identify issues for the survey. A team (either insiders or consultants) interviews managers and employees on an informal basis to identify issues of current concern in the workplace.

Albrecht & Associates, a San Diego consulting firm, has developed a list of contributors to quality of work life. The list provides a good ckecklist for the open-ended interviews; questioning employees or managers about each of these factors often reveals important issues for the survey:

Factor	Desired condition
Job	Worthwhile; challenging; contributes to organization
Work conditions	Safe; humane
Pay and benefits	Adequate; decent
Job security	Reasonable assurance that job will continue
Supervision	Positive, supportive, competent treatment
Feedback	Contributions recognized and appreciated
Growth opportunities	Chances to develop work skills; increasing responsibilities
Advancement opportunities	Chances for promotion based on merit performance; access to training; visibility to management

Factor	Desired condition
Social climate	Positive, stable, humane values and human interactions in the workplace
Justice	Supervisors treat everyone fairly and reasonably; no racist, sexist, or classist treatment

2. Perform a "rating scale" survey of all the employees in the relevant division or unit.

Basic issues such as those in the preceding list are turned into a rating scale for employees, with an emphasis on any issues or problem areas identified in step 1. For example:

How well do these statements describe your work?

	True				False
My job makes a worthwhile contribution to the company.	1	2	3	4	5
My job challenges me.	1	2	3	4	5

If possible someone with a knowledge of questionnaires should design the survey. Test the proposed questions on a small group of employees to make sure questions are clear and meaningful. Use all relevant managers to implement the survey—they should participate in each step. Questionnaires should be anonymous.

Note: Two commonly used job satisfaction questionnaires are available to the public. The Minnesota Satisfaction Questionnaire is available from the University of Minnesota Industrial Relations Center, Minneapolis, Minnesota 55455; and the Job Descriptive Index is available from the Department of Psychology, Bowling Green State University, Bowling Green, Ohio 43403.

3. Analyze and present results. The results should be tabulated and summarized quickly, and then pre-

sented to management. Questions raised by management and any ambiguous or important results are identified for step 4.

4. Mixed groups of 5 to 15 employees are interviewed. The leader asks a series of open-ended questions derived from step 3 and records employee's responses. 20% of the employees should be interviewed in this manner. The format is somewhat like a focus group, although it need not be as formal or lengthy. Participants should be assured of anonymity (a good reason not to have managers be the group leaders).

5. Analyze and present the results. The interview notes are checked for recurring themes, which are ranked based on frequency and intensity. A summary report is presented to management for possible action. Note that the survey and interviews will build employee expectations, so be prepared to respond to problems identified in the study!

6. *Optional.* Repeat the study. Repetition of the study once or twice a year alerts management to changes in employee attitudes. It accustoms employees to the study so that it does not generate worries or unrealistic expectations. But some organizations will prefer to do the study on a one-time basis only when problems (productivity, turnover, quality) are pressing.

Reference

Karl Albrecht. *Organization Development.* Englewood Cliffs, NJ: Prentice Hall, 1983. (The list of factors is from page 77.)

PART 6

PRODUCT DEVELOPMENT AND INNOVATION

AMANA PRODUCT/MARKET PLANNING MATRIX

Applications

- Identifying product development opportunities.
- Systematizing the search for new product ideas.
- Presenting new product opportunities visually.

Procedures

1. Draw the matrix. If you have many products, use separate matrices or lists for each product family.
2. Enter current products into the "Present Products/Same Markets" cell of the matrix.
3. Fill the rest of the cells with new product ideas (a brainstorming session is helpful).
4. Evaluate the opportunities identified and pursue those that have merit.

Cross-Reference

Marketing Decisions—a good tool for joint product-planning efforts by technical and marketing staff.

Amana Refrigeration uses a product/market planning matrix when deciding what types of new products to develop. The roots of Amana's matrix are found in Ansoff's product/market expansion grid (see illustration). Ansoff's grid identifies four strategies—market penetration, market development, product development, and diversification.

Amana has added more cells to the matrix (see the second illustration) because it found that product development focuses on improving old products and

ANSOFF'S
PRODUCT/MARKET EXPANSION GRID
(The Original Product/Market Matrix)

	Current Products	New Products
Current Markets	**1** Market penetration strategy	**3** Product development strategy
New Markets	**2** Market development strategy	**4** Diversification strategy

developing related products. Diversification into unrelated products and markets is unusual and risky. Amana has integrated the matrix into its product planning to ensure that all possible opportunities are considered.

INSTRUCTIONS

To use the matrix, first lay out a table like that in the Amana Product/Market Planning Matrix and fill in the current products and markets. Amana lists microwave ovens to appliance stores in the first cell, "Present Products/Same Markets," since it currently sells microwave ovens through appliance stores.

Defining markets: The marketing department should provide a breakdown by segments, such as type of buyer, geographic area, or distribution channel.

The next and more difficult step is to fill in the rest of the cells. Amana tries to specify opportunities for each category even though every opportunity is not necessarily pursued. There is usually a variety of existing proposals that can be entered, and if these

AMANA PRODUCT / MARKET PLANNING MATRIX

	Present Products	Improved Products	Related New Products	Unrelated New Products
Same Markets	Microwaves to appliance stores	Less expensive microwaves	Combination microwave & electric oven	?
New Markets	Microwaves to department stores	Built-in refrigerators	Commercial microwave ovens	?

do not fill all the cells of the matrix, ask the product development and marketing people to go back to the drawing board. A brainstorming session is a good way to identify opportunities.

Problem Situation: If you have a long product line, you cannot fit all the current products and markets on a single matrix. Use the matrix as a tool for presenting the concept to your staff and associates, but switch to lists when it comes to recording the information. Create a list for each of the cells of the matrix. Another solution is to do a separate matrix for each family of products or product line.

The final step is to select some of the opportunities for development and introduction. Most companies have a standard procedure for selecting projects, but no standard procedure for identifying opportunities. Use the matrix to identify opportunities that might not have been considered otherwise, then feed all those opportunities into the standard evaluation process. Typically, this means product development or marketing managers select the most promising for market research and technical review, followed by formal proposals to senior management.

Benefits: Helps identify opportunities that might not have been considered otherwise. In a simple experiment I found that business school students who use the matrix for case studies come up with more and better new product ideas than students who do not.

IMPLICATIONS OF THE AMANA MATRIX
(illustrated by examples from Amana)

Present products X same markets.

Create more demand through sales training, advertising, etc.

Present products X new markets.

Find new markets or distribution channels for products. Only 25% of microwave ovens are sold through traditional appliance stores, so Amana is taking microwaves to new markets such as Montgomery Ward and Wal-Mart.

Improved products X same markets.

Amana is looking at built-in refrigerators which would be sold to builders and kitchen remodelers—new markets for Amana. Small changes in a current product will often make it useful to a new market. One source of ideas for this cell is what your *indirect* competitors are doing.

New related products X same markets.

Market research often holds clues to this category of opportunities. New products that solve customers' problems do well. Microwaves are considered inferior for baking; a combination electric and microwave oven will address this problem.

New related products X new markets.

Opportunities in this category require more work but are often bigger. Amana has been very successful with a production-line spin-off of their microwave ovens for commercial markets.

Reference

"Amana's Analysis." *Management Briefing: Marketing* (April 1987). The Conference Board.

DRUCKER'S SEVEN SOURCES OF INNOVATION

Applications

- Systematizing your organization's search for innovative ideas.
- Identifying specific areas in which to look for innovation.
- Prioritizing your organization's innovation efforts.

Procedures

Use the hierarchical list of sources of innovation to identify opportunities, create an innovation program, and allocate staff, or to review your organization's current emphasis. Review discussion of each source for specific ideas and warnings.

Peter Drucker argues that firms must learn to "practice systematic innovation" much as they have already learned to take a systematic approach to research and invention. While entrepreneurs are usually good innovators, established companies often have difficulty identifying opportunities for innovation in their industries. Innovations typically exploit change, and Drucker has identified the areas in which a firm should look for change in order to find opportunities for innovation.

INSTRUCTIONS

The sources of innovation are listed in the table below. Note that some are internal and some external to the firm. Most R&D departments focus on new knowledge and process needs, as these are the most likely to be monitored by scientific staff. One of the benefits of Drucker's model is that it draws attention to other sources of innovation that can be more practical and less difficult to pursue.

Sources of Innovation

Focus of monitoring effort	
Within the company	Beyond the company
Unexpected events or results	Population changes
Incongruities	Perception changes
Process needs	New knowledge
Unexpected changes in industry/market structure	

Assign responsibility for monitoring each of these areas to individuals and insist on periodic reports to ensure that the organization recognizes and exploits opportunities from all possible sources. Drucker's seven sources of innovation are ranked from most important to least important in the following discussion. This may be helpful in deciding how to assign responsibility and where to place your emphasis. It is also productive to rank the sources according to your organization's current emphasis. Often companies throw most of their resources at the areas near the bottom of this list rather than at the top!

Sources of innovation

1. *The unexpected.* Unexpected success indicates a shift or trend that opens up a new or larger market for the organization. Its cause should be identified and new products or services developed to exploit the opportunity. Unexpected success is *usually ignored by management*—after all, reporting systems try to identify and explain problems, not successes. Unexpected success may initially be viewed as an inconvenience or problem.

Example: Some pharmaceutical companies viewed early requests for their products from veterinarians as an inconvenience and let other companies develop what has become a significant market.

An unexpected failure, one that occurs despite the care, planning, and experience of good management, also indicates a change that innovation could turn into opportunity. Because the cause is likely to be unexpected or surprising, analysis and number crunching is not likely to identify it. Management should "go out, look around, and listen" to find the cause.

An unexpected or sudden external event may create an important opportunity. However, if the organization's current expertise cannot be applied to exploit the event, it is probably not a viable opportunity for innovation. (*Note*: Large organizations are especially suited to exploiting outside events because of the expertise and resources they can mobilize.)

2. *Incongruities.* When things are not as they ought to be, when something does not make sense, it usually indicates an important change that has yet to be recognized. Incongruities are often noticeable to insiders, yet they are often ignored because they do not conform with accepted views of the world.

The organization should cast a wide net in its search for useful incongruities. Incongruous economics in an industry (such as growth without profits) are a potential source, as are incongruities between facts and assumptions and between product benefits and customer expectations. Also look at internal incongruities in a system or process.

Observations: Opportunities arising from incongruities are usually greatest for a small and well-focused organization such as an entrepreneurial company. Innovations should be kept simple and straightforward.

Monitoring incongruities requires a qualitative approach. However, survey research can help identify incongruities between perception of management and customers. (*Hint*: Look for problems that organizations have been unable to solve despite concerted effort.)

3. *Process need.* Process needs are usually quite obvious, so when a bottleneck or weak link in a

process is addressed by an innovation it is rapidly accepted. Process-oriented innovations sometimes take advantage of new knowledge to replace a cumbersome process with a better one. Some process needs are created by demographic trends. For example, Bell Telephone developed the first automatic switchboard in 1910 after projections indicated that by 1925 every adult woman in America would be needed to staff manual switchboards.

Three constraints should be considered in evaluating a process need: The need cannot be met unless the need is clearly understood, the necessary knowledge is available, and the solution is consistent with how the users prefer to work.

4. *Structured change.* A stable industry or market structure can shift suddenly and unexpectedly, requiring members to innovate in order to adapt to the new context. These changes create visible, dramatic opportunities for outsiders and threaten established insiders.

To predict change in industry structure, look for rapid growth, inappropriate segmentation strategies by leaders, a convergence of technologies, or rapid change in the way firms do business in the industry.

Industries or markets that are dominated by one or a few suppliers are appealing targets for innovators. The established firms are not used to challenges and will be slow to recognize changes in industry structure.

5. *Demographics.* Changes in population size and structure, such as an increase in education level, age, or the size of a particular group, are clear and predictable. They can happen quite quickly and have a dramatic impact on markets. But businesses seldom monitor demographics closely or consider it in routine decision making. Because demographic changes are readily apparent yet generally neglected by decision makers, they present many opportunities for innovation.

Example: None of the leading fast-food restaurants have developed specialized menus for the growing number of middle-aged and elderly Americans on restricted diets. An outsider could come into the market with specialized food and service to take advantage of this rapidly growing group.

6. *Perception.* A shift in the way people see themselves creates opportunity. Changes in perception are not readily recognized by established companies, and innovations based on perceptual shifts usually have little competition.

Perceptual change can be difficult to diagnose—facts do not change, only their meaning does! Unexpected success or failure may indicate a change in perception, and opinion research can often identify and quantify changed perceptions.

Example: William Benton investigated the shift in the 1950s which led most Americans to describe themselves as "middle class" rather than "working class." He discovered that people believed their children had the opportunity to better themselves through education, an insight that led him to buy Encyclopaedia Britannica and market it to the newly self-proclaimed middle class.

Warnings: Timing is everything. If an innovation anticipates the perceptual change it will not find a receptive market. But a delay may give away the opportunity to a competitor. Also, some fads appear to be important perceptual changes at first, and of course basing an innovation on a fad is trouble. Because these risks exist, Drucker advises keeping perception-based innovations specific and starting small.

7. *New knowledge.* Drucker places this source of innovation at the bottom of his list because it is hard to manage, unpredictable, expensive, and characterized by long lead times. However, most organizations currently emphasize new knowledge over other sources of innovation because it is so conspicuous and exciting. Note that knowledge-based innovations often fail because a breakthrough in one area usually needs breakthroughs in other areas in order to be applied. The required convergence of new knowledge in multiple areas, both technical and social, makes it difficult for organizations to successfully introduce knowledge-based innovations.

Knowledge-based innovations require entrepreneurial management and with it can sometimes be very successful. Hewlett-Packard and Intel are examples of companies that consistently produce successful knowledge-based innovations. But other companies without a strong technical focus and a history of leadership in research are advised to look hard at other sources of innovation before choosing to pursue a knowledge-based strategy.

Note: Knowledge-based innovation depends on the "bright idea." Bright ideas are hard to manage— they are by nature nonsystematic and, like gambling, resistant to systematizing. Companies like HP play a numbers game; they can afford to have many people thinking so they come up with more bright ideas than most competitors.

Reference

Peter F. Drucker. *Innovation and Entrepreneurship: Practice and Principles*. New York: Harper & Row, 1985.

HONEYWELL PRODUCT
DEVELEOPMENT TACTICS

Applications

- Eliminating redesign to achieve cost and time savings in product development.
- Managing a multidepartmental product development team.
- Diagnosing problems with a company's product development process.

Procedures

1. Gather a team from all the departments responsible for product development and introduction.
2. Cross-train the members so they understand the role each department plays.
3. Use the seven tactics to define how the group works together, how it interacts with the rest of the company, and how it will be evaluated.

Cross-Reference

Financial Decisions—useful in designing multidepartmental teams for turnaround projects and acquisitions.

At Honeywell, many problems and delays in product development were eliminated by doing away with the usually sequential product development cycle. Instead, Honeywell switched to a method that uses a design team made up of people from every department involved in product development and introduction.

Problems often arise when a new product moves from stage to stage in its development cycle. The scale-up team finds problems that were overlooked in the lab; the quality-control group requires changes in specifications; the marketing department demands new performance criteria, and so forth. In this method, however, everyone has his or her say the first time around, so redesign should not be necessary.

Red Flag: Does it work? Not necessarily. Problems often arise when cooperation and consensus are required of so diverse a group. Therefore Honeywell developed seven tactics for managing a product development team. Use them as a checklist in designing a team for your own company or for finding the cause of problems and delays in your company's product development efforts.

Tactics for managing a product development team (Source: The Conference Board)

1. *Parity*. Each individual and department involved has equal input.

2. *Frozen specification*. The team settles on firm specifications in advance. This means market research must precede design.

3. *Consulting gurus*. Technical gurus should be kept *off* the team, contributing in a consulting role only.

4. *Simple rules*. The team must be evaluated simply (i.e., according to how well it achieves scheduled milestones).

5. *Championship*. Necessary support and recognition can be provided through championship by a high-level manager.

6. *Risk*. By eliminating punishments and other organizational deterrents, risk taking can be encouraged.

7. *Communication*. The team must communicate freely with the rest of the organization (i.e., don't send them to a remote location without a

mechanism to stay in touch daily with their peers).

Idea: Cross-train members in each others' specialities to increase their understanding of the entire product development process and facilitate cooperation. Honeywell has had good luck with this technique.

Be sure the rules are clear to both the participants and the organization as a whole. Follow through— check with team members periodically to see if the tactics are being followed. One way to do this is to give them a rating sheet with each tactic listed down the left-hand side and space to evaluate conformity to the tactic on a 1 to 10 scale to the right. At the bottom, leave space for comments and complaints. Make sure the forms are returned anonymously.

Benefits: Honeywell reported 30% to 60% reductions in average product development times in various departments as well as substantial cost savings through the use of these tactics. Product quality is also likely to benefit.

Reference

Clint Larson, "Team Tactics Can Cut Product Development Costs." *Journal of Business Strategy* (September–October 1988): 22–26

JACKSON'S TIME CHART

Applications

- Managing the many aspects of developing and launching a new product.
- Informal control and planning for time-sensitive product development projects.
- Scheduling of tasks in product development and entrepreneurial activities.

Procedures

1. Break the project into specific processes.
2. List all the steps or tasks required for each process and the time each will require.
3. Using a large time chart for each process, draw the steps, working from the last to the first (group consecutive activities; show concomitant activities as overlapping on the timeline).
4. Use the chart to estimate the time required for the process and to plan daily and weekly activities.
5. *Optional.* Prepare a critical-path diagram for the more complex processes to identify which tasks are critical to on-time completion.

Cross-Reference

Organization and Human Resources

This method is a simplified form of project scheduling. It was developed by Mary Anne Jackson when she left Beatrice to found a start-up children's food company. To successfully manage the 20 processes required for the startup and product development she adapted a project scheduling approach, but dropped the formal, quantitative models of PERT/CPM and other project scheduling procedures. Her method is qualitative and hands-on and can be used more like a glorified calendar than a formal project model. However, it is a good first step toward more formal project scheduling and can be used to identify which processes need formal models and which don't. It is especially suited to product development, where many lengthy processes need to be coordinated, but is also useful in all types of project management.

INSTRUCTIONS

1. Start by defining the various processes that are required to complete the project. How a process is defined is really a matter of convenience. A narrow definition is appropriate for lengthy, complex tasks which are easier to manage when broken down into many simpler tasks. Most projects have at least a few natural breakdowns, such as:

- Benchtop demonstration
- Scale-up to production volumes
- Federal approvals and safety tests
- Consumer research for feedback on features
- Preparation of instruction manuals or specifications
- Adaptation to automated in-lab equipment
- Marketing plan

and so forth, depending on the type of product under development. Formal project scheduling usually breaks down a project into separate activities, emphasizing those that occur consecutively. But in this method, start with natural processes (which are often simultaneous or at least overlapping in time). Leave the identification of specific activities until step 2.

2. List all the steps or tasks required for each process and the time each will require. Be specific—identify every discrete activity. Prepare a table listing activities and the time they will take. Group related activities and make sure you understand the order in which they must be performed.

3. Using a large time chart for each process, draw the steps, working from the last to the first. Group consecutive activities together to make it easier to show one starting when another ends. Use solid horizontal lines to represent the time needed for each activity. If some activities can be pursued simultaneously, draw overlapping lines for them.

If your list of processes includes some that must be completed *after* others are completed or partially completed, start with these processes. Complete their time charts first, then take the ending dates for earlier process charts from the later process charts, so that you diagram the entire project from end to beginning.

Note: Define the time lines in days or weeks, but do not *date* them until every chart is done and the total time required is clear. Then you can set a start and end date.

4. Use the chart to estimate the time required for the process and to plan daily and weekly activities. It is helpful in planning and coordinating activities, especially when the work of multiple people or departments must be coordinated. The chart can be prepared with the appropriate departmental managers, then consulted by the project manager to coordinate the departmental activities.

5. *Optional*. Prepare a critical-path diagram for the more complex processes to identify which tasks are critical to on-time completion. A critical-path diagram is prepared as follows:

   a. Identify the immediate predecessor activity to each activity (if a predecessor is requisite). Assign all activities code letters to use in labeling the diagram.

   b. Diagram the process by connecting each activity by a line to its required predecessor, starting at the end of the process. Each activity is represented by a solid line, and circles are used to signify the beginning and end of activities. (Dotted lines connect the end of one activity to the start of another with a "dummy activity" if necessary to connect all branches to the final circle, which represents the end of the process.)

c. Label the activity lines with the appropriate code letters and add the time required for each activity next to the line.

d. Examine the diagram to see how many separate paths can be followed from the beginning circle to the ending circle. Add up the activity times along each of these paths and clearly mark the path with the longest total time. This is the critical path—it determines the length of the process, and delays in any activity on this path have the greatest impact on the timing of the process.

Reference

Tom Richman. "The New American Start-Up." *Inc.* (September 1988): 54–64.

JAMES RIVER COST/PERFORMANCE MATRIX

Applications

- Identifying cost and performance requirements for a drawing-board product.
- Comparing competing products on the basis of their value to the customer.
- Evaluating new products by comparing them to market norms for performance and value.
- Developing a quality- or performance-based strategy in industries where innovation is traditionally cost-oriented.

Procedures

1. Rate products in a market or market segment on the basis of overall quality of the product and the services associated with it. (Estimate quality for your new and proposed products as well.)
2. Estimate cost per unit for each of the products.
3. Plot the products on a cost/performance graph. Add lines for average performance and cost, and fit a parity line to the data using linear regression, eyeballing, or conjoint analysis.
4. Identify the products that fall significantly above the priority line (winners) and below it (losers). Map proposed products to see where they stand relative to current products.

Cross-Reference

Marketing Decisions

James River Corp., a paper manufacturer, faces a competitive industry in which many sales are com-

modity-oriented and price is typically very important. The tendency in industries like this is for
competitors to focus on price and volume. Innovation often centers on cost reductions. But because
scale has an impact on cost in paper manufacturing,
many smaller mills have found it difficult to compete.
Some, however, have differentiated their products on
the basis of quality and have targeted segments with
specialized needs (Strathmore Paper and James River
are two excellent examples of the success of this
strategy).

James River has developed a product planning
tool that helps ensure every new product offers a
competitive combination of quality and price. This
method focuses attention on performance, but does
not break performance down into the many individual attributes that most marketing studies delineate.
Instead, the method puts performance in the context
of price to create a value map. James River's Cost/
Performance Matrix defines performance from the
customer's perspective—determined through a formal survey or informal interviews. The other dimension of the matrix, price, is represented by
manufacturing cost since cost is the best predictor of
pricing strategy in the long run in price-sensitive
markets. R&D or manufacturing can often provide
good estimates of the relative cost position of competing manufacturers, and product characteristics
provide additional information about the unit costs.

INSTRUCTIONS

1. Survey customers to obtain rankings of overall
product and service performance on a 1 to 10 scale.
(James River uses a consultant, which lends objec-
tivity to the questions about competitors' products.)
Ask customers to provide overall ratings of your
product and its major competitors. If the product is
in the planning stages, a focus-group format should
be used rather than a telephone or written survey.

Idea: A formal research study may have already
been done by marketing, showing which product
attributes customers value most and how they rate
each competing product on each attribute. You can
use this data by weighting attribute ratings by impor-

tance ratings, summing weighted ratings to give a single performance rating for each product, then scaling this rating to the 1 to 10 scale of the matrix.

Although market research is helpful in evaluating customer perception, a formal study is not required. Quizzing customers, the sales force, and distributors provides a quick approximation of each product's performance score. *Caution*: Technical staff have a tendency to define performance according to objective laboratory measures, but these should not be used in the matrix unless there is clear evidence that customers use the same measures!

2. Estimate cost per unit for your own product proposal and for each competing product. James River collects as much information as possible about the manufacturing facilities of competitors to provide a basis for these estimates. In other industries, distribution channels, marketing programs, and other costs might also be relevant to cost analysis. Prices are often a good clue to product costs as well, and the sales force and distributors will have a good idea of standard markups and any competitive pressures that might suppress prices abnormally. Public companies may release data on revenues and earnings by segment. Finally, where the economies of scale are important and quantifiable, cost can be deduced from volume or share. (Combustion Engineering estimates competitor costs in a formal meeting of a multidepartmental team of managers. See Combustion Engineering's Competitor Analysis in the marketing decisions section.)

3. Plot each competing product on a graph with performance on the vertical and cost on the horizontal scale. Draw a vertical line at average competitor cost per unit and a horizontal line at average performance. The intersection of these two lines represents the average value offered by current products and provides a general target for new product development.

4. A diagonal line can be drawn to represent the various combinations of cost and performance that are equal trade-offs from the customer's perspective. This is called the parity line.

Note: Estimate the slope of this line by performing a linear regression on the paired cost/performance

COST / PERFORMANCE MATRIX

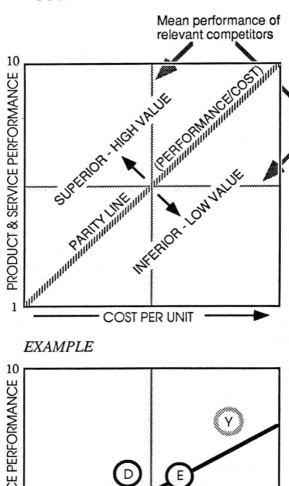

Mean performance of
relevant competitors

EXAMPLE

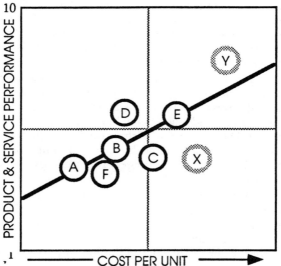

data for the products in this market or fitting a line by eye. Another approach is to do a market research study in which trade-offs are presented to customers and the customers are asked to identify combinations of price and performance that offer equal value. *Warning*: With new product introductions the parity line can move over time.

Products below the parity line probably need improvement or cost reductions to bring them up to or above parity. Any new product offering should be aimed *above* the parity line.

Example:

The sample matrix illustrates a hypothetical paper market with six major products at present, plus two product proposals that R&D considers feasible from a development and production standpoint. The proposed products are labeled X and Y. X will offer high cost and performance, and Y will offer very high cost and performance in an effort to differentiate them for the high end of the market. R&D and marketing expect product X to be successful because it is closer to existing products in both cost and performance, but they are not certain that the market will accept Y because it is considerably beyond competing products in both performance and price.

The matrix indicates that the opposite will probably be true. Although X is closer to current products, it falls below the parity line. Customers will probably view it as offering no more value than product C, which has a lower cost position. Product Y lies well above the parity line and should be perceived as a good value despite its high cost.

Reference

Management Briefing: Marketing (October 1987). The Conference Board.

MARRIOTT TRADE-OFF ANALYSIS

Applications

- Finding out what new service or product features customers want.
- Exploring customers' willingness to pay more for a feature or trade another for it.
- Sorting and ranking combinations of possible features and prices from the customers' perspective.

Procedures

1. Recruit participants as you would for a focus group. (You may want to replicate the study two or three times, just as in focus-group research.)
2. Prepare a series of cards for each participant, specifying different combinations of services or features and prices.
3. Have participants identify equivalent cards for trade-off analysis.
4. You can also have participants rank cards in order of preference.
5. Interpret the results as input to product development and pricing decisions, being careful to keep in mind that the study is qualitative, not quantitative.

Cross-Reference

Marketing Decisions

Marriott uses an informal form of conjoint analysis to explore customer preferences and gather insight into the value placed on various services and combinations of services. Whenever a new service or feature is developed, it can be explored using this method to see how it could be combined with existing services. The information generated is also useful in pricing decisions and cost management. For example, if costs have to be reduced, the data will give some guidance to management by steering management toward the features that are less valuable to customers. According to Frank Comacho, Vice-President, Corporate Marketing Services at Marriott,

> Customers may be asked to indicate trade-offs involving site selection, room size, reservation systems, and room service. Then, if costs must be reduced or new features added, a rough guide showing cost versus preference exists upon which to base decisions.

The method is especially useful for service marketers, as most services are a variable combination of specific service features. It may also be appealing to product marketers as a quick, inexpensive way to explore alternative configurations for new products or product/service combinations.

INSTRUCTIONS

1. Select a cross-section of customers to participate. Selection and recruiting is analogous to the process used in putting together a focus group.

2. Prepare a series of cards for each participant. Each card lists (and describes if necessary) a group of three to six individual services or features. Each card also indicates a price for this combination.

Note: Before preparing the cards, you must have thought through the options you want customers to evaluate. Prepare a list of questions as you would in designing any opinion research study. Limit the number of options and if you must include a large number *test* them on several people to make sure there are not too many to handle.

3. Ask customers to create trade-offs by indicating which cards are of equivalent value in their minds. This analysis can be used to find out what services and features have to be added to justify an x% increase in price. It can also be used to develop responses to a competitor's challenge or a perceived

weakness; for example, it can be used to identify a low-cost combination of small room and features that compensate for a larger room. In fact, any of the standard methodologies used in trade-off analysis are applicable here, except that the researcher should bear in mind the unusually small sample sizes and stay away from questions that require detailed quantitative analysis, cross-tabulation, and so on.

4. Ask customers to rank the alternatives by preference. Ranking gives useful information about trade-offs by indicating which combinations of services/features and price are better or worse. It can also be used to explore how much customers are willing to pay for a new combination or new service. For example, one card can have a standard service package at a standard price, and several others can add a new service to the package at varying prices.

Note: This is a good tool for qualitative product development and exploration of customer preferences.

Because it is qualitative, it is a lot easier to prepare and analyze than a full-blown quantitative conjoint analysis, and it should be less expensive as well. Furthermore, it is better suited to the exploratory research of product development, and since it brings the respondents together in a focus-group like setting, it can be combined with a traditional focus-group session or a moderator can lead a discussion afterward to explore the reasons behind responses.

Warning: The trade-offs and rankings made by respondants should be summarized in tabular format. But this gives the impression of a quantitative study. Be sure to include a note on the summary that explains quite clearly that it is qualitative and discourages management from relying on the numbers.

Reference

Management Briefing: Marketing (April–May 1988): The Conference Board.

NFO PRODUCT ANALYSIS

Applications

- Clarifying customer perception of a product's attributes to help decide how to improve it.
- Identifying the product attributes that are in greatest need of attention from R&D.
- Graphing product attributes to illustrate their importance and your product's strength on each.

Procedures

1. Survey consumer attitudes to obtain rankings of the importance of product attributes and evaluate your product on each. Also obtain an overall rating of your product.
2. Perform stepwise linear regression to find out which attributes are most important to the overall product ratings.
3. Graph the importance scores and the mean ratings for each attribute.

Cross-Reference

Marketing Decisions

The cost of adding multiple regression analysis to a study is minimal, but the information gained will provide R&D much clearer product development direction.
> - Richard Cain, NFO

Adapted and reprinted from *Marketing News*, published by the American Marketing Association. Richard F. Cain. "Give R. & D. Clearer Direction for Product Development," Sept. 26, 1988, 22:20.

Richard Cain, research manager for NFO Research of San Francisco, recommends this procedure to make data from product testing more useful for R&D. The problem is that tests usually have directional ratings of multiple product attributes, and it can be difficult to deduce from the results which of the attributes deserve the most attention from R&D. NFO prescribes stepwise linear regression to provide more specific information to R&D, and Mr. Cain recommends that product development managers request a similar analysis from their marketing departments or research firms.

INSTRUCTIONS

1. Do a survey of consumer attitudes to identify all the product attributes of importance to consumers and rank your product on each attribute. Use the following rating scale:

much too much of x	$+2$
slightly too much of x	$+1$
just about the right amount of x	0
not quite enough of x	-1
not nearly enough of x	-2

Also be sure an overall rating of the product is included. (The linear analysis will treat this rating as the dependent variable and individual attribute ratings as independent variables, ignoring possible colinearity between attributes.)

2. Use one of the standard computer programs for performing stepwise regression (a forward selection-type program is probably best). If your survey research firm cannot do this, fire them, because it is an unnecessary hassle for you or your staff to input all the data into a spreadsheet or statistics program and do the analysis yourself. (Also order a correlation matrix from your research firm to allow you to consider interactions among attributes when the analysis is done.)

Stepwise regression with forward selection will introduce variables into the regression model one at a time, starting with the most important variables, and can stop adding variables once a certain level of statistical significance is reached. The output might look like this for a study of apple pie:

Step	Regressor added	R^2
1	Amount of fruit	.58
2	Filling consistency	.66
3	Topping color	.69
4	Sweetness	.71

Note: R^2 is the coefficient of determination. As the model improves—better explains the consumer's overall ranking of the pie—R^2 approaches 1.

3. Prepare a graph showing the relative importance of each attribute to the regression model and the product's directional rating on the attribute. The importance of an attribute is defined as the attribute's Type II sum of squares divided by the total of all attributes' sum of squares. (Type II sum of squares is a measure of the power of each independent variable in the model.) Use the sum of squares ratio on the vertical axis and use the mean score of the attribute's rating on the horizontal to represent how well your product does on that attribute.

In this simplified example, the pie has too little fruit—its major problem—and also would benefit from a less thick filling and a darker crust. Any attributes that fall into the upper left or upper right of this graph are priority items for R&D. (*Idea*: Draw

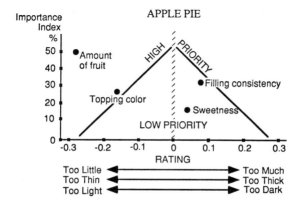

a triangle on the graph to create high-priority and low-priority zones. This clarifies priorities when many attributes are plotted.)

4. Check the correlation table and look at the distribution for each directional rating before reaching a final conclusion. This model might overlook an attribute because it correlates closely with a more important attribute, but if a large percentage of respondents have rated the product poorly on a lesser attribute you may want to consider fixing it anyway.

Technical Note: Regression isolates attributes which are characterized by an *imbalance* between the two tails of the directional rating. For example, if 20% said there was too little fruit and 20% said there was too much, the results cancel out—graphically the result is an upside-down U which is approximated by a straight line of 0 slope in linear regression. In this case the model would not indicate a need for change, but there might be an opportunity to segment the market with two products differentiated on this attribute. If, however, there was an imbalance—many more people said there was too little fruit for example—then the attribute would be significant in the results.

Reference

Richard F. Cain. "Give R&D Clearer Direction for Product Development." *Marketing News* (September 26, 1988): 22. (Published by the American Marketing Association.)

PEARSON'S FIVE STRATEGIES FOR INNOVATION

Applications

- Encouraging and sustaining innovation throughout the organization.
- Creating a culture which values and encourages steady improvements in products and services and also in other business systems.

Procedures

Use the five strategies in combination for an innovation program—introduce procedures and tactics suggested by them. Or use them as a checklist to identify weak areas in your organization and to understand why some competitors in your industry are more innovative than others.

Cross-Reference

Leadership Skills and Methods

Here are five strategies from Andrall Pearson, president of PepsiCo during a period marked by innovation in soft drinks and fast food, and now a professor at Harvard Business School. He argues that innovation is the key to the success of superior competitors like PepsiCo and that a systematic approach to innovation is required. In his words,

Competitive success is built on a steady stream of improvements in production, finance, distribution, and every other function, not just a big hit in sales or marketing or R&D.

Pearson's five strategies are designed to keep a company innovating and improving its operations by fostering the values, incentives, and opportunities needed for innovation to flourish. They may appear obvious, as they are simple ideas, but few companies really do all five well. Apply these five strategies to make your company more innovative or use them as a model for understanding why some competitors innovate better than others.

Innovation strategies

1. *Begin with the right mind-set.* Organizations must place high value on improving performance on a regular basis. Make change a way of life at your company through involving senior management, setting high goals, focusing hard on competitors, and experimenting frequently and continuously. Frequent experimentation spreads the word that risk taking is encouraged and it spreads the risk around.

2. *Unsettle the organization.* Organizational structure and procedures—bureaucratization—stifles innovation and limits cross-fertilization of ideas by building vertical and horizontal barriers to communications and collaborations within the company. Use task forces superimposed over the organizational structure and headed by senior managers. Spin off businesses into small divisions and encourage managers to be entrepreneurs, or take other steps to make sure people are able to break out of the organizational structure to produce and pursue innovations.

3. *Be hardheaded about your strategy.* Use the organization's strategy to keep innovation focused on well-defined areas. To avoid a lot of wasted energy don't let efforts become too diffuse. But make sure the strategy is realistic. A U.S. manufacturer pursuing the low-cost position may never be able to displace Japanese competitors, no matter how competitive it becomes. A more realistic strategy might be to become the low-cost producer in a protectable segment of the market. Realistic and focused strategies channel innovation into productive areas.

4. *Look hard at what's already going on.* Pearson: "I firmly believe the best backdrop for spurring innova-

tion is knowledge—knowing your business cold." Look for opportunities and ideas by looking at your operations and at your customers and competitors. Specifics to look for include:

- Successful ideas and strategies that can be extended.
- New ways to segment markets.
- Differences between your business systems and the competitors' that could be turned into competitive advantage.

Smaller competitors are a good source of ideas—they often come up with innovations that a big company can turn into successes.

5. *Go for broke.* Good ideas don't always work the first time. Persistence is required to work out bugs and build consumer acceptance. Underspending on new ideas is a more common cause of failure than overspending.

A corollary of this is that companies need to be selective in order to avoid spreading resources too thin on the implementation stage.

Tip: Pick the one or few innovations with the best prospects and push those hard; hold the rest until next year. This is especially true for any innovations that must be introduced to customers. New-product launches generally have different and greater marketing needs than existing products.

Reference

Andrall E. Pearson. "Tough-Minded Ways to Get Innovative." *Harvard Business Review* (May–June 1988).

ROSENAU'S R&D CHECKLIST

Applications

- Identifying critical issues for planning or evaluating R&D proposals.
- Incorporating management judgment into evaluation of new products and new research projects.
- Presenting evaluation criteria in a graphical format.

Procedures

1. Develop a list of issues that may be important for evaluating a proposed product or research project.
2. Rank each issue based on its importance to the success of the project and your company's strength in the area.
3. Plot the issues on a graph or sort them in a spreadsheet program to identify critical issues—those important issues on which the project is weak.

Cross-Reference

Strategic Planning Decisions

Many books on R&D offer checklists of issues for evaluating new product ideas. But Milton Rosenau of Rosenau Consulting (a Santa Monica firm specializing in technology management) finds these lists overly general and simplistic. Different issues are important for different products and companies. The problem: Which issues deserve the most attention in any specific case?

INSTRUCTIONS

1. Develop a list of issues for evaluating a research proposal or new-product proposal. The objective is to list every issue that might be important to the future success of the project. Use one of the many published lists as a source (Rosenau's book, referenced below, has a list of 54 issues). Or compile your own by brainstorming with your managers or product development team to identify issues of relevance to your company.

Useful device: Start with a list of general issues based on the functional divisions of your company. This list might include issues such as financing, development, manufacturing, distribution, marketing, sales, service, social impact. Then break each area down into the specific issues from the area that seem relevant to this project. For example, brainstorming on the marketing area might produce the following list: product life-cycle, advertising, packaging, pricing, image, market needs.

An advantage of this approach is that you can delegate the task of listing relevant subissues to the managers specializing in each relevant area. The marketing manager, for example, could easily compile a list of all the relevant criteria under the marketing heading.

2. Rank evaluation issues on two scales:

a. How *important* is the issue to success of the new product?

b. How *strong* is the new product on this issue, based on its characteristics and the company's resources?

For example, advertising is an important issue for a new consumer product. If the company is primarily in industrial sales and has little experience with advertising, the product development proposal would receive a high rating on the importance scale and a low rating on the strength scale.

Use a numerical scale (0 to 5 or 0 to 10) for the ratings, with the high end of the scale equal to very important or very strong. (*Idea:* Have as many managers as possible rate the issues and calculate the mean ratings.)

3. The results may be graphed to summarize the findings.

R&D ISSUE GRAPH

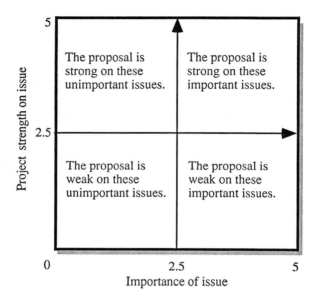

From Rosenau, *Innovation: Managing the Development of Profitable New Products,* Van Nostrand Reinhold, 1982.

The issues which fall into the lower-right quadrant of the graph are especially important to the project in the view of those managers polled. In addition, they are issues on which the company and/or product is currently weak, and obviously deserve special attention. Any project plan should discuss each of these in depth. Their impact on success should be evaluated carefully, and strategies to overcome weaknesses on these issues should be developed. For example, the industrial company discussed above should explore licensing and distribution options with established retailers before developing the proposed retail product in order to overcome its weakness in consumer advertising, which was rated as important to the success of the product.

Note: The graph is useful in presenting the method to managers or summarizing results. But if many issues are rated, the graph may become too cluttered to work with. Try using a PC-based spreadsheet program to sort the list of issues by their two scores. Do a primary sort from highest to lowest on importance and a secondary sort from lowest to highest on strength. The most critical issues will be at the top of this list.

Caution: Rosenau warns that no checklist can substitute for judgment when evaluating R&D proposals. At best a checklist is a useful aid to good judgment.

Reference

Milton D. Rosenau, Jr. *Innovation: Managing the Development of Profitable New Products*. Lifetime Learning Publications (Van Nostrand Reinhold), 1982.

SHELL SCENARIO FORECASTING

Applications

- Making long-term decisions concerning where to allocate R&D funds and expertise.
- Developing a variety of forecasts for use in contingency planning.
- Evaluating current technology strategies to see how vulnerable to environmental changes they are.

Procedures

1. Collect historical data on organizational and environmental variables relevant to attainment of technological objectives.
2. List specific technological objectives and make sure they remain the focus of analysis in the following stages of the analysis.
3. Select the variables which are most important to attainment of objectives, going back to step 1 if new variables are identified for which historical information has not already been collected.
4. Evaluate the potential impact of each variable on the organization, either in an informal management roundtable or by using MacNulty's Matrix Analysis.
5. Create a surprise-free scenario, two extreme-case scenarios, and several intermediate scenarios.
6. Study the potential impact of each scenario on the achievement of technological and other organizational objectives. Modify current tech-

nology strategies or prepare contingency plans in order to prepare for threatening scenarios.

Cross-Reference

Strategic Planning Decisions, Financial Decisions

Royal Dutch Shell began using scenario forecasting in the early 1970s and now uses this method to produce three groups of forecasts: Long-term, medium-term, and operating. The long-term forecasts go out 20 years and medium-term provide 5 year projections. Operating forecasts focus on more narrow issues of interest to specific operating companies or investments, and their terms vary. Long-term scenarios are revised on a 5-year cycle and others are usually revised annually. Not every firm needs as many or as long-term forecasts as a large oil company does, but many managers of technology-driven organizations or departments can adapt the basic methods of scenario forecasting to their needs. R&D requires long-term strategies, so long-range forecasting is especially applicable to this area. There is a strong argument for doing the forecasting within the R&D wing of the organization, as it will produce scenarios that are much more relevant to technology decisions than do general business forecasts.

While Shell is often credited with introducing this particular approach to scenario forecasting, it has been highly developed by C. Ralph MacNulty, a forecaster who has worked with many European and U.S. companies. The instructions presented here largely follow her methodology.

The method produces one forecast that extends current trends—a suprise-free scenario—and two alternatives that assume extreme variations from the current situation. Michael Martin, an academic studying R&D planning, reports that the method is especially useful for generating forecasts of variables that are relevant to technology strategies. *For example*: relevant variables for some R&D departments include rate of technical development, federal regulation, and patent filings by competitors.

INSTRUCTIONS

1. Collect historical information.

Quantitative forecasts should be based on historical data extending at least as far into the past as the forecast extends into the future. At a minimum, long-range forecasts need ten years of historical data unless the industry is less than ten years old (in which case the definition of long-term should be shortened!). The researcher should collect relevant qualitative information as well as any relevant numbers that are available. Qualitative information about technological processes and environmental, political, social, and demographic events may be useful in building scenarios.

Note: Many organizations already monitor their environment and maintain useful databases (but you may need to supplement these with technical information). If your organization does not have an applicable database, building one for scenario analysis is a lengthy process. Consider using a consultant or committing a staff member to the project full time for a month.

2. Identify organizational objectives.

Technical objectives and goals provide a context for scenario development and use. List them (and define them if they are not already clear) in order to focus the scenario analysis on issues of relevance to your organization's objectives. Scenario building is a frustrating process without clear objectives to keep it focused.

3. Select key variables.

What variables affect the organization's pursuit of its objectives? Understanding these variables is the key to building accurate and useful scenarios. Relevant variables include factors in the organization's environment (price of energy, supplies of a computer chip) and factors within the organization (R&D funding levels, licensing revenues, average time required for process scale-up).

4. Evaluate variables.

How do these variables affect the organization's attainment of its technological objectives? How might these variables interact? Examination of the data collected in step 1 and discussion with knowledgeable managers and scientists can shed light on the likely direction and impact of each variable.

Note: If dozens of variables are identified and in-depth analysis of them appears necessary, delegate steps 3 and 4 to staff or a consulting firm—but keep close tabs on the work to see that it remains focused on the objectives and questions that are important to you.

5. Select scenarios.

Some practitioners start with this step, but the four preliminary steps used by MacNulty create a strong foundation for scenario building and increase the probability of realistic and useful forecasts. Managers often delegate the data collection and analysis in the first four steps, which is acceptable, but management participation is essential at step 5.

Scenarios include the following:

Surprise-free scenario. Assumes current trends continue. Extrapolates indefinitely based on current standards and current values of relevant variables.

Example: A PC manufacturer's surprise-free scenario might indicate continued incremental increases in sales and a gradual decline in sales growth as the product matures.

Two extreme scenarios. Two scenarios are constructed to represent the most extreme deviations from the surprise-free scenario in either direction. They should be based on reasonable assumptions about the variables identified in step 3, and the combination of factors needed to create these extremes should be described in a qualitative or quantitative model.

Example A: A rapid increase in oil prices plus increased home usage of PC's leads to an explosion in home electronic shopping. PC sales grow very rapidly.

Example B: A Japanese manufacturer introduces hand-held PC's the size and cost of calculators. They replace the CPU of a PC. Peripheral sales grow to serve this new market, but sales of traditional PC's fall drastically.

More moderate variations. While the two extreme scenarios are fairly unlikely, events are likely to deviate from the surprise-free scenario and toward one of the extremes over time. By combining elements of the surprise-free and extreme scenarios the forecaster can develop several variations that are more plausible and hence more useful for technology planning.

Example: Oil prices do rise, but not enough to inhibit shopping by auto. Electronic shopping grows moderately. It takes five years to miniaturize PC's, work out the glitches, establish industry standards, and develop special software and peripherals. The moderate forecast is therefore that PC sales grow slightly faster for several years, then level off and decline slowly after five years.

MacNulty's matrix analysis

MacNulty uses a lengthy, formal procedure for generating scenarios. It is probably not necessary in most technology planning applications, but it is a useful option when trouble is encountered in step 4 or 5. An impact matrix is constructed with all the organizational variables listed across the top and all environmental variables down the side. A team of three to seven upper managers and a moderator fill in each cell of the matrix with a consensus opinion of the impact of each environmental variable on each organizational variable. The moderator asks a question such as, "If oil prices increase, will our PC sales increase, stay the same, or decrease?" Managers respond in writing using the following scale:

1   high increase

2   medium increase

3   low increase

4   no change

5   low decrease

6   medium decrease

7   high decrease

The answers are compared and any significant differences are worked out in discussion. The method produces a wealth of information about specific impacts of variables. Some firms analyze hundreds of variables, so a systematic approach is necessary. The completed tables guide staff in creating scenarios that reflect management's view of each variable. *Keep in mind:* the process is cumbersome and lengthy, and many users prefer an informal approach to scenario construction for this reason.

6. Study the implications of each scenario.

How well would the organization achieve its technological or product development goals under each scenario? Usually one or more of the scenarios would prevent the organization from performing as desired. When the implications of each scenario have been identified, the organization has two viable responses.

First, technology strategies can be modified to make the organization less vulnerable to a scenario (an attractive alternative only when the scenario is considered likely). For example: if the scenario in which hand-held PC's threaten traditional PC sales is likely, the organization could shift resources to hand-held PC product development.

Second, the organization can monitor key variables to detect any deviations from the surprise-free scenario in their earliest stages. Contingency plans should be developed for rapid response once a scenario appears likely. This approach is more common since it is difficult to assign a high probability to long-term scenario forecasts. The plans' main value is in identifying *possible* futures rather than in predicting a specific future with great accuracy. Unfortunately no method currently exists for that purpose!

References

Nagy Hanna. *Strategic Planning Management: A Review of Recent Experience.* Washington, D.C.: The World Bank, 1985. (Pages 31-32 discuss Royal Dutch Shell's scenario forecasting.)

C. Ralph MacNulty. *Managing Technological Innovation and Entrepreneurship.* (pp. 93–99) Reston, 1984.

STEELE'S SEVEN MISCONCEPTIONS

Applications

- Identifying false assumptions that may hinder completion and commercialization of R&D projects.
- Evaluating project proposals.
- Training research staff to consider issues of market adoption, scale-up, and production in the product development phase.

Procedures

Review projects to look for any of the seven misconceptions listed below. Distribute the list of misconceptions to R&D staff for consideration when preparing proposals.

Cross-Reference

Strategic Planning Decisions

After 29 years of experience in nurturing innovative activity at General Electric, I am still amazed by how fragile and improbable a process innovation really is.
> - Lowell Steele, General Electric

Lowell Steele developed this checklist of common misconceptions about innovation because they often compromise R&D projects and make innovation difficult to manage. Use the checklist to screen proposals for false assumptions. It is a simple and useful tool for identifying basic misconceptions behind research programs before money and effort are wasted on them. Given the low success rate of R&D, any new tools for screening or improving proposals are worthwhile. Note that Steele's checklist includes misconceptions that are typically *not* part of the technical and financial analysis of R&D proposals. This makes it a useful tool for focusing attention on nontechnical hurdles to successful commercialization of a technical idea. *Training application*: It might be useful to ask R&D staff to discuss the list of misconceptions and decide whether any of them characterize previous or current R&D programs at your company.

INSTRUCTIONS

Evaluate proposals by looking for any of these misconceptions in the justification or market analysis sections. The list of misconceptions might also be useful in defining or evaluating strategies for R&D and product development.

1. *The best possible technology should be implemented.* Wrong. The goal should be technology that is good enough, rather than the best possible. Providing capability in excess of current expectations can lead to excessive costs and hinder adoption. Pursuit of technical perfection ignores the fact that there must be a trade-off among performance, cost, and product life. Better to optimize this trade-off, developing a technology that is just good enough to do so.

2. *"Good enough" is determined rationally.* Wrong. Convention and consumer expectations must determine what is good enough. Sometimes the market demands technology that is better and fancier than that needed to solve the problems, and sometimes the market will not accept a technology even though it may be better. In Steele's words, "Widely shared beliefs, even if mistaken, do much to shape technical effort." An R&D effort that defines its goals in technical terms without regard for "widely shared beliefs" may produce a product failure.

3. *Innovations are generally successful.* Wrong. Many managers assume an innovation has a decent chance of success, but this may be because successes are publicized and remembered and failures are not. Failure rates are actually high, and innovations have to provide significant advantages over the old technology. Furthermore, they must chase a "moving target" as marketers of the old technology cut costs and improve their products to defend their market.

4. *Murphy's Law does not apply to technical innovation.* Wrong. The benefits of a new technology are usually recognized (otherwise it would never have been noticed), but problems are likely to be uncovered with further research or testing. For example, GE invented a synthetic wool fiber, but discovered later that it dissolved in dry-cleaning solvents. Of course, even though problems will be encountered, they can sometimes be overcome, and dealing with them is part of the natural evolution of a technology.

5. *The more novel the idea, the better.* Wrong. A radically new technology can produce dramatic successes, but most successes are advances on existing technology. Extensions of conventional technology are less risky and time-consuming, and therefore generally more cost-effective. Possibilities for improving existing technologies are often overlooked, and the difficulty of introducing a radically new technology is often underestimated.

6. *Technical success is the major hurdle an innovation has to cross.* Wrong. Successful introduction is dependent primarily on the existence of the requisite infrastructure. The key question to ask is, "Assuming the technology works, what stands in the way of adoption?" Often physical or economic aspects of distribution and marketing, consumer behavior, regulations, the availability of raw materials, and other factors stand between an innovation and its market.

7. *Routines, standards, precision, and similar constraints are not important in technology development.* Wrong. Although contrary to the preferences of creative developers, a structured development climate imposes standardization and produces innovations that are more likely to be suitable for scale-up and production.

Reference

Adapted from Lowell Steele, "Managers' Misconceptions About Technology." *Harvard Business Review* (November–December 1983): 133–40. (I have reworded and summarized the misconceptions for clarity. Many illustrative examples from GE can be found in the original article.)

TEXAS INSTRUMENTS' OST PLANNING SYSTEM

Applications

- Fostering innovation in a technology-based company.
- Translating the company's objectives and strategic and tactical plans into an R&D program.
- Giving long-range and risky projects a chance along with short-term projects.

Procedures

1. Assign operational managers responsibility for reviewing and ranking R&D project proposals at tactical, strategic, and operational levels.
2. Reward all managers for promoting R&D projects to encourage them to propose projects for review.
3. Set an R&D budget for each level of the objectives, strategies, and tactics (OST) program. Have each proposal subjected to competitive review and prioritized at each level, working up from tactical to operational levels.
4. Promising ideas that are too undeveloped to be funded through the OST reviews should receive seed funding through designated "venture" managers.

Michael Martin, *Managing Technological Innovation & Entrepreneurship*, © 1984, pp. 307–314. Adapted by permission of Prentice-Hall, Inc. Englewood Cliffs, NJ.

Cross-Reference

Leadership Skills and Methods

As Texas Instruments grew in size it developed a planning system that maintains the innovative spirit of its entrepreneurial years. TI's OST method of planning has proven very successful at encouraging managers to innovate and helping upper management identify and support the most promising inventions. While application outside of TI has been limited, there is no good reason why other companies could not adopt similar procedures for a planning cycle to see how well the OST model fits their organizations.

INSTRUCTIONS

1. Assign operational managers responsibility for reviewing and ranking R&D project proposals at tactical, strategic, and operational levels. A committee is needed for each level. Higher-level managers sit on higher-level committees.

In OST, operations managers have a responsibility to generate and champion innovation and also to be responsible for evaluating R&D proposals on either the tactical, strategic, or operational level. They wear both operating and R&D hats, which keeps them more idea-oriented than the typical operations person. The company's strategic planning generates a number of objectives; a manager is assigned to each. Each objective has several strategies, and each strategy has a number of tactics; managers are assigned to these as well. A hierarchical system exists in the sense that research proposals work their way up one of the branches of the objective-strategy-tactic tree.

2. It is essential to the OST method that managers be recognized and rewarded for their contributions to OST and their willingness to identify and champion new product ideas. Reward all managers for promoting R&D projects to encourage them to propose projects for review. In general operating managers are judged by their contribution to operat-

ing results. But in OST, additional criteria must be devised to create an incentive for operating managers to put on their R&D hats. The dual role will require more time and effort of managers and will also require them to look farther ahead than next period's operating results. Recognition of their participation in the OST program is a minimum first step, and financial incentives or promotions are at the other end of the spectrum.

3. Set an R&D budget for each level of the OST program. Have each proposal subjected to competitive review and prioritized at each level, working up from tactical to operational levels. Every proposal is screened and given a priority ranking, first at the tactical level, then at the strategic level, and finally at the corporate-objectives level. The strategy manager reviews tactical selections and objectives managers review strategy-level decisions, sometimes revising the rankings of proposals.

Long-term and risky proposals which are not appealing at the tactical level have a second chance when upper-level managers review them. Relationships between projects originating in different parts of the company are recognized at the strategic or operational levels, making it easier to take advantage of synergies.

Note: Projects which received funding in earlier periods are reviewed and ranked routinely along with the new proposals. Problems in their development or changes in strategies and tactics may lead to a changed ranking for an ongoing project.

Upper management establishes spending levels at the tactical, strategic, and operational levels, and projects are funded at each level based on their ranking. A project that conforms well with tactics will receive tactical funding (unless it is not consistent with strategies and objectives). Unfunded projects are kept in a backlog for review when more R&D funds become available.

4. Promising ideas that are too undeveloped to be funded through the OST reviews should receive seed funding through designated "venture" managers. TI found that the OST program inhibits some entrepreneurial projects, both when champions are

young and have little experience in the OST process and when the project does not fit clearly within established strategies and tactics.

At TI this problem was addressed by creating an informal secondary source of funding for projects. It provides low levels of funding for feasibility demonstrations and idea development. Review is by one of a number of experienced managers whose main criterion is simply that the idea be a good one. A project given seed money for a feasibility study may later succeed in the OST program. Of course, there must be no penalty for the failure of a project that has received seed funding.

References

Michael J. C. Martin. *Managing Technological Innovation and Entrepreneurship.* Reston, 1984.

"Texas Instruments Shows U.S. Business How to Survive in the 1980s." *Business Week*, (September 18, 1978): 66–92.

Nagy Hanna. *Strategic Planning and Management: A Review of Recent Experience.* Washington D.C.: The World Bank, 1985.

PART 7

SALES MANAGEMENT DECISIONS

BINDICATOR TERRITORY PERFORMANCE ANALYSIS

Applications

- Developing an objective measure by which to compare the performance of sales territories.
- Setting sales goals based on the potential of a territory rather than on last year's performance in that territory.
- Evaluating the coverage of lead-generating advertising by territory.

Procedures

1. Break down your company's sales by SIC code.
2. Define territories by the states or counties within them.
3. Choose a statistic to represent the potential market size for each territory.
4. Calculate total market potential per territory.
5. Calculate the contribution of each territory to your company's sales.
6. Calculate the ratio between actual sales and potential contribution for each territory.
7. Plot the data on a graph.
8. *Optional*: Calculate sales leads versus sales potential per territory and plot this on a second graph.

Cross-Reference

Marketing Decisions

Bindicator, a manufacturer of instruments for measuring raw-material levels in bins, needed better measures of sales territory performance in order to improve its marketing. Its nationwide sales force operated out of approximately 30 territories, and management wanted a better way to compare territory performance and allocate resources. The method the company used was developed in cooperation with Market Statistics and used Market Statistics' database. But this method can be applied successfully in house by many organizations using other sources of data.

The following instructions use readily available census data (which, however, is not kept as current as Market Statistics' data). See *County Business Patterns* published by the Bureau of the Census, U.S. Department of Commerce, for each state of interest. Another inexpensive alternative is to use data from Market Statistics that is published annually in *Sales and Marketing Management* magazine.

INSTRUCTIONS

1. Assign SIC codes to each customer in order to determine the percent of sales from each industry group. (Three digit codes are used in *County Business Patterns*, so do not bother to break sales down by five digit codes if this is your source!) Aggregate the sales figures for the last few years if there is significant year-to-year variation.

Shortcut: If your company has many small customers, analyze a random sample of accounts and assume the industry composition of the sample applies to all sales. Make sure the sample includes all areas, as industry representation will probably vary with geographic location.

2. List the counties or states that compose sales territories. This may require some map work if you do not normally define territories by county or state borders.

3. Select a statistic that best represents sales potential from those available. In *County Business Patterns* you have a choice of total payroll, total number of employees, number of businesses, and number of businesses by size class based on number of employees. Counts of businesses are provided for each of these categories, by SIC code, county, and state. For example, an organization like Bindicator that sells to large manufacturing and processing companies might select number of establishments with over 50 employees in designated SIC codes as their measure of sales potential.

4. Sum the chosen statistic for the appropriate SIC codes in each territory. Total the territory figures by SIC code, weight each SIC code by its percent contribution to your sales, and then sum across all SIC codes. When you have done this for each territory, find the total for all territories, then calculate each territory's percent of the total.

5. Using actual sales figures, calculate each territory's percent contribution to your company's total sales. Use last period's sales figures, a three-year average, or the most recent figure from a trend line fitted to several years of sales data for each territory. (The latter is more difficult but preferable when there is consistent growth within territories and growth rates differ significantly between territories.)

6. For each territory, divide the percent of actual sales (step 5) by the percent of expected sales (from step 4). A negative number indicates the territory's performance is below average, and a positive number suggests it is above average. (*Warning*: the results are only as good as the statistic used to represent market potential.)

7. The data can be plotted on a graph with the horizontal axis representing percent of expected sales and the vertical representing percent of actual sales. Deviations from a diagonal line indicate over-performing and underperforming territories. A logarithmic scale on each axis makes this graph clearer.

Sales Leads: Bindicator also plots percent of sales leads per territory versus percent of expected sales to see whether lead-generating advertising is covering territories evenly. They found that some underper-

TERRITORY SALES PERFORMANCE
(*Versus Potential*)

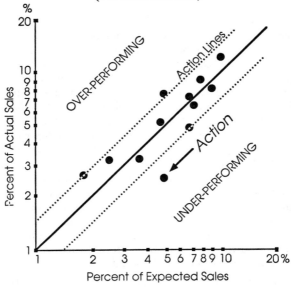

SALES LEADS PER TERRITORY
(*Versus Potential*)

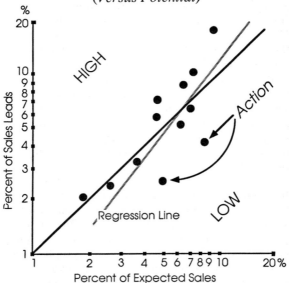

forming territories did not have adequate sales support. (Not surprising since advertising is usually allocated based on sales history.)

Reference

Karsten Hellebust. "Bindicator Finds a Fair Measure of Sales Territory Performance." *Sales and Marketing Management* (November 11, 1985).

BLAKE-MOUTON SALES GRID

Applications

- Improving selling style by examining underlying assumptions.
- Analyzing selling style for training exercises and evaluations.
- Analyzing performance of individual salespeople.
- Mapping and planning the sales cycle for complex sales.

Procedures

1. Evaluate the salesperson's concern for the customer on a 1 to 9 scale.
2. Evaluate the salesperson's concern for the sale on a 1 to 9 scale.
3. Map the salesperson's style on the Grid and identify which of the five generic styles describes it.
4. Use the Grid as a training and sales tool.

Options: Use the Grid to teach selling styles or to evaluate style and performance of salespeople. Categorize customers and prospects according to the sales style that they prefer. It is also possible to map the life cycle of a complex sale on the Grid and use the Grid to develop strategy for complex or lengthy sales.

Cross-Reference

Organization and Human Resources

Left to their own devices, most salespeople fall into a standard style of selling that is most comfortable for them. Quotas and other quantitative measures of performance do not provide direct feedback about the effectiveness of selling style, so salespeople

and managers tend not to evaluate the appropriateness of style as often as they should.

This is a powerful tool for analyzing the performance of individual salespeople, training salespeople
to identify and improve their selling styles, or planning long-term sales efforts for complex sales. The
use of the Grid in planning is rare, but I have seen a
case in which the consultative positioning strategy of
a computer company dictated a true "9,9" sales style.
In this situation, plans need to include specifications
for sales style, and an assessment of current style
combined with special training is generally
necessary.

INSTRUCTIONS

The Grid uses Concern for the Customer on one
dimension and Concern for the Sale on the other.
These represent the two most important dimensions
of sales style. The traditional hard sell is a totally

SALES GRID

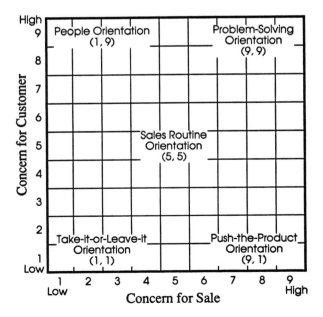

sales-oriented style, with no customization of message or approach. The other extreme is a personal style, in which a long-term personal relationship is developed and forms the basis of any sales. The concept of consultative selling, involving a long-term, problem-solving relationship with a client company, is represented on the Grid as a combination of high concern for both customer and sale.

To plot a particular selling style on this Grid, first rate the salesperson's concern for the customer on a 1 to 9 scale (1 equals low, 9 equals high). (It may be helpful to rate a group of salespeople at the same time in order to add a comparative element to the rating.) Next, rate the salesperson's concern for the sale on a 1 to 9 scale.

Note: It is preferable to *observe* salespeople in action before rating their selling styles.

Use the two ratings to map each salesperson's style on the Grid and identify the generic strategy that best describes him or her. The strategies are indicated on the exhibit, and their definitions are as follows:

People-oriented. Builds a personal relationship with the customer. Motivated by desire to be liked. Customers purchase out of friendship.

Problem-solving–oriented. Studies customer's needs and sells products that satisfy these needs. Can involve building a consultative relationship with the customer in which the customer purchases because salesperson can solve problems better than others.

Sales technique–oriented. A well-rehearsed presentation that combines problem solving, personality-oriented appeals, and sustained nudging to produce sales.

Take-it-or-leave-it. Allows the product to "sell itself" without making an effort to get to know the customer or to push the product to the customer. Passive selling style.

Push-the-product–oriented. Aggressive style. Tries to take charge of the customer and create pressure to purchase through hard-sell tactics. Emphasis on product features rather than personal relationship or customer needs. (May include reference to customer needs and problem solving, but in a generic and not always credible manner.)

Identifying the current styles of the people in your sales force may provide useful clues to what makes some more effective than others. Companies often look at top performers for lessons in how to sell, and in many cases the top performers are successful because their style ranks higher on one or both dimensions of the Grid, than other salespeople's styles.

When salespeople are first asked to evaluate their own sales style on the Grid, "83 percent...see themselves as 9.9 oriented" (referenced book, page 177). But after salespeople go through a training seminar based on the Grid, the percentage drops to 33. Blake and Mouton explain this "50 percent reduction in self-deception" as a result of a better understanding of personal sales style developed through self-examination and feedback from peer evaluations (feedback is provided in role-playing exercises in their seminars). It is apparently important to provide structured evaluation in sales training to help salespeople reach a realistic understanding of personal sales style.

The 9,9 style is as popular with Blake and Mouton as with their seminar attendants—they consider it the most effective style and the only one that works well with all types of buying behavior (referenced book, page 16). The Grid can be used to help salespeople adjust their style toward this ideal. Here are some of the characteristics of the 9,9 sales style:

- Has expert knowledge of the product
- Gains in-depth knowledge of the customer
- Creates customer involvement in sales interview
- Helps customer make a reasoned purchase decision
- Gives customers free and spontaneous help

However, the Grid is not prescriptive. Salespeople should be encouraged to identify and develop the style that is most comfortable and effective for them, and to try to stick to this personal goal in most selling situations. They should also recognize that they probably have a backup style which is used in difficult and tense situations. This too can be modified by targeting an ideal backup from the Grid. According to Blake and Mouton, any combination of styles is possible when selecting an ideal and backup style, but clearly styles that are closer to 9,9 are preferable and, in general, the 1,1 style is going to be ineffective.

Reference

Robert R. Blake and Jane S. Mouton. *The Grid for Sales Excellence: New Insights into a Proven System of Effective Sales* (2nd Ed.). Austin, Texas: Scientific Methods, Inc., 1970.

(Thanks to Walter Barclay of Scientific Methods for corrections and permission to reprint the Grid.)

DELPHI SALES FORECASTING

Applications

- Incorporating judgment into quantitative forecasts of sales and future events in the market.
- Increasing the accuracy of sales forecasts by sales managers and salespeople.
- Creating accurate sales forecasts using non-expert forecasters.

Procedures

1. Prepare a factual briefing and alternative sales forecasts.
2. Select a group of salespeople and sales managers and distribute the material to them through a group coordinator.
3. Keep group members apart. Have each member review the briefing, select a forecast, and communicate their selection to the coordinator. The coordinator summarizes group opinion, conveys this to members, and asks them to rethink their opinion and revise it if they see fit. Members again communicate their opinions and their reasoning to the coordinator, who sends out the new results along with a summary of the reasons. Repeat at least three times to reach consensus or near-consensus.

Cross-Reference

Useful in many areas, including Marketing Decisions and Strategic Planning Decisions

This method applies the Delphi Technique developed by the Rand Corporation to sales forecasting. It is especially applicable for annual sales projections by sales management and salespeople and can increase the accuracy of these forecasts. It is also applicable to the task of anticipating outcomes of strategic alternatives for sales and marketing plans.

American Hoist and Derrick has found the method a useful supplement to purely quantitative projections when incorporating judgments into sales forecasting. And a number of academic studies have tested the accuracy of forecasts and found that the Delphi method can increase the performance of a group significantly (see the references for more on both topics).

INSTRUCTIONS

1. Define the forecasting task clearly. Prepare a short briefing on the situation—it might include previous year's sales figures, major trends, market shares, new product plans, marketing strategies, and any relevant demographic and economic projections that might be available from the government, a trade group, or a custom survey. It is also preferable to identify approximately four alternative forecasts from which group members will choose. For example, research staff could prepare high and low projections and two or three intermediate projections.

2. Select groups of approximately six sales managers, salespeople, and staff for each forecast needed. For example, a company with five geographic areas might use five groups for area forecasts and one or two more for any special groups such as government sales. The overall forecast can be built up from the individual forecasts, or a separate group can be used for the overall forecast and the results compared with the composite of area forecasts. The groups do *not* need to be assembled. You can communicate with them through the regular mail, or through electronic mail if your company has one of these systems. But if they are all in one place for a meeting the method can be implemented in an hour or two.

Note: You will also need to assign an individual manager or staff member to coordinate each group's communications since group members *are not permitted* to discuss their opinions with each other.

3. Each member of a group is asked to review the briefing (and alternative forecasts if included). Then members select the forecast they think is most accurate and communicate it to their group coordinator (usually in writing; by filling in a questionnaire).

The coordinator summarizes the group's opinions and reports them to each member of the group. If alternatives were given to the group, the number favoring each alternative is provided to group members. But the summary is written so as to conceal the opinions (and sometimes even the identities) of individual group members.

Now the group members review the summary of group opinions and again report their opinions to the group leader. This time, members provide brief explanations of their reasoning. The coordinator again summarizes opinion and adds a summary of the main reasons behind the various group opinions. This gives group members an understanding of the various arguments and helps them think through the validity of their opinions.

The coordinator should repeat the process three or more times. The goal is to continue until all members of the group converge on a single forecast. In some cases time, or the stubbornness of a group member, will not permit consensus, and a majority vote must suffice.

Note: See Pfizer's Sales Forecasting for a related method that is used for projecting the impact of multiple sales and marketing variables on future sales.

References

S. Basu and R.G. Shroeder. "Incorporating Judgments in Sales Forecasts—Application of the Delphi Method of American Hoist and Derrick." *Interfaces* (May 1977): 18–27.

Christopher Orpen. "The Relative Accuracy of Individual, Group, and Delphi Process Strategic Forecasts." *Handbook of Business Strategy: 1986/1987 Yearbook*, ed. W. D. Guth (Chapter 20). Warren, Gorham & Lamont, 1986.

DOYLE'S SALES-FORCE MOTIVATION MODEL

Applications

- Assessing and improving sales-force motivation without changing compensation or recruiting policies.
- Improving sales-force performance for complex, lengthy, and other difficult sales.
- Choosing between incentive and nonincentive compensation plans.

Procedures

Assess sales task clarity and modify policies, procedures, and information systems to increase it if it is low. Measure task clarity before designing a compensation plan or when evaluating the cost-effectiveness of an incentive system.

Cross-Reference

Organization and Human Resources; Manufacturing and Operations. Task clarity can also be a powerful motivator in other jobs.

Steven Doyle of SXD Associates developed this method while doing research for his dissertation at Harvard Business School. His research evaluated the impact of various motivators on the performance of sales forces at transportation service and business product companies. Surprisingly, he discovered that something he calls "task clarity" had a greater impact on motivation than compensation method or ego drive, the two motivators generally thought to account for sales performance. He has extended this finding in work for companies in other industries, and it is probably applicable to most sales forces. It is helpful in developing nonmonetary and nonrecruiting solutions to sales performance problems, which means it can save money and time. It is also useful for selecting the appropriate type of compensation package for a sales force.

Sales task clarity is the obviousness of the relationship between a salesperson's efforts and reported results. It varies significantly. A door-to-door canvasser collecting cash and checks for a lobbying group receives rapid and unambiguous (although not necessarily positive) feedback concerning performance. Task clarity is generally high. But a salesperson for a company like Digital Equipment Corp. is one of many customer contacts during a lengthy sales cycle involving multiple decisionmakers and influencers and complex products and concepts. This salesperson's task clarity is liable to be considerably lower.

In Doyle's model, task clarity is a function of the impact the individual has on sales results (higher equals clearer), the speed with which results or performance feedback occurs (quicker equals clearer), and the accuracy of performance feedback (more accurate equals clearer). The DEC salesperson's individual impact on the sale may not be clear to him or her, the lengthy sales cycle could delay feedback for a year, and reporting procedures might fail to credit the salesperson fully for his or her individual contribution. These are the reasons why the computer salesperson's job may tend to be low in task clarity.

Use this simple model to improve motivation by improving on one or more of the three contributors to task clarity. Policy changes; modifications or additions to performance reports; more rapid or frequent reporting; changes in the structure and design of sales teams; and many other tactics can be used to improve task clarity.

Measure task clarity either by making a judgmental assessment (through observation and discussions with salespeople) or by administering a questionnaire. The assessment should have one or more questions for each of the three factors contributing to task clarity and can take the form of a rating scale.

Another implication of the model is that incentive compensation is a more effective motivator when task clarity is high. (*Tip:* Consider task clarity when selecting a compensation method and either increase task clarity before using incentives or stick with straight salary. There is no point in wasting money on commissions when task clarity is low.)

References

Benson P. Shapiro and Stephen X. Doyle. "What Counts Most in Motivating Your Sales Force." *Harvard Business Review* (May–June 1980): 133.

_____. "Make the Sales Task Clear." *Harvard Business Review* (November–December 1983) 72, 76.

MACKAY ENVELOPE'S CUSTOMER QUESTIONNAIRE

Applications

- Building a strong relationship between salesperson and customer contact.
- Developing a database on decisionmakers at client companies and prospects for planning sales strategy, improving service performance, reducing account turnover, and providing transition information for new salespeople.
- Evaluating the personal relationship between customer contact and salesperson.
- Training the sales force to listen to customer needs as part of a shift toward consultative or partnership selling.

Procedures

1. Develop a list of questions about customers, including aspects such as biographical information, attitudes toward their company, their company's performance, and issues facing their company.

2. Create a customer file for use in developing sales strategies. Require salespeople to maintain files on prospects as well as customers to keep the salespeople focused on account development.

3. Refer to the file to tailor service, sales calls, entertainment, and gifts to the contact's preferences and the customer's needs and policies.

Adapted from *Marketing News*, published by the American Marketing Association. (Noris Tolson, "Good Sales Team Knows Customers Inside and Out," November 21, 1988, Vol. 22, pp. 5, 11.)

Also use to evaluate the customer/salesperson relationship and to brief a new salesperson.

Cross-Reference

Leadership Skills and Methods

Harvey Mackay of Mackay Envelope developed this method to improve the effectiveness of his sales force. Although the method is unsophisticated from an analytical point of view, it has the advantage of making the sales force gather and use information about customers. And it gives management a unique tool for assessing the relationship between customer and salesperson.

INSTRUCTIONS

1. Develop a list of questions about your customers and the kind of relationship you want your sales force to develop with your customers. Mackay Envelope uses a list of 66 questions in each of the following categories.

Biographical:	Education, career history, interests, life style, vacation preferences, family, birthday, favorite lunch spots, political views, etc.
Attitudes toward company:	Views on their company's performance and goals, the industry, issues facing their company.
Company performance:	Growth, profitability, trends in purchasing, purchase of your company's products/services, strategic issues and plans, major competitors and challenges.

Sources of this information include SEC filings, discussions with secretaries and associates, and conversations with the decisionmaker at lunches and special events.

2. Create a customer or prospect file with this information. Refer to it when developing a strategy to

land new accounts. Mr. Mackay subscribes to the theory that "by making ourselves Number Two in many places, sooner or later we'll be Number One in some." A detailed prospect file is a good interim goal for the salesperson who might otherwise become frustrated with the pursuit of the number two position.

3. Use the file to strengthen existing customer relationships by tailoring entertainment, gifts, and conversation to the decisionmaker's personal interest and adapting your company's service to the needs and goals of the organization.

Use customer files for sales management. Managers should review files periodically to evaluate the customer relationship. Lack of personal information is a clear indicator of a mismatch between salesperson and customer. Company information may suggest strategies for improving service to the customer as a way to increase your share of the customer's business.

Files are also valuable for training new salespeople and for orienting them to take over existing accounts. Mackay believes the effort of collecting all the information trains salespeople to listen better, which makes them better at handling the customer's business.

Example:

Du Pont Electronics uses similar methods, both to improve customer relationships and to facilitate development of products for the specific needs of major customers in the computer, auto, defense, and home electronics industries. Norris Tolson, director of sales, stresses that "there is no substitute for thoroughly knowing the customer in today's selling world."

Du Pont Electronics has applied a variety of methods, including field work by managers and inclusion of salespeople in product development, to deepen the customer relationship. The company also has regional electronics centers that provide meeting rooms, teleconferencing facilities, and labs for customers to use. These services give Du Pont Electronics many opportunities to learn more about the customer's business and technical needs, bringing the concept of client research beyond the personal relationship and toward a complete business relationship.

The sales function is evolving toward partnership selling and a consultative approach in many industrial and business-to-business markets. Du Pont Electronics has achieved considerable success with this approach, and so has Mackay Envelope. The customer questionnaire is a good way to initiate a push toward a more personal and problem-solving style of salesmanship in any company, as the salespeople are usually the biggest obstacle to implementation of this strategy!

References

Harvey B. Mackay. "Humanize Your Selling Strategy." *Harvard Business Review* (March–April 1988).

Norris Tolson. "Good Sales Team Knows Customers Inside and Out." *Marketing News* (November 21, 1988.)

MCKINSEY CUSTOMER PROFITABILITY MATRIX

Applications

- Allocating sales force-effort based on account profitability.
- Developing sales and marketing strategies that target the most profitable types of customers in a market.
- Providing detailed cost data for customer price negotiations.
- Finding out how profitable the largest, most demanding customers really are.

Procedures

1. Analyze costs per customer, including presale costs, production costs, distribution costs, and postsale service costs.

2. Calculate the net price and net revenues for each of the customers included in the cost analysis.

3. Graph the customers on a cost/price graph. (Use circles proportionate to annual net revenues.) Add lines to represent average cost and price and include a diagonal break-even line. The matrix indicates which customers fall into standard categories of buyer behavior: carriage trade, bargain basement, passive, and aggressive.

4. Develop strategies and support systems to help the sales force and the marketing department target customers in the category or categories considered most desirable in your current situation.

5. Repeat the analysis periodically to identify changes in account profitability and renew the sales profitability strategy.

Cross-Reference

Marketing Decisions

Companies often price on the basis of average product cost, but prices rarely reflect the total costs of providing the product or service to a *specific* customer. A study by Elliot Ross of McKinsey, in collaboration with Harvard Business School faculty, indicates that the cost of servicing individual customers varies by as much as 30%, making some customers profitable to work with and others unprofitable. The study went on to identify *types* of customers based on their buying behavior and average profitability, making it possible to predict the profitability of each customer type and tailor strategy toward the most profitable customers. The customer profitability matrix helps companies analyze their customers for profitability and develop strategies that target the most profitable groups of customers.

INSTRUCTIONS

1. The hitch is that you must first analyze costs per customer in more detail than most cost-accounting systems allow; you need to calculate total costs of servicing each customer over a period of time. There are different approaches to this problem, depending on how far you want to go with the method. To start, try working with a small, random sample of accounts to limit the amount of homework needed, or just perform the analysis on the national or "A" accounts. A more involved alternative is, of course, to hire a large consulting firm such as McKinsey to do the analysis.

Identify and allocate costs as well as possible in the following categories:

Presale costs	Differences in customer buying-processes, location, and need for customized engineering and other presale services make a big difference in per-sale costs per customer.
Production costs	Some firms do custom designs for their customers, which obviously affects production costs per customer. But other factors—packaging requirements, timing, set-up time, fast delivery requirements—may also vary by customer. Inventory and accounting procedures can make it difficult to estimate these costs on a per-customer basis.
Distribution costs	The customer location and the mode of shipment can vary significantly from customer to customer. The logistics or transportation department usually can identify per-customer distribution costs easily, although they are rarely asked to.
Postsale service costs	Training, installation, support, repair, and maintenance costs usually vary, and warranty and contract terms can differ as well, making the cost of postsales service an important variable for per-customer cost analysis.

2. Calculate the net price of your products or services to the same customers for which you per-

formed the cost analysis. Make sure that any discounts, returns, and so forth are taken into account. In many companies these items are not reported on weekly or monthly account-by-account revenue reports; they appear later as adjustments. Also collect a gross-sales-per-year figure for each customer analyzed.

3. Plot the data for each customer on a graph with net price on the vertical axis and cost on the horizontal axis. Represent each customer with a circle proportional to gross sales (or to revenues from that customer as a proportion of your company's total revenues). Add lines to represent average price and

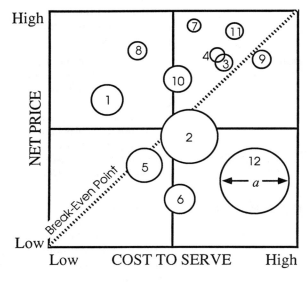

CUSTOMER PROFITABILITY MATRIX

a = % of Sales or Total Sales per Year

(This matrix indicates that two large accounts are unprofitable and that there are few passive accounts.)

cost, and a diagonal line to show the break-even point where cost equals price.

The resulting matrix shows which customers have high costs in relation to the price they pay and which customers are producing high net profits for your company. It divides customers into four groups based on where they stand relative to the average cost and price lines. Quadrants are labeled "passive," "carriage trade," "bargain basement," and "aggressive," reflecting the fact that there is a typical buying behavior for each quadrant of the matrix. Customers can be divided into these four groups according to how high or low net price and cost are:

Carriage trade	High cost, high net price. Willing to pay a high price for superior products and services. Often place small, custom orders.
Bargain basement	Low cost, low net price. Price-sensitive; less concerned about quality or service.
Passive	Low cost, high net price. Less concerned about quality or service but not very price-sensitive either. Buying behavior is passive either because the product is insignificant to this customer, or extremely significant, or not readily available from other sources.
Aggressive	High cost, low net price. Command high quality and service and low prices, often because they buy in large quantity. Strong negotiators and technological leaders often fall into this category as well.

4. Interpret the matrix and develop strategies and support systems to help your company manage its customers for profitability. Most companies have customers in all four categories. Sometimes a company's most prized accounts—large volume, high-profile

customers—are breaking even or losing money when a careful cost analysis is performed, while many of the smaller accounts may be far more profitable.

On the strategy level, a company can define itself based on the type of customer it pursues. For example, a company positioned in the high-price/high-quality end of the market should focus on customers in the upper-left section of the matrix, while low-price/low-service providers looking for high volume and a favorable cost position in their markets should target customers in the lower left of the matrix. Note that customer buying-behavior may vary depending on who makes the purchase and what it is, and changes in the customer's organization or operations may also move them from one quadrant to another.

Idea: Survey decision-makers in your markets to identify their company's buying behavior in terms of service needs, negotiation, and the other variables related to net cost. Look for relationships between net cost of serving a customer and other variables, such as size, age, location, and organization, that will help you define and target profitable segments for account development.

On the tactical level, pricing should reflect per-customer costs to the extent that they can be estimated. Information systems may need to be modified to provide the information necessary for negotiation and discount decisions as well as for establishing base prices.

5. Repeat the analysis. Cost structures change over time and so do customers. For example, a reorganization may change the way a customer buys your product, altering the cost of serving that customer and requiring a change in your pricing tactics. Account profitability strategies, like any strategies, should be evaluated every year or two, and up-to-date information will be needed for this purpose.

Example: The method has not been widely applied, so nonproprietary examples are scarce. But the inventors of the method describe several examples in the referenced article, including the case of an electrical-products division of a large company that competes in a mature, commodity-oriented market. It applied this method and began to focus on the more profitable customers, shifting its sales and product-line strategies in the process. The company reported a resulting shift from a 5% loss to a 10% profit.

Reference

Shapiro, Rangan, Moriarty, and Ross. "Manage Customers for Profits (Not Just Sales)." *Harvard Business Review*. (September–October 1987).

PFIZER'S SALES FORECASTING

Applications

- Developing planning guidelines that incorporate the expertise of local managers in a specific market or country.
- Selecting the most productive and cost-effective way of allocating sales effort and expenditures.
- Making sales-force and marketing decisions in the context of local markets rather than on a unilateral or average-response basis.

Procedures

1. Meet with local managers to identify the issues of concern to them in planning the sales and marketing strategy for a product in their local market.

2. Have staff collect historical information to identify any clear trends between sales-force size, spending on promotion, and other variables, and the sales response in the local market.

3. Prepare a short report summarizing the findings from step 2, adding a profile of the product and market.

4. Write a series of questions asking what sales response to expect with modifications in the current sales and marketing variables. Bring the managers back for a meeting in which they fill out a questionnaire based on these questions.

5. Summarize their answers and give the group the summary. Hand out blank questionnaires again and have the managers answer them after reviewing the summarized results. Repeat both steps until consensus is reached.

6. Prepare a report summarizing the consensus from the meeting or have staff build a spreadsheet model based on the results. Use to evaluate alternative sales plans and strategies.

Cross-Reference

Marketing Decisions

Pfizer's international operations require management of sales forces and promotional efforts in many countries, each with unique needs and constraints. Davey William, Director of Field Force Development at Pfizer International, uses a modification of the Rand Corporation's Delphi Technique to forecast the response of sales to differing levels of resource allocation. The method incorporates management judgment in decisions concerning sales-force size and structure and resource allocation. By including management judgment it produces decision guidelines tailored to the needs and constraints of each separate market. This is especially important when U.S. companies compete in international markets, as decisions that are optimal in the U.S. are often suboptimal in other countries.

Pfizer uses the method to develop PC-based decision support systems for local sales management. But the method can easily be used to produce manual decision guidelines and plans as well. It is applicable to regional markets within the U.S. as well as to international markets, and could also be applied SBU by SBU or subsidiary by subsidiary to develop sales plans for an entire company.

Pfizer asks, "How much sales-force effort should we put behind each of our products in each of our market segments?" The question is answered by asking managers to help estimate the sales response to differing levels of effort allocated in various ways in each segment.

INSTRUCTIONS

1. Identify a specific market for study. Pick a single product in the market (the analysis must be

done product by product). Meet with managers in the local market to identify the issues they consider to be high priority. Issues may be far-reaching, including such items as new competitors, regulations, fear of an economic downturn. They may also be quite focused on issues of sales-force management, such as whether to hire more salespeople and how much to spend on advertising support. The more focused issues are of more importance in this method, so try to encourage managers to elaborate on these.

2. Apply historical data to develop a picture of the effect sales efforts have had on the history of sales in the market under study. This may be as simple as looking through your corporate records for relationships between sales and coverage by territory, sales and advertising by product, and so forth. Or, in some industries, there may be extensive industrywide data that support some generalizations. However, do not be surprised if meaningful information is hard to find. In many industries there is little hard evidence for relationships between sales efforts and response.

3. Prepare a short report describing any clear quantitative or qualitative evidence concerning the impact of sales efforts on sales results. Add to this a brief profile of facts about the product and market. Pfizer includes the following in this profile:

- Product profile
- Profiles of competing products
- Sales history
- Promotional program history
- Future promotional plans
- Market characteristics

Send the report to each of the managers who attended the original meeting (Step 1).

4. Have the managers attend a meeting to answer a series of questions concerning the effects of various promotional and sales strategies on sales revenues over the next three years. Questions should be designed to explore the response of sales to varied levels of resource allocation. Answers should be made anonymously on paper and without discussion.

Generate your questions by first listing the different variables of concern for the product and market. Size of sales force, spending levels on print advertising, promotion, telemarketing, direct mail, and other issues may be deemed relevant. Issues raised in step 1 may suggest questions. The best source of questions is often the annual sales or marketing plan, which identifies marketing variables and establishes allocation levels for them. Using the planned allocations (or last year's allocations if the plan has not been written yet), define two or three higher and lower alternatives for each variable. For each alternative, write a question asking what the impact on sales would be over the next three years.

Example: Last year there were 23 salespeople in France. Ask your French management team for estimates of the percent increase in sales over the next three years if there were 28 salespeople. If there were 33 salespeople. And ask what percent decrease, if any, the managers would expect with 18 and 13 salespeople.

There are no formal rules for these questions, but they should cover the range of options that managers are likely to consider in developing their sales and marketing plans.

If you want to use the responses to build a quantitative model, as Pfizer does, then you also have to include "second-order" questions that ask managers to evaluate the *combined* effect of the resource allocation decisions to find out how individual decisions interact. For example, if five new salespeople were added *and* the promotion budget were increased by 10%, what percent increase would there be in sales? If there are many marketing variables, combine them into a smaller number of plausible scenarios to reduce the complexity of the questions.

5. Summarize the answers quickly and disseminate them to the group (in the same meeting). After the group has reviewed the answers, each member fills out the questionnaire again, as in step 3. Again, the questions should be answered privately and anonymously. Summarize the answers from the second questionnaire, disseminate them to the group again, and have them fill in the questionnaire a third time. Repeat until a consensus is reached, usually after three rounds. (Consensus does not have to be absolute—small deviations in answers can be averaged by

the manager or moderator who is running the meeting.)

6. Let the managers go back to their work—they may be growing impatient by now! Have staff or a consultant integrate any useful historical data from step 2 with the managers' views from the questionnaire summary. The main purpose of this integration is to make sure there are no contradictions between historical facts and management perception. If there are, it may be necessary to decide which source is correct through further research and discussions with managers.

At Pfizer, analysts go on to build a PC-based spreadsheet model based on the answers. The impact of differing allocation decisions provides the basis for formulas in the spreadsheet. The spreadsheet can then be used by managers to model the effect of various scenarios and see which one gives the best response for the money.

If you have staff that are skilled at model making, let them try their hands at turning the answers into mathematical functions and building a formal model. However, many managers will prefer just to summarize the findings of the questionnaire in written form and send it to managers as a reference tool for sales and marketing plans. (In either case, calculate the predicted sales response for each option on a cost basis to facilitate comparison of returns.)

Many of the useful conclusions from it are too obvious to require a computerized model. For example, the results will indicate which of the variables at management's command is expected to have the greatest impact on sales. This is obviously where resources should be spent. Also, answers to the second-order questions may reveal (for example) that spending extra on telemarketing *and* new salespeople will produce only slightly more than spending extra on telemarketing alone; the conclusion is clear in this hypothetical case—adding salespeople is not cost-effective.

Group decision-making techniques

The Delphi Technique was developed to eliminate negative aspects of group problem solving such as self-censorship and domination by one or a few of the group members. Conventionally a Delphi group never meets. The moderator sends a questionnaire to participants, summarizes results, sends them back with another questionnaire, and so on until individual responses converge on a common opinion. Pfizer's method brings the group together to shorten the process—it would take weeks to reach consensus through the mail.

Pfizer's method borrows elements of the Nominal Group Technique. In this method, the group does meet but members silently write down their ideas. Next, each member presents his or her ideas in turn (but, obviously, not anonymously). There is no discussion during these presentations. The moderator records the ideas on a chalkboard. After each member's ideas have been presented the group discusses and clarifies the ideas. Then group members rank-order the ideas anonymously. The moderator sums the rankings and the idea with the highest rank is chosen.

Keep in mind: Because it requires group discussion of each idea, the Nominal Group Technique is not as useful for complex issues requiring answers to many questions as is the Delphi Technique.

Reference

Management Briefing: Marketing. (June 1987). The Conference Board.

PRODUCT/MARKET CERTAINTY MATRIX

Applications

- Adjusting long-term sales forecasts to reflect the risk associated with each product or service.
- Analyzing revenue projections to identify their sensitivity to risk.
- Identifying the product sales forecasts that are least likely to be accurate.

Procedures

1. Categorize each product on the market and product dimensions of the matrix.
2. Prepare a 3 × 3 matrix labeled with product and market categories. List the appropriate products for each cell.
3. Sum the product forecasts for each product in a cell and enter this total in the cell. Fill in all the cells of the matrix with sales-forecast figures in this manner.
4. Adjust these figures for risk, referring to your firm's historical experience or using the risk factors conventionally used with the model.

Cross-Reference

Marketing Decisions—useful for marketing plans and strategies

The Product/Market Certainty Matrix is, like the Amana Product/Market Planning Matrix, an outgrowth of Ansoff's Product/Market Expansion Grid. (See Amana's method in the product development and innovation section for background information.) However, this method adds the concept of risk to come up with an innovative application for sales forecasting.

The probability of achieving a sales forecast for a product will tend to be lower if the product is new or if it is to be sold to a new market. However, most sales forecasts are not adjusted for risk, and as a result resource allocation and financial projections can be way off for high-risk products. Use this method to build up risk-adjusted forecasts of product sales for a one-year or five-year plan. It is especially useful for companies with frequent product introductions.

INSTRUCTIONS

Start by categorizing each product (or service) by the following criteria:

Market: Existing; new but related to existing; or new/unrelated.

Product: Existing; new but related; or new/unrelated.

Draw a 3 × 3 matrix (see exhibit) with product categories on the horizontal axis and market categories on the vertical. Enter all the products in the appropriate cells of the matrix or on nine separate lists if there are too many products to put on the matrix. Write down the sales projections for each product and sum all projections within each cell to obtain totals for each cell. Write these nine totals in the cells of the matrix.

Estimate the probability that these projections will be correct. If you have historical data from many products, use it to find out what percent of the time forecasts were close to performance in previous periods. If you break out the historical data into the same nine groups, you will be able to calculate the percentage of accurate forecasts your firm produced for each of the categories. However, many companies will find that they do not have a large enough sample of product histories or that they have not saved the forecasts (incorrect forecasts have a way of disappearing).

PRODUCT/MARKET
CERTAINTY MATRIX

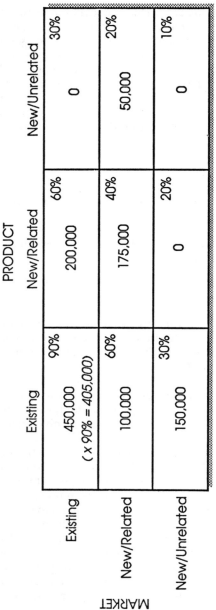

Alternative: Use conventional percentages for the cells. These range from 90% accuracy rate for the existing product/existing market cell to 10% for the unrelated product/unrelated market cell. The conventional percentages appear in the exhibit.

Now that the matrix shows sales forecasts and probabilities for each cell, you can use it to see how risky those sales forecasts really are. Calculate a total forecast—the sum of all the product forecasts. Then calculate a risk-adjusted total by multiplying each forecast in the matrix by the percent figure appearing in its cell before totaling the matrix forecasts. If all the projections are for existing products and markets, the risk-adjusted total will only be 10% lower than the first total. But if higher-risk products are included, the risk-adjusted total may be considerably lower. Use this figure as a pessimistic forecast to model the impact of lower sales on financial performance. If the effect would be catastrophic you might consider a more conservative financial strategy.

You can also use the matrix to identify high-risk projections and plan follow-up as needed. You can probably reduce the risk of a five-year projection for an unrelated product in an unrelated market by reassessing it a few months after introduction. More information may allow you to up the risk factor from 10% to 20% or more—this is a judgment call for management. (*Key point:* It does not make sense to live by a forecast for five years, or even one year, if it only has a 10% chance of being correct! Better to treat these forecasts as temporary and permit them to be modified whenever new information is available.)

REILLY'S LAW OF RETAIL GRAVITATION

Applications

- Determining the drawing power of two competing stores.
- Evaluating proposed store sites.

Procedures

1. Find the distance between stores and the population of each store's trading area.
2. Calculate the drawing power of each store using Reilly's formula.

Cross-Reference

Marketing Decisions

This tool has been used for many years by large retailers to estimate the drawing power of proposed stores based on population data and distance from competing stores. A whole class of complex computer models is now being developed based on Reilly's Law, and applications are increasing. Price Chopper supermarkets and Super Value stores are both said to use gravity models in selecting new store sites. Therefore, executives may find it useful to understand the formula and be aware of its uses and limitations.

INSTRUCTIONS

1. Find the distance between the stores and the population of each store's trading area. If you are using the method to evaluate a proposed store site, take the distance between the store site and the

nearest major competitor. Estimate the trading area—the area within easy reach of the proposed store site where you expect most of your customers to come from. Obtain or estimate the total adult population for your trading area and the trading area of the nearest competitor.

Note: In many cases it is best to measure distance in terms of drive time or walk time between stores.

2. Plug these three numbers into the following formula. (Define the store with the largest population as a and the smaller as b.)

$$Db = \frac{d}{1 + \sqrt{\dfrac{Pa}{Pb}}}$$

Db = drawing power of store b in the direction of store a

d = distance (or drive time) between store a and store b

Pa = population of store a's trading area

Pb = population of store b's trading area (make b the *smaller* area)

The answer gives the estimated drawing power of the store in the smaller area in the direction of the other store. Subtract this number from the total distance for the drawing power of the large-area store toward the small area.

Example:

You are considering opening a new store which is a 21-minute drive away from your large downtown department store. The population of the downtown area is 800,000 and the population of the new suburban site is 200,000. Your concern: The new store will pull customers out of the downtown area in large numbers, cannibalizing the business of the old store. The formula is computed as follows:

$$Db = \frac{21}{1 + \sqrt{\dfrac{800,000}{200,000}}} = \frac{21}{3} = 7$$

The result, 7 minutes, indicates that the new store should draw customers from up to a 7-minute drive in the direction of the old store (and the old store should therefore draw customers from up to 14 minutes in the direction of the new store). This result suggests that the core of the old store's market will not be affected by the new store.

Should you believe the result? Reilly's Law is a bit mysterious. Why should it be true? Although it generally provides a better estimate than a guess, market research and an analysis of driving and shopping habits should also be performed before deciding to build the new store! What if the downtown area no longer has a strong pull on shoppers, despite its larger population, because many good stores have moved to malls in outlying areas? Then the drawing power of the new store will be underestimated. The prediction of Reilly's Law is a useful hypothesis which can be verified or modified through more expensive and time-consuming methods.

Reference

William J. Reilly. *The Law of Retail Gravitation*, 2nd ed. New York: Pilsbury Publishers, 1953. (The original formula as presented by Reilly in this book is still referred to in a variety of published applications, both general and applied.)

SALES COST-CONTROL CHART

Applications

- Tracking sales and marketing costs by product, territory, or salesperson.
- Identifying unusually high or low costs for further investigation.
- Creating standards for expense-to-sales ratio analysis and computerizing the identification and analysis of deviations from the norm.
- Reducing the number of computer forms and statistics that sales managers have to review in order to keep track of expenses.

Procedures

1. Review historical data, marketing plans, and industry norms to establish target expense-to-sales ratios for marketing expenses and various component expenses.
2. Define a range within which cost ratios fluctuate under normal circumstances.
3. Create control charts to graph the fluctuations in cost ratios.
4. Investigate cost ratios that fall beyond the established control limits.

Cross-Reference

Marketing Decisions

This method is an antidote to the foot-high computerized expense and revenue reports that arrive on managers' desks monthly or weekly in most companies. Depending on the flexibility of your MIS department, you can either ask them to replace the reports with control charts or have your staff summarize the reports in charts for you. Sales managers out in the field can also use cost-control charts to track some of the sales expenses, such as entertainment and travel, that rarely make it into official computer reports.

INSTRUCTIONS

1. Most companies collect detailed information on marketing expenses, breaking down expenses into sales force, advertising, research, promotion, administrative, and other costs depending on the company and industry. Companies with large sales forces typically generate monthly reports detailing these expenses by territory or area as well. And sales managers often collect statistics on costs incurred by individual salespeople, such as entertainment and travel costs. If these latter costs are not currently available in accounting reports, they can easily be collected from expense sheets or vouchers.

First, historical statistics from company records should be reviewed to translate costs for each period into a cost-to-sales revenues ratio by dividing costs by revenues for the company or, if you are tracking area or territory costs, for the area or territory in question. Second, a series of cost-to-sales ratios should be averaged for each cost and for each area or territory. These averages can be used as targets, or they may be modified slightly to reflect goals based on industry norms if you feel your company's costs are not in line with industry standards.

Create a target cost-to-sales ratio for each cost you want to track and also for each geographic or functional area you want to track.

2. Define a range around the target cost ratio that you consider acceptable. Both a lower and an upper limit should be set. This can be done statistically, for example by doing a variance analysis and setting the limits of the range so as to include 95% or 99% of the historical figures. It can also be set judgmentally by picking limits that seem reasonable to management. The latter is preferable in my opinion, since the object is to identify ratios that need management's attention—an issue which should be left to management judgment anyway.

Example: Entertainment expenses typically hover at 5% of sales. In some territories they average one to two percentage points higher due to differences in the client base of these territories. This does not concern management. But every now and then a sales representative goes to town on the company credit cards, pushing a territory's ratio three or more points higher than usual. So management sets the upper limit at 7.75% to detect these problem situations. For the lower limit, management is concerned that some reps do not entertain customers enough, and wants a tighter range. The lower limit is set at 4%.

3. Create a control chart for each cost ratio and each geographic or functional area you want to track. This control chart can be maintained by staff or can be turned into a computer report. Either way, the system should be designed to provide rapid exception reporting. Whenever a cost ratio moves beyond the upper or lower limit, management should be notified.

The control chart consists of a graph with time on the horizontal axis (divided into weeks, months, or quarters depending on management needs and preferences) and the cost ratio on the vertical axis. The target for the ratio is indicated by a bold horizontal line, and the upper and lower limits are also indi-

SALES COST-CONTROL CHART

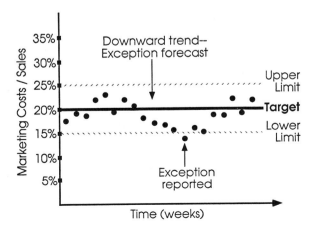

cated by lines. The chart is updated every period by plotting the latest cost ratio. Whenever the ratio moves beyond the limit, management is notified.

Note: You might also want to be notified when a cost ratio moves in the *same direction* on the chart for a number of periods in a row. The more periods an upward trend is observed, for example, the less likely it is due to chance; it indicates a likely exception in the future.

4. The control chart is of little use unless reported fluctuations in costs are investigated. Investigation should always be based on the understanding that costs can fluctuate beyond the control limits for *two* reasons:

1. Due to a real problem or a lack of control over costs.

2. Due to chance.

Any limit will be exceeded occasionally just by chance, so management must be careful to avoid a punitive tone to investigations. Look for possible causes or underlying problems. Talk to the relevant managers or salespeople. And if no good reason for the exception can be found, see what happens next period. If the exception is repeated next period, the chances of it being a random occurrence are almost nil.

Idea: Some companies create revenue control charts as well, using sales quotas as the target and setting limits a few percentage points above and below. Then sales by territory, area, or even customer can be plotted every period on the revenue control chart.

If you track revenues in this manner, you will have comparable statistics on actual versus target costs *and* revenues for each period and territory. You can graph both cost and revenue performance of each territory by expressing the cost-to-sales ratio as a percent of the target ratio and expressing period revenues as a percentage of the target revenues. Then create a graph with expense attainment (as a percent) on the verticle axis and sales quota attainment (as a percent) on the horizontal. (100% is in the middle of each axis, representing the targets.) A diagonal line from the origin will indicate points at

which cost and revenue variations are equivalent.
Positions below the diagonal are desirable; positions
above it are not.

COST/REVENUE
CONTROL CHART

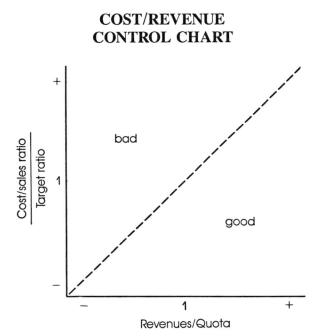

PART 8

STRATEGIC
PLANNING
DECISIONS

ADL LIFE-CYCLE MATRIX

Applications

- Developing or evaluating strategies of business units.
- Managing a portfolio of businesses and product lines.
- Basing strategies on life-cycle stage and competitive position (especially relevant in high-tech or other industries where life cycles are short or volatile).

Procedures

1. Identify strategy centers—ADL's version of the strategic business unit.
2. Determine which stage of its product/industry life cycle each strategy center is in.
3. Determine which of ADL's competitive position categories applies to each strategy center.
4. Plot strategy centers on the matrix.
5. Interpret the matrix for developing strategy-center strategies or for overall portfolio management.

Cross-Reference

Marketing Decisions

This method was developed by the consulting firm Arthur D. Little for use in portfolio planning and strategy development. It is based on the product life-cycle model but adds a second dimension—competitive position. Because many factors contribute to the determination of both life-cycle stage and competitive position the matrix has considerable depth to it. In this respect it is similar to the GE Matrix. It is especially useful for companies with product lines in rapidly evolving markets, including most technology-oriented companies, because product life cycles have such an impact on these companies. Consumer-goods producers may find it a useful tool for the same reason.

INSTRUCTIONS

1. Identify strategy centers, ADL's term for strategic business units, for analysis. Strategy centers are "natural businesses" having a well-defined market for their products or services and independent strategic objectives. The method can be applied to each of a company's strategy centers for a full portfolio analysis or to a single center to assess its strategic options.

Note: ADL defines strategy centers as having products that have common competitors and customers; being affected similarly by changes in price, quality, and style; and being close substitutes for each other. Strategy centers should also have the potential to operate as stand-alone businesses if divested. These criteria tend to produce more narrowly defined business units than BCG's strategic business units (see Boston Consulting Group Matrix, this section).

2. Next, identify the strategy center's industry maturity. The industry life cycle model postulates a four-stage cycle, moving from embryonic or introductory through a growth stage, into a mature and then a decline stage. In practice, industries may stay in growth or maturity for a long time, or may start to decline and then return to growth due to product innovation or changes in the environment. There are numerous references to this model in the marketing literature and most managers are familiar with it. Use the following table as a guide to determining the appropriate stage or consult the references for more detailed information. In selecting a stage, pick the one that best fits the strategy center, but do not be surprised if a center exhibits some characteristics that are inconsistent with this stage.

3. Define the current competitive position of the strategy unit. Competitive position is defined as follows at ADL:

	INTRODUCTION	GROWTH	MATURITY	DECLINE
GROWTH RATE	Rising slowly	Accelerating	Leveling	Declining
SALES	Low	Rising	Peak	Declining
COSTS/CUSTOMER	High	Average	Low	Low
PRODUCT LINE	Very short	Growing	Diversified	Shrinking
PROFITS	Negative	Increasing	Can be high	Declining
COMPETITORS	Few	Increasing	More but stable	Declining
TYPICAL PRICING	Cost-plus	Penetration	Competitive	Cut
ENTRY BARRIERS	Technology	Competitors	Competitors	Overcapacity
TYPICAL ADVERTISING	Awareness and education	Mass-market awareness	Differentiation and segmentation	Reduced

Dominant. A strong leader. Rare. Technological leadership or partial monopoly usually necessary.

Strong. Significantly greater share than any competitor and able to pursue strategies fairly independent of competitors. Not found in all industries.

Favorable. Several competitors share leadership of their market, or one leads, but only by a little.

Tenable. A weak number two or worse. A specialized niche competitor.

Weak. Too small to survive in the long term given the nature of the industry. Or larger competitors that have fallen on hard times through serious mistakes or problems. In either case, needs to improve to survive.

4. Plot the strategy centers of your company on a table with the rows corresponding to competitive position categories and the columns corresponding to life-cycle stages. Some users simply write the names of the centers in the appropriate cells, while others use circles proportionate to the centers' sales, profits, or another financial indicator of the strength of the units.

5. Interpret the matrix. It provides a simple way to visualize the portfolio in terms of the strength and life-cycle stage of each business unit. A portfolio consisting of strategy centers that are in general strongly positioned but in mature and declining markets indicates a need to diversify into growth markets, for example.

ADL has also developed a number of specific strategy tools that can be used for a more sophisticated analysis of the matrix. One of these is the concept of natural strategic thrusts, as illustrated on the accompanying Life-Cycle Matrix. The idea behind this model is that a firm should build up the strategy centers that fall above a lower-left to upper-right diagonal line—the businesses with stronger competitive positions in more youthful markets. Below this line, management needs to take a more selective approach and be willing to abandon nonviable businesses.

ADL LIFE-CYCLE MATRIX

Another tool that may be of interest to some readers is the generic-strategies model. ADL has identified 24 generic business strategies, covering specific strategies such as backward integration, licensing abroad, and unit abandonment. They are linked to one of 16 basic strategic thrusts, producing a total of 384 options, which is about 380 more than can be addressed in this format. See the Hax and

Majluf reference or contact ADL directly for information about the generic strategies model and a variety of other strategy tools based on the Life-Cycle Matrix.

References

Arnoldo C. Hax and Nicolas S. Majluf. *Strategic Management: An Integrative Perspective* (pp. 183–208). Englewood Cliffs, NJ: Prentice Hall, 1984.

Philip Kotler. *Marketing Management: Analysis, Planning and Control.* 5th ed. Prentice Hall, 1984. (Chapter 11 provides a detailed and authoritative review of the product life cycle.)

Noel Capon. "Product Life Cycle." In Benson P. Shapiro, Robert J. Dolan, and John A. Quelch, *Marketing Management: Strategy, Planning and Implementation*, Volume II. Richard D. Irwin, Inc., 1985.

(Thanks to Arthur D. Little, Inc., for permission to reproduce the exhibits and to David Shanks of ADL for his helpful input.)

THE BOSTON CONSULTING GROUP GROWTH SHARE MATRIX

Applications

- Developing market share strategies for a portfolio of products based on their cash-flow characteristics.

- Representing a firm's product portfolio so as to highlight its strengths and weaknesses.

- Deciding whether to continue investing in unprofitable products.

- Allocating a marketing budget among products so as to maximize long-term cash flow from them.

- Measuring management performance based on the performance of a manager's products in the marketplace.

Procedures

1. Identify the unit of analysis, being careful to define the market realistically. Can be used for products, business units, or other units of analysis.

2. Gather statistics on annual sales, competitors' annual sales, anmd market-growth rate for each product or business unit to be analyzed.

3. Calculate relative market share (the revenues of a unit divided by the revenues of its largest competitor).

4. Plot the products/business units on a graph using relative share and market-growth rate. Divide the graph into quandrants to create the growth/share matrix.

5. Evaluate the portfolio based on BCG's assumptions concerning cash flow within the matrix

and performance of products/units in each quandrant.

Cross-Reference

Marketing Decisions—for product portfolio analysis; "Organization and Human Resources"—for performance evaluation.

The Boston Consulting Group developed its famous Growth/Share Matrix to help diversified companies maximize portfolio performance by identifying which products to invest in, which to milk for investment funds, and which to eliminate from the portfolio. Although most managers are aware of the BCG matrix, few are familiar with the logic behind it or realize that it is still a useful tool for strategic planning and product management.

The matrix assumes that cash-flow potential of a product is related to the overall growth rate of its market, to its share of the market relative to competing products, and to its current size. Since these are generalized measures, they allow comparison of widely differing products and markets.

The experience curve (in which costs go down with number of units produced) justifies the assumption that high market share relative to competitors is advantageous. The product life-cycle model (in which a product moves from introduction through growth, maturity, and decline stages) justifies the assumption that high growth is desirable. Other arguments also favor high share (economies of scale, tactical strength of leadership position) and high market growth (higher sales growth and higher profits). These arguments lead to the cash-flow predictions in Exhibit 1. The Growth/Share Matrix depends on these cash-flow assumptions.

INSTRUCTIONS

1. Identify the unit of analysis. Usually the method is applied to individual products, and they are looked at in the context of their entire markets. But sometimes a product category is subdivided (example: models). Markets may also be subdivided

GROWTH SHARE MATRIX

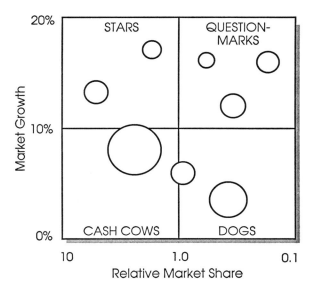

From "The Experience Curve—Reviewed," *Perspectives*, Number 135, © 1973, The Boston Consulting Group, Boston, Massachusetts.

(examples: geographic areas, segments). The matrix has also been used to analyze strategic business units, divisions, entire companies, and even countries. As long as the cash-flow assumptions of the model appear valid, the matrix may be used for whatever unit of analysis is important in decision making.

Note: The Norton Company uses a hierarchical approach in which matrices are first prepared for strategic business units, then product lines, and finally for individual products. By starting with a large unit of analysis, Norton is able to take a broad strategic view of its portfolio supplemented by in-depth analysis of areas in need of attention. (See Abell and Hammond, p. 141.)

2. Gather the necessary statistics on the products to be analyzed:

- Annual sales for each of your company's products (in dollars or units, most recent period).

- Annual sales of the largest competitor to each of your products (same unit and period).

- Annual growth rate in each of the products' markets (percent growth in total market revenues or unit sales over most recent period).

3. Calculate relative market share by dividing most recent annual sales of each product by the annual sales of its largest competitor.

Relative share is 1, where your company's product has as large a share of its market as its main competitor. If your product has a smaller share than its largest competitor its relative share is less than 1. If it is larger than the next largest competitor its relative share is more than 1.

Note: You do not need to know market share to calculate relative share. Nor do you need data on any competitors except the largest, even if there are many competitors with a larger share than your product.

4. Plot each product on a graph with market-growth rate on the vertical and relative market share on the horizontal.

A log scale is usually used for relative share, and relative share increases to the left, not the right. The graph is customarily divided into quadrants by a vertical line at relative share equals 1.0 and a horizontal line at market growth equals 10%.(*Alternatives*: Divide the growth axis at the industry average growth rate, a weighted average of the growth rates of all products in the portfolio, or a corporate hurdle rate.)

Draw a circle around each product's plot with diameter proportionate to the product's recent annual revenues. (Some users make the *area* of the circle relative to revenues—a more accurate but complex approach.)

Hint: Plot sales on a bar chart that is half as long as your growth/share matrice's horizontal axis. Trace the bars to obtain appropriate circle diameters.

5. Evaluate the product portfolio based on the quadrant each product falls into. Products are categorized according to the quadrant where they appear in the matrix. High growth, high relative-share products are stars. Low growth, high relative-share prod-

ucts are cash cows. Low growth, low share products are dogs, and high growth but low share makes a product a "troubled child" or question mark.

The cash-flow assumptions of the model lead to the following conclusions about each of the quadrants:

Stars   High growth and high share. Strongly positioned in the growth phase of the product life cycle. Although cash flow is strong, it may not be sufficient to finance the rapid growth. Expected to throw off excess cash later when the market matures and growth slows.

Question marks   Low share of a growing market suggests weak cash flow and considerable cash needed to maintain share. Investment in a question mark may increase share and create a future star, but investment is risky.

Cash cows   Dominant products in a mature market produce excess cash which can be invested in stars or question marks.

Dogs   Low-share products in slow-growth markets. Cash flows are low and often negative due to the weak competitive position. If investment is required to maintain the share of a dog, it might be better to divest it and reallocate the funds to a question mark or star.

Managers usually cannot control market growth but can invest to maintain, lose, or build market share. Market share strategies for each product should reflect the need for future cash cows. Question marks can be transformed into stars by investing in share growth, then allowed to mature into cash cows through a share-maintenance strategy. Unprofitable dogs can be dropped to divert funds to question marks or stars, and efforts can be concentrated on the most promising question marks. (Share strategies should produce a cash flow from the lower left to the upper right of the matrix.)

6. Follow the movement of products over time. A time series makes it possible to identify the direction of each product's movement within the growth/share

matrix. Prepare several matrices on the same scale, one for each of the last two or three years, and superimpose them. Trace them onto a single matrix or use directional arrows to indicate movement on a copy of the most recent year's matrix. In the following exhibit a growth/share matrix illustrates three-year trends with arrows.

Idea: According to Bruce Henderson, founder of BCG, matrices "may be even more useful to evaluate management performance." The manager of a product or a portfolio of products can be evaluated based on how products move within the matrix over time. Any product that does not move rapidly toward 100 percent of the relevant market share is presumably mismanaged." (See The Rule of Three and Four in this section for further explanation of his thinking.)

Example:

The Mead Corp. has adopted this method in its annual strategic-planning process. Its Business Strategy Matrix looks slightly different because different terms are used, but the underlying logic and computations are the same. Mead's choice of terms may be more palatable to some than the terms used by the Boston Consulting Group (what manager wants to be responsible for a "dog"?).

Mead has also developed guidelines which are useful in strategic analysis of products in each quadrant. These are displayed in the following table.

Cautions: Not applicable where experience curve and economies of scale are irrelevant to product cost. Assumes units of analysis are independent; if resources are shared among business units, cash-flow data and assumptions should be questioned. How markets are defined can change the outcome of the analysis dramatically by altering relative share and market growth. Not useful where balancing cash flow is not an important objective (i.e., where external funding is planned).

References

Abell and Hammond. *Strategic Market Planning.* Englewood Cliffs, NJ: Prentice Hall, 1979. (Chapter 7, "The Use of the Growth-Share Matrix in Strategic

STRATEGY IMPLICATIONS OF THE MEAD MATRIX

	SWEEPSTAKE	SAVINGS ACCOUNT	BOND	MORTGAGE
Life-Cycle Stage	Growth	Development	Maturity	Maturity
Cash Flow	Negative	Self-financing	Positive	Probably positive
Risk	High	Medium	Low	Medium
Profit	Low	High	High	Low
Cost-Effective?	No	Yes	Yes	Probably not

From Francis J. Aguilar, *The Mead Corporation: Strategic Planning.* Boston, Harvard Business School, case 9–379–070. Reprinted by Permission.

Mead Corp. Business Strategy Matrix

Planning," provides an in-depth discussion of the matrix. See pages 195–209 for a case study of Electro Industries, Inc. and their use of the matrix in market analysis and planning.)

Francis Aguilar. *The Mead Corporation: Strategic Planning.* Harvard Business School Case 9-379-070.

Bruce Henderson. *The Logic of Business Strategy.* Cambridge, MA: Ballinger, 1984. (Evaluating management performance, p. 68.)

(The Growth Share Matrix is reproduced with permission from "The Experience Curve—Reviewed," *Perspectives*, Number 135, © 1973, The Boston Consulting Group, Boston, Massachusetts.)

CAPSUGEL CRISIS-MANAGEMENT CHECKLIST

Applications

- Responding to a crisis.
- Evaluating and improving current crisis-management plans.

Procedures

1. Develop a list of possible crises that could affect your business and industry.

2. Use the checklist to see whether your company is prepared for these possible crises. Develop a forecasting mechanism to make sure a crisis is recognized as early as possible.

3. Reduce the potential damage of future crises by making strategy conform to the approaches described in the checklist.

4. When a crisis occurs, consult the checklist to help develop contingency plans and guide reaction to the problem.

The ten-point checklist is used as a basis for creating crisis-response plans and policies at Warner-Lambert's Capsugel Division. Crisis planning was adopted at Capsugel after the Tylenol tampering cases devastated the market for capsules and created public suspicion of capsulized over-the-counter medications and their manufacturers. Management at Capsugel identified a number of policies and tactics that helped it and other companies in this market survive and maintain a positive public image. Their ten-point checklist and associated planning procedures may also help other companies survive crises.

Any organization can find itself in a crisis. Johnson & Johnson's Tylenol disaster, Union Carbide's Bhopal disaster, the Rushdie/*Satanic Verses* incident, and NASA's disastrous 25th space shuttle mission are obvious examples. A recent survey of CEO's indicates that 70% of *Fortune 500* companies and 20% of *Inc 500* companies have adopted crisis planning. These, and the many other organizations that have yet to address the issue, will find Capsugel's method to be of interest.

INSTRUCTIONS

1. The first step in crisis planning is to anticipate possible crises. Try listing all the conceivable disasters that could befall your company and its industry. If the list is long, go back over it and rank them by how likely they are to occur. All may seem quite improbable, but some are bound to be more likely than others. Second, ask how significant the impact of each disaster might be. Try ranking them based on impact. Now take the most probable and the ones with the greatest potential impact and focus on them in your disaster forecasting and preparation.

Note: This step is the hardest for most CEO's, and the temptation is to delegate the task until it disappears. As Gerald Meyer, former chairman of American Motors, puts it: "Most executives don't like to think about crises.... They equate a crisis with bad management; things like that just don't happen on their watch."

2. Review the Capsugel checklist to see whether your company's policies, procedures, and philosophy violate any of the ten items. Make appropriate changes.

Focus especially on forecasting methods (see items 1 and 6 on checklist). Many companies do not systematically look for signs of crisis. Use the list developed in step 1 above and think of events and information that could foretell each of the possible crises. Assign someone in publicity or strategic planning the job of monitoring the environment for early indicators of a crisis. Make sure the staff responsible for this function has direct communication with upper management and is not afraid to relay false alarms, since no crisis forecasting system can be very accurate.

3. Integrate crisis preparation into strategic plans. Some of the items on the checklist are long term in focus. They will do no good if not acted on until after a crisis has been identified. But if implemented as part of the planning criteria, they will provide protection against unforeseen events and make strategy more robust. Items 2, 7, 9, and 10 are especially relevant to strategic planning.

4. *Crisis response.* If you are in the midst of a crisis, whether large, like Capsugel's, or of more modest proportions, the checklist may also be useful. Several of the items focus on how you respond during the crisis. Advice includes:

- Don't overreact
- Stay close to the market
- Watch your competition
- Be prepared to give up some of your market
- Don't assume a hostile environment
- Develop a contingency plan

See the checklist for specifics.

Crisis-management checklist

1. *Look for signs that may foretell a crisis.* This task should be formalized and regularly reviewed by the chief executive. Ask yourself what events could have the worst impact on your organization.

2. *Have an alternative product or technology standing by.* Initiate product development now so that an almost-ready replacement will be in the pipeline.

3. *Speed is of the essence.* Your reactions in the first day or two of the crisis will establish consumer attitudes toward your company and product. Make sure your side of the story is included in the initial news coverage of the crisis.

4. *Don't overreact.* Make one person responsible for managing the crisis and have everyone else continue to take care of their work.

5. *Stay close to the market.* Market surveys and direct communications with customers are

important. You need to track attitudes during the crisis.

6. *Watch your competition.* Crises can create opportunities for you or your competitors.

7. *Be prepared to give up some of your market initially.* According to Charles Hoover, vice-president of Capsugel, "It's ridiculous to think that you can manage a crisis with no damage. The idea is to minimize the damage, not eliminate the possibility of damage."

8. *Don't assume a hostile environment.* Many companies "clam up" in a crisis, which raises suspicions and leads to reduced confidence in the company and product. Do not act confrontational. (Include a PR person as well as a lawyer on your planning committee!) *Example*: Tenneco Oil's crisis-policy statement includes the following: "When we must take a dose of bad publicity, it is better to release accurate information fast and as fully as possible."

9. *Build goodwill before the crisis.* A strong positive image will help you through crises.

10. *Develop a contingency or crisis plan in advance.* This will allow you to react effectively in the first hours of a crisis.

References:

Management Briefing: Business Finance (January 1987). The Conference Board. (Based on a presentation by Charles Hoover of Capsugel at a Conference Board marketing conference.)

Paul Holmes. "Surviving Crisis." *Relate: Supplement to Adweek's Marketing Week* (March 27, 1989). (See page 10 for a description of the survey by The Goldman Group. Quotes from Gerald Meyer and Tenneco are also from this source.)

CITICORP INTERACTION ANALYSIS

Applications

- Identifying common needs of different business units in large or diversified companies.
- Eliminating duplication of effort and "reinventon of the wheel."
- Integrating activities of strategic business units to achieve strategic objectives and economies of scale.

Procedures

1. Identify key resources for each business unit. Prepare a table to identify overlap.
2. Identify key concerns (issues and tasks) for each business unit. Prepare a table to identify overlap.
3. Assess overall interdependence of business units and evaluate strategic and organizational implications.

Cross-Reference

Organization and Human Resources

This method has been used at Citicorp as part of its strategic planning process and is favored by Hax and Majluf in their book *Strategic Management.* A number of other companies have begun to use the method, and it is applicable for many more.

Strategic planning often works from the bottom up, with individual business units preparing their own plans for approval of senior management. It also works from the top down, with senior management preparing plans and objectives for business unit managers to pursue. But neither model necessarily coordinates the activities of different business units so as to take full advantage of any common needs and objectives. Add this method to your planning process to look at questions of interaction between SBU's.

INSTRUCTIONS

1. Identify key resources for each business unit. Prepare a table to identify overlap.

Business unit managers should be involved in this step. Identify the key resources—those upon which the strategy of the business unit depends. If the resources are plentiful and cheap, then they need not be of concern for this analysis. But if access to any important resource is an issue or if it is unusual or special in any way, be sure to include it.

The tabular format shown here is used to present the information and highlight any common resource needs, illustrated with an example from Citicorp.

2. Identify key concerns (issues and tasks) for each business unit. Prepare a table to identify overlap.

The identification of major concerns is in most cases already performed at each business unit as part of its strategic planning. If not, see King's Strategic Issue Analysis or World Bank Strategic Issue Management for methods to use in identifying issues. As in step 1, it is a good idea to assemble the business unit managers to develop this list. Different business units may use different terms to talk about the same problems, and discussion among managers will help them identify common concerns.

The second tabular format shown is used by Citicorp to identify shared concerns.

3. Assess overall interdependence of business units and evaluate strategic and organizational implications.

At Citicorp there are obviously many shared resources and concerns. The analysis indicates a high level of interactions is possible (and probably already takes place to some degree). A high degree of coordination among SBU's is needed in companies like

Resource	Strategic Business Unit		
	Individual banks	Institutional banks	Capital markets
1. Potential sharing of the same markets generates overall interdependence	X	X	X
2. Capital base resources	X	X	X
3. Transferable human resources	X	X	X
4. Account relationship officers		X	X
5. Global communications network	X	X	X
6. Treasury funding activities	X	X	

Concern	Strategic Business Unit		
	Individual banks	Institutional banks	Capital markets
1. Servicing major client's needs	X	X	X
2. Domestic markets	X	X	X
3. Major international markets	X	X	X
4. Industries		X	
5. Regulatory barriers	X	X	X
6. Foreign bank and nonbank entry	X	X	X
7. Market segmentation	X	X	X
8. Product/service packaging and delivery	X	X	X
9. Marketing	X	X	X
10. Funding costs	X	X	
11. Interest credit liquidity risk assessment	X	X	X

Citicorp, which according to Hax and Majluf is why Citicorp uses a complex matrix organization.

A matrix organization is one way to formalize the interaction and interdependence of SBU's. Creation of "liaison" managers who operate between two SBU's to coordinate a shared resource or help unify the SBU's activities addressing a common concern is a less drastic organizational solution.

In addition to the organizational implications, look also at strategic implications of interdependence and interactions. Can individual SBU's obtain a resource more efficiently by joining forces? Can an issue facing several SBU's be addressed by a coordinated multi-SBU effort, thereby giving competitive advantage to SBU's whose competitors do not have "sister" businesses to assist them?

References

Antoinette M. Williams. *A Strategic Planning Process: The Case of Citicorp and Its Commercial Finance Subsidiary*. Masters thesis, Sloan School of Management, MIT, May 1983.

Hax, Arnoldo C. and Majluf, Nicholas S., *Strategic Management: An Integrative Perspective*. Englewood Cliffs, NJ: Prentice Hall, 1984.

DOW-CORNING STRATEGY MATRIX

Applications

- Implementing strategies that require coordination of multiple operating units or SBU's within the organization.
- Generating strategic plans that are more action-oriented and easier to implement.

Allocating limited organizational resources to competing strategic objectives.

- Creating momentum and commitment for a new strategic direction, as in a turnaround situation.

Procedures

1. Generate specific strategies through the organization's normal strategic planning process or by fiat from upper management.
2. Assign a manager to each strategy. Strategy managers should prepare an initial report describing the strategy and how they propose to implement it.
3. Assemble strategy managers and operational managers at a meeting. Strategy managers present their initial plans at this meeting and describe the resources they want operational managers to commit to their strategies.
4. Following this meeting, strategy and operations managers allocate operational resources to strategy projects through negotiation.
5. Strategy managers prepare final plans for approval of upper management.
6. Strategy managers take responsibility for the implementation of their strategies, coordinating with operational departments as necessary.

7. Strategy managers report on the progress of their strategies at quarterly meetings with upper management.

Cross-Reference

Leadership Skills and Methods

Strategic planning has gotten a bad name lately because companies find that implementing strategy is a major hurdle, since managers have to answer to short-term performance measures that conflict with long-term strategy objectives, and because many strategic plans are more descriptive than prescriptive. Gary Reiner of the Boston Consulting Group, the firm many credit with inventing strategic planning, recently declared in the *New York Times* that "planning is passé."

At Dow-Corning, however, planning is not passé. Strategic objectives, generated by senior management, are translated into practical implementation plans by operating managers in a process that builds commitment to plans and ensures effective implementation throughout the organization.

Organizational objectives and strategies often cut across boundaries within the organization, requiring coordination by multiple managers and competing for attention and funds with other projects of concern to each operating manager. Dow-Corning gives responsibility for a strategy's implementation to a single manager, who becomes its champion and advocate as it crosses operational boundaries; he or she negotiates with operation managers for access to the resources needed to implement the strategy. Dow-Corning's strategy matrix is an effective method for ensuring implementation of important strategies.

INSTRUCTIONS

1. Formulate specific strategies. Senior management is responsible for generating strategies based on the organization's objectives. Most organizations already generate strategies through periodic strategic-planning efforts.

Strategies typically cover a wide range, from specific to general. "Learn to listen to our customers" is a very broad strategy while "build our market share in products X, Y, and Z by targeting smaller companies in the Midwest and South" is very specific. Some strategic plans produce a few very broad strategy statements, but these are not good input for the Dow-Corning Strategy Matrix. Break them down into component strategies or define them more narrowly. For example, "Listen to our customers" could be divided into "Develop a consultative approach to selling through retraining the sales force and calling on more managers" and "Improve customer service and locate responsibility for the function with the sales, repair, and training teams that have direct contact with the customer."

2. Assign managers to strategy management positions, one to each strategy. (If your company is large enough to bear the extra cost, they should *not* continue to hold their operational or staff responsibilities.) Ask them to review their strategies and work with upper management to clarify any ambiguities or problems. Have them begin work on a strategic plan that will be the basis of the company's implementation of their strategy by preparing the following:

1. Background (a competitive position or context analysis)

2. Specific strategies and tactics for implementation

3. Required company resources (the costs)

4. Performance forecast (the results)

3. Call an off-site meeting attended by the managers who control each operational unit of the company, such as manufacturing, marketing, sales, purchasing, logistics, customer service, and so on. Also have each of the strategy managers at this meeting. Have the strategy managers present their plans, complete with tactics, needs, and anticipated results, to the operations managers. The operations managers control the resources such as funds, personnel, equipment, and expertise needed to implement each strategy, and are responsible for allocating

those resources among competing strategies. As a result, strategy managers have an incentive to develop credible and persuasive proposals for this meeting.

4. After the meeting, operations managers and strategy managers negotiate to resolve the final sections of the plan, and strategy managers write their plans for presentation to upper management. The final sections are

5. Balance resource requirements against availability

6. Finalize the tactical plan, including a calendar and budget

7. Set operational goals (which will be used to measure performance)

Upper management has no direct involvement in this process unless the negotiations break down, in which case involvement may be necessary to mediate a dispute.

5. Strategy managers develop their final plans over the next month after operating managers have made allocation decisions.

6. Strategy managers maintain responsibility for the strategies throughout the year, working with operations managers and staff to see that the plans are implemented. Where coordination between different operational functions is required the strategic managers fill the role of coordinator. Note that this creates a matrix organization in which anyone working on the implementation of a strategy will be partially responsible to the strategy manager as well as to their normal operational manager.

7. Strategy managers report on their progress relative to the plan's goals in quarterly meetings with upper management.

Examples:

The method has been adopted in similar form at IBM, Intel, Shell Oil, and Federal Express. Velsicol Chemical (a subsidiary of Northwest Industries) first used the method in 1979 as part of a turnaround effort by its new manager, Howard Beasley. Problems included environmental problems caused by Velsicol products and overcapacity in its industry. Implementation of strategies to overcome these problems and gain market share required coordination and commitment from multiple operational units. Reorganization was considered too disruptive. The strategy matrix was adopted because it was the quickest and least disruptive way to focus the organization on its new strategies.

Velsicol initially adopted a cost leadership strategy, a product differentiation strategy, and a market focus strategy. These generated more specific strategies for strategy managers to pursue. The method helped Velsicol's turnaround and led to a company that focuses on agriculture (most chemical companies have a broader focus) and pursues differentiation or cost leadership strategies with different products.

References

Naylor, Thomas H. *The Corporate Strategy Matrix.* New York: Basic Books, 1986. (The Velsicol case is described on pages 176–192.)

Reiner, Gary, "Getting There First: It Takes Planning to Put Plans Into Action." The *New York Times*, (March 12, 1989): Forum.

(Reiner describes another method that addresses the problems with traditional strategic planning: Panasonic's Technology Platform planning process.)

GENERAL ELECTRIC MATRIX

Applications

- Evaluating business units based on their strength in the market and the attractiveness of their market.
- Representing a firm's business unit portfolio so as to highlight its strengths and weaknesses.
- Matrix-based strategic planning where broad and flexible definitions of industry attractiveness and business strength are desired.

Procedures

1. Define the critical success factors you want to use in evaluating industry attractiveness and business strength.
2. Assess the impact (positive, negative, or neutral) of internal factors on business strength and external factors on industry attractiveness.
3. Assess the importance of factors and develop summary measures of strength and attractiveness.
4. Plot the business unit (usually with a portfolio of businesses) on the GE matrix.
5. Interpret the strategic implications of the matrix using A. T. Kearney's strategic options.

Cross-Reference

Financial Decisions

The Attractiveness/Strengths Matrix was developed at GE in the 1970s in response to problems they saw with the Boston Consulting Group Growth/

Share Matrix.* It provides a similar comparison of industry attractiveness and business strength, but where the BCG matrix measures attractiveness by growth rate and strength by relative market share, the GE matrix uses a large number of factors to measure these variables. And because it uses multiple factors, it can easily be adapted to the specific interests of management or the oddities of a particular industry by changing the factors and their emphasis.

INSTRUCTIONS

The matrix is drawn by identifying critical internal and external factors, then weighting these to create measures of business strength (internal factors) and market attractiveness (external factors). The following instructions provide a step-by-step approach to this task. As with the BCG matrix, it is important to define the unit of analysis carefully before starting to collect data. Focus on meaningful strategic business units and define markets carefully.

1. Define factors. Select the important factors for evaluating business (or product) strength and market attractiveness. In GE's terminology, business strength factors are "internal" and market-attractiveness factors are "external." Here is a list of factors to guide your selection (you may want to drop some of these and add some of your own):

Internal factors	External factors
Advertising	Cyclicality of sales
Breadth of product line	Demographics
Customer service	Entry barriers
Distribution	Environmental issues
Financial strength	Exit barriers
Image	Market concentration/
Management strength	structure
Manufacturing	Market-growth rate
Market share	Market size
Marketing	Political issues
New-product	Profitability
development	Regulation

*Developers included William Rothschild at G.E. and consultant Mike Allen of McKinsey.

Internal factors	External factors
Perceived quality	Resource availability
Repair and support	Social issues
Sales force	Technological advances

This step is very important—if important factors are overlooked, the analysis will not be valid. And trivial factors should not be included because they will sidetrack the analysis and waste time. A management team can be used to identify factors, perhaps through the use of brainstorming, the Nominal Group Technique, or Crawford Slip Writing (see "General Decision-Making Tools"). (Note: William Rothschild says this is an early list of factors, and that G.E. tried many when he worked with them. The point is to pick factors that work for your situation.)

2. Assess the impact of external and internal factors. Starting with the external factors, review the list (using the same group of managers) and rate each factor according to how attractive or unattractive it is. (*Tip:* For factors having a similar impact on all competitors, evaluate impact in general; but where a factor impacts competitors differently, compare the impact on your business with the impact on key competitors.)

Use a five-point rating scale:

1   very unattractive
2   unattractive
3   neutral impact
4   attractive
5   very attractive

Example: A highly cyclical pattern of sales might be ranked 2, unattractive.

Now, for the internal factors, do a similar rating using the following scale:

1   severe competitive disadvantage
2   competitive advantage
3   equal to competitors

4   competitive advantage

5   severe competitive disadvantage

In rating your business on the internal factors, comparison with a competitor is generally necessary. Pick the strongest competitor overall as a basis for comparison rather than switching to the strongest on each specific factor, or else your ratings will be artificially low.

3. Assess the importance of external and internal factors and develop summary measures of strength and attractiveness. Now that you have established a rating for each factor, you need to decide how important each factor is to a general assessment of your business's position. There are two approaches to this task:

Qualitative Assessment. Review and discuss the list of internal factors and their ratings. Judge how strong the business is on the basis of the factor ratings using the following scale:

Business strength

High
ᴍedium
Low

Now evaluate the attractiveness of the industry based on the ratings of external factors. Decide whether industry attractiveness is high, medium, or low.

Quantitative assessment. The following instructions should be applied to the list of internal factors and the list of external factors separately, in two steps.

Rank the factors by importance, placing the most important at the top of the list (there may be many ties). Now assign a weight to each factor, using fractions that add to 1 or percentages that add to 100%. This is easier said than done. A helpful trick is to start by giving all factors the same rating, which is equal to *1/number of factors*, then adjusting up or down to reflect rank. If you do this on a computerized spreadsheet showing the sum of ratings, you can keep adjusting them until the total is correct.

Next, multiply each factor's ranking on the 1 to 5 scale (from step 2) by its importance weight. *Example*: Market share confers a competitive advantage on your firm relative to its primary competitor; the managers gave this internal factor a 3. It was considered one of the most important factors and was assigned a weight of .2. To calculate this factor's weighted score multiply .2 by 3, which equals .6. Total the weighted scores for both the internal and external factors (keeping the two lists separate). The totals will be somewhere between 1 and 5, with 1 representing low industry attractiveness and low business strength, and 5 representing high industry attractiveness or business strength.

4. Plot the business on the GE matrix. Construct the matrix by labeling the horizontal axis of a graph "Industry Attractiveness" and the vertical axis "Business Strength." Divide the graph into grids by dividing each axis in thirds with two lines. Label the grids high, medium, and low on each axis (high to the left and top). If you used the quantitative method of rating (step 2B), superimpose a 1 to 5 scale on each axis.

GE MATRIX

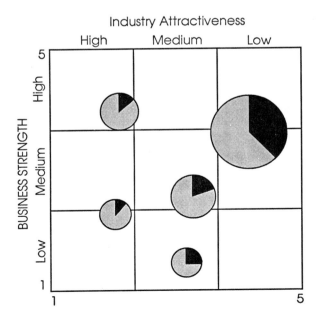

Now take the overall score of the business for each group of factors and plot it on the matrix. The external factors are plotted on the horizontal industry-attractiveness axis, and internal factors on the business-strengths axis. Repeat the analysis for other business units or for competitors of the business unit you are studying, depending on the strategic interests of management.

The analysis can also be performed for several time periods to observe the movement of businesses within the matrix.

Idea: When plotting a portfolio of business units, each in a different market or industry, represent each business as a circle with diameter proportionate to the total sales in its market and draw a pie-shaped wedge within the circle to represent the business's market share. Otherwise share information will not be visible on the matrix since it is combined with other internal factors in the business strength assessment.

5. Interpret the matrix. The strategic implications of the matrix for portfolio planning are presented in the following table, based on the thinking of the consulting firm A. T. Kearney, Inc., of Chicago.

Industry attractiveness	Business strengths	Suggested strategies
High	High	Grow Seek dominance Maximize investment
Medium	High	Identify growth segments Invest strongly Maintain position elsewhere
Low	High	Maintain overall position Seek cash flow Invest at maintenance level
High	Medium	Evaluate potential for leadership via segmentation Identify weaknesses Build strengths

Industry attractiveness	Business strengths	Suggested strategies
Medium	Medium	Identify growth segments Specialize Invest selectively
Low	Medium	Prune lines Minimize investment Position to divest
High	Low	Specialize Seek niches Consider acquisitions
Medium	Low	Specialize Seek niches Consider exit
Low	Low	Trust leader's statesmanship Focus on competitor's cash generators Time exit and divest

Forecasting

This method can also be used to forecast the industry attractiveness and business strengths of a portfolio of business units. Have a team of managers assess each factor, as above, except that they should try to anticipate the impact and importance of each factor at some point in the future. Then build up an overall score for strength and industry attractiveness, as above, and plot a projected matrix.

Caution: Bruce Bunch of G.E. observes that the matrix is a time-consuming planning tool, and its use at G.E. is currently limited as a result.

References

Arnoldo Hax and Nicolas S. Majluf. *Strategic Management.* Englewood Cliffs, NJ: Prentice Hall, 1984.

Royal Dutch Shell Company. *The Directional Policy Matrix, a New Aid to Corporate Planning*, 1975.

William E. Rothschild. *Strategic Alternatives: Selection, Development and Implementation.* Amacom, 1979.

(Rotchschild was one of the developers of the GE Matrix.)

Rothschild. *Strategic Thinking.* Amacom, 1976. (Currently available through the author, Norwalk, CT.)

(Thanks to Bruce Bunch of G.E. and William Rothschild, now a management consultant, for their comments.)

HARRIGAN-PORTER END-GAME ANALYSIS

Applications

- Identifying the appropriate strategy for a company in a declining market.
- Developing viable alternatives to the "harvest" strategy for mature and declining markets.
- Evaluating company or business unit strategy on a matrix tailored to overcrowded, competitive, declining-growth industries.

Procedures

1. Analyze industry structure and determine whether it will produce an orderly and potentially profitable decline phase.
2. Analyze your competitive strengths to see whether they match remaining pockets of demand.
3. Select the appropriate strategy using the End-Game Matrix.

Here is one of the pleasant examples of academic research that has immediate value to managers. Kathryn Harrigan of Columbia and Michael Porter of Harvard studied nearly 100 companies in declining markets to develop a model of strategic alternatives and a matrix to help identify which alternative is appropriate in any given situation. Their tools will be helpful to companies facing stagnant or declining markets and will also apply to divisions and product lines that are entering the final stage of their market life cycle.

ENVIRONMENTAL ATTRACTIVENESS

Structural factors	Hospitable
1. Conditions of demand	
Speed of decline	Very slow
Certainty of decline	100% certain, predictable patterns
Pockets of enduring demand	Several or major ones
Product differentiation	Brand loyalty
Price stability	Stable, price premiums attainable
2. Exit barriers	
Reinvestment requirements	None
Excess capacity	Little
Asset age	Mostly old assets
Resale markets for assets	Easy to convert or sell
Shared facilities	Few free-standing plants
Vertical integration	Little
"Single product" competitors	None
3. Rivalry determinants	
Customer industries	Fragmented, weak
Customer switching costs	High
Diseconomies of scale	None
Dissimilar strategic groups	Few

INSTRUCTIONS

1. Analyze industry structure to determine whether it will produce an orderly and potentially

Inhospitable

Rapid or erratic

Great uncertainty, erratic patterns

No niches

Commodity like products

Very unstable, pricing below costs

High, often mandatory and involving capital assets
Substantial
Sizable new assets and old ones not retired

No markets available, substantial costs to retire
Substantial and interconnected with important
  businesses
Several large companies

Several large companies

Strong bargaining power

Minimal
Minimal

Several in same target markets

profitable decline phase. Three areas are key in this analysis: conditions of demand, exit barriers, and determinants of rivalry. The table above, reproduced from the referenced article, shows what to look for in analyzing each of these factors. Use the table to assess each factor and see whether the environment will be hospitable or inhospitable during the decline phase.

Note: You may find a combination of negative and positive factors, in which case you will have to decide which will be most important and use judgment to decide whether on balance the industry will be hospitable or not.

2. Analyze your competitive strengths to see whether they match remaining pockets of demand. It is important to identify the nature of demand during the decline phase. Demand will fall but usually remains strong in certain pockets. Evaluate the strength of your company or business unit in these pockets—a strong competitor overall may not be strong in the specific areas that will count during decline. Also do a careful comparison of your

END-GAME MATRIX

	Has competitive strengths for remaining demand pockets	Lacks competitive strengths for remaining demand pockets
Favorable industry structure for decline	Leadership or niche	Harvest or divest quickly
Unfavorable industry structure for decline	Niche or harvest	Divest quickly

Source: *Harvard Business Review,* July-Aug. 1983, page 119. Copyright © 1983 by the President and Fellows of Harvard College; all rights reserved.

strengths and your competitor's strengths in the specific areas where demand will continue. Business strength must be defined relative to competitors.

3. Select the appropriate strategy. Harrigan and Porter identify generic strategies that are appropriate for each of the four combinations of competitive strength/weakness and favorable/unfavorable industry structure. (See the End-Game Matrix.) The strategies are:

Leadership. The goal is to be one of only a few remaining companies and to build (or maintain) market-share leadership. This position allows the company to make relatively high profits under favorable market conditions, and requires both competitive strength and a favorable industry structure. If these conditions exist, a company may achieve leadership by encouraging competitors to leave the market through aggressive pricing or an information campaign to inform them of the situation, by helping them leave by reducing their exit barriers (i.e., buying them out), and by raising the stakes through new product introductions. Once the position is established, a harvest strategy can be pursued.

Niche. In this strategy the company identifies a segment which has more favorable characteristics than the rest of the market and moves rapidly to become a leader in it. Withdrawal from the rest of the market is pursued. Within this niche the company pursues a leadership strategy, as previously described.

Harvest. The object of this strategy is to maximize cash flow while disinvesting. Therefore, new investments, including advertising and other investments in awareness and goodwill, are cut to an absolute minimum. Services may be cut, product lines shortened, and less profitable types of customers dropped as part of this strategy. But note that problems can arise as customers lose confidence in the business and employees lose motivation—who wants to work on a sinking ship? For these reasons it is not always possible to harvest a business fully.

Quick divestment. Pursue this strategy when you think you can get more for a business before, or in the early stages of, decline than you will be able to through a harvest strategy or later divestment. In many cases, an alert management recognizes clear signs of decline before all potential buyers have and can therefore get more for a business than management thinks it is worth. But recognize that the decision to divest quickly must be made under uncertainty—it is possible that your negative assessment of the situation will prove wrong.

Reference

Kathryn Rudie Harrigan and Michael Porter. "End-Game Strategies for Declining Industries." *Harvard Business Review* (July–August 1983).

KEPNER-TREGOE DRIVING-FORCE ANALYSIS

Applications

- Defining an organization's basic strategic mission from which decisions of product, market, and geographic scope follow.
- Focusing an organization on a single, clear mission to unify its management and strategy.
- Providing a foundation for strategic planning.

Procedures

1. Identify the organization's current driving force(s) from the list of alternatives.
2. Select a single driving force (the same or a new one) to guide organization strategy and to develop a mission statement based on it.
3. Review and modify mission statements of business centers and staff departments to make them consistent with the organization's driving force. Make strategies and resource-allocation decisions consistent with the mission statements.

Idea: Use Driving-Force Analysis as a preliminary to more detailed strategic-planning efforts.

Cross-Reference

Leadership Skills and Methods

Driving-Force Analysis is an antidote to the weak, vague mission statements and lack of unifying vision that plague many larger organizations. For example,

Whitney MacMillan, Chairman of Cargill Inc., claims that "the concept of Driving Force was a key to gaining clarity about our strategic direction." A variant on strengths/weaknesses analysis, Driving-Force Analysis identifies a single basic strength for the organization to focus on and exploit in future strategic decisions.

Use Driving-Force Analysis to make management determine what underlying strategic focus, if any, has guided the organization's decisions in the past and agree on a single, well-defined strategic direction to guide future decisions.

INSTRUCTIONS

There are nine basic choices from which management selects a driving force for the company or division. Select a force that best describes the organization's current direction or mission. In some cases a company is going in more than one direction, and two or three forces from the list are necessary to describe current conditions. But in most cases a single force has dominated the organization in recent years. It is especially helpful to assemble a group of managers for this task, letting them hash out differences in their views of the company, in the hope of arriving at a consensus.

Driving force is "the primary determinant of the scope of future products and markets" according to Benjamin Tregoe and John Zimmerman (see the references). To identify an organization's driving force, ask managers why the organization makes and sells certain products or services and not others. Selecting a new driving force affects future choices of product and market scope. It is essential for those who set strategy (the executives and board in most cases) to agree on the driving force before making product or market decisions. Select a driving force from one of the options enumerated in the list.

Integrate a driving force into the organization's planning process through the mission statement. Use Driving-Force Analysis to write a mission statement, either independently by the CEO or in collaboration with other managers. Then have division and subsidiary managers do an independent Driving-Force

Analysis to prepare their own mission statements. They may select the same driving force, or possibly a different but compatible one. In most cases the CEO will want to review these choices before approving the mission statements.

Driving forces

1. *Products/services offered.* Committed to a category of products. New products will be similar to old; new markets will be pursued as a way to sell more of the products. Diversification into novel products not a good idea. Example: Boeing.

2. *Market needs.* Dedicated to current markets and customers. Open to new products or services if they are needed by the market. Expands only into similar markets. Example: Merrill Lynch.

3. *Technology.* Technology-driven. Develops and markets products or services that take advantage of technological resources and tries to be a technology leader. Example: Texas Instruments.

4. *Production capability.* Manufacturing facilities and production expertise are the organization's greatest strengths. A variety of products and markets are possible as long as they exploit the production capability. Example: U.S. Steel. *Note*: A service company can fall into this category as well. Example: UPS.

5. *Method of sale.* A strong sales and distribution capability is exploited to offer a variety of products or services, possibly including other company's products. Expansion into unrelated sales and marketing channels does not make sense. Example: Book-of-the-Month Club.

6. *Method of distribution.* Distribution channels are the main determinant of product and market focus. When, where, and how products are sold is strongly influenced by distribution issues. Example: MacDonald's.

7. *Natural resources.* The natural resources the organization controls, processes, distributes, and sells are its key focus. New products and

markets that utilize the company's access to natural resources are the most appealing to these companies. Example: Standard Oil.

8. *Size/growth.* Growth targets are beyond those attainable in the current product/market scope, and the organization pursues new products and markets to achieve its goals. Usually a short-term driving force. Sometimes organizations adopt this driving force in order to become smaller rather than larger. Example: Boise Cascade Corp., 1960s.

9. *Return/profit.* Although returns are important to every business, few place such a high priority on them that they adopt new products or markets because of contribution to returns and for no other reason. A diversification strategy is driven by return/profit objectives (and assumes only one strength—superior management—which is no doubt the rarest!). A company which shifts its product or market focus to escape from a declining industry adopts this driving force temporarily. Example: ITT.

References

Benjamin B. Tregoe and John W. Zimmerman. *Top Management Strategy: What It Is and How to Make It Work.* New York: Simon & Schuster, 1980. (See especially Chapters 3 and 4.)

Arnoldo Hax and Nicholas Majluf. *Strategic Management: An Integrative Perspective.* Englewood Cliffs, NJ: Prentice Hall, 1984.

KEPNER-TREGOE STRATEGIC IQ TEST

Applications

- Measuring the extent of an organization's orientation toward strategy and implementation of strategy.
- Identifying areas in which strategy is subservient to other considerations.
- Generating discussion of the role of strategy among division and department managers.

Procedures

1. Review the list of 14 statements to see which are true of your organization.
2. Analyze and discuss the results, focusing on statements which do not apply and therefore indicate a lack of strategic focus.

Many organizations have adopted some of the techniques of strategic planning. Many have strategic-planning staff and prepare annual strategic plans. Yet research by Benjamin Tregoe and John Zimmerman of Kepner-Tregoe, Inc., led them to believe that strategic planning has not really taken root in many cases. They developed a series of questions which reveal the extent of an organization's strategic focus. Use them as a checklist to measure the extent to which an organization has adopted the strategic-planning approach. Also use them to see whether all the managers participate in strategic planning and share a common view of strategy and goals by asking your managers to answer these questions and then compare and discuss their answers.

INSTRUCTIONS

1. Take the Strategic IQ Test. Answer these questions yourself, or ask your management team to "take

the test," and then discuss the results in your next meeting.

Strategic IQ test

1. The direction of future organizational development is clearly defined by upper management.   Yes ☐   No ☐

2. Each manager knows details of strategy.   Yes ☐   No ☐

3. Each manager agrees on details of strategy.   Yes ☐   No ☐

4. Each manager has a common view of new products/markets based on strategy.   Yes ☐   No ☐

5. The organization's strategy is the most important factor in evaluating opportunities.   Yes ☐   No ☐

6. Strategy is developed independently of long-range planning.   Yes ☐   No ☐

7. Strategy determines plans and guides resource allocation.   Yes ☐   No ☐

8. Strategy is based on analysis and assumptions, not plans.   Yes ☐   No ☐

9. Strategy guides acquisitions, capital expenditures, and systems development, not vice versa.   Yes ☐   No ☐

10. Each division or subsidiary has a clear strategy.   Yes ☐   No ☐

11. Each division/subsidiary strategy is completely consistent with the organization's strategy.   Yes ☐   No ☐

12. Each department has a clear strategy.   Yes ☐   No ☐

13 Each department strategy is completely consistent with the organization's strategy.   Yes ☐   No ☐

14. The organization and its divisions or subsidiaries are evaluated on the basis of strategic performance as well as operating performance. Yes ☐ No ☐

2. Evaluate the responses. "Yes" is the correct answer if you are dedicated to the concept of strategy-based management, as Kepner-Tregoe and other management consulting firms are. Any negative responses indicate areas in which strategy is subservient to other concerns. Although this may be acceptable to some managers, at least make sure that in these cases other concerns do not work against achieving strategic objectives. Also look for differences in the perceptions of different managers. Some managers may feel that their departments or divisions have clear strategies that are closely aligned with the organization's, while others may not. And managers often respond negatively to the questions concerning agreement on strategy. The IQ test can provide a good vehicle to reveal and hash out disagreements.

Reference

Adapted from Benjamin Tregoe and John Zimmerman. *Top Management Strategy: What It Is and How To Make It Work*. New York: Simon and Schuster, 1980.

KING'S STRATEGIC-ISSUE ANALYSIS

Applications

- Focusing the efforts of staff, analysts, or consultants on questions of real importance to the strategy decisions of upper management.
- Making strategic-planning efforts of staff or consultants support and build on the judgment of executives (as opposed to prescriptive strategic planning).
- Obtaining consensus on strategic decisions by encouraging all decision makers to use a common information base.
- Prioritizing issues for analysis and monitoring issues and threats on a continuing basis.

Procedures

1. Strategic issues are identified by management.
2. Management and staff collaborate to define each issue formally.
3. Analysts build a model of the issue that identifies relevant subissues.
4. Management reviews the model and makes improvements.
5. Staff gathers information on each subissue to build an "information model" for management.
6. Management uses the information from the issue analysis to aid in decision making.
7. If desired, strategic-issue management can be used to monitor issues regularly and identify high-priority issues for strategic-issue analysis.

William King, a professor at University of Pittsburg's Graduate School of Business, developed SIA to improve on the organization's ability to make judgments about important issues and to integrate issue analysis into the regular planning process. His method helps managers and analysts cooperate and achieve consensus. It can also be adapted to individual decision making as the discipline it provides is valuable.

Note: This strategic-planning method does not produce any prescriptions. It collects and organizes information for use in decision making but does not have any specific formulas or models of the decision process. For those executives who want to make their own strategic decisions, this method provides a good vehicle for utilizing staff time and expertise in a helpful but nonintrusive manner.

INSTRUCTIONS

1. Management lists strategic issues. These are situations and pressures of importance and whose outcomes are uncertain enough that analysis is indicated. Formally, they are defined as:

- Having outcomes important to the organization's performance;

- Having uncertain or controversial impact;

- Requiring different strategies depending on their outcome.

The question, "Will there be a recession next year?" would be a strategic issue for most companies, especially if a recent slow-down in the economy made recession a real possibility. The outcome is likely to be important to an organization's performance, but the exact impact is probably uncertain, and different strategies would be required depending on whether there is a recession and how deep and long it is.

2. Management and staff cooperate to make a formal statement of the issue. Clarifying questions are explored. This step ensures that analysts understand management's concerns, and it adds depth and clarity to the issues.

3. Analysts build a strategic-issue model. This is a diagram illustrating all the subissues that relate to the strategic issue. The theory behind it is that any big question can be better understood by breaking it down into a series of smaller questions.

King uses the example of a firm which is concerned that another may enter its market. The strategic issue in this case is the threat of entry. The extent and nature of the threat can only be understood by looking at such questions as whether there are economies of scale in this market, how much capital it takes to enter, whether the new competitor would have any cost advantages, and so forth. Some of these subissues may have to be broken down even further, as is cost advantages in the table, page 401.

4. Management reviews the model to improve or clarify it, making sure all important subissues are identified. This step allows management to examine the analytical model before staff time is invested in analysis and makes sure it is focused on valuable questions.

Idea: If resources are limited, prioritize the issues and explore the most important. For example, if the firm concerned with threat of entry thinks its potential competitor has a cost advantage, it would see this as a key issue needing immediate analysis and verification.

5. The previous steps lead to agreement on specific subissues that require detailed research. Now analysts or staff from appropriate departments are delegated the task of information gathering. Questions that require expertise or time unavailable within the organization can be farmed out to consultants or research firms. Relevant information is added to the strategic-issue diagram or put into a briefing paper. This information and the issue model itself form an information model that provides a solid foundation for management judgment and decision making.

6. Now managers can use the the strategic-issue model to help them evaluate the impact of the issue and develop a strategy that takes the issue into account. According to Professor King, "When each participant in the planning process is forced to deal with each issue in the specific terms of the strategy-issue model rather than in vague and undefined terms, real consensus is possible." (See the referenced article by King, page 48.)

Strategic Issue	Subissue	Subissue
	Economies of scale	
	Product differentiation	
	Capital required	Experience curve effect
		Proprietary technology
Threat of Entry	Cost advantages	Access to materials
		Subsidies
	Access to distribution channels	Location
	Government policy	Lower fixed costs

7. *Idea*: Use a technique called Strategic Issue Management to make issue analysis an ongoing process. Advantage: Early warning of change or threats through continuous monitoring.

  1. Assign appropriate managers or analysts strategic issues or potential strategic issues to monitor.
  2. Review issues in periodic meetings. Rank them as follows:
      a. Urgent. Immediate attention.
      b. Will have an impact. Attend in next planning cycle.
      c. May have an impact. Continue to monitor.
      d. False alarm. Drop.
  3. Do an immediate strategic-issue analysis on urgent issues and develop an appropriate strategic or tactical response. Postpone analysis of other issues.
  4. Review issues and assignments to keep monitoring up-to-date and relevant.

References

H. Igor Ansoff. *Implanting Strategic Management.* Englewood Cliffs, NJ: Prentice Hall, 1984.

William R. King. "Using Strategic Issue Analysis." *Long Range Planning* 15(4) (1982).

LORANGE'S DIVISIONAL PLANNING MATRIX

Applications

- Helping division-level planners consider their options from the corporate as well as divisional perspective.

- Encouraging divisions to handle risk in a manner that reflects the strength of the parent company instead of pursuing an overly conservative strategy appropriate to a company the size of the division.

Procedures

1. Rate the division's business/product lines on the basis of how attractive their markets are.

2. Rate them based on how strong their competitive positions are in their markets.

3. Rate them based on how well they fit into the overall corporate context, including risk posture, strategic objectives, and the activities of other divisions.

Cross-Reference

Financial Decisions

This method was developed for large companies in which product-line planning takes place in multiple divisions. Peter Lorange argues that divisions display risk-taking behavior appropriate to small companies, but inappropriate to the larger parent company (a large company can afford more risk in its portfolio than a small company). Lorange found that divisional managers and small business managers have a similar aversion to risk. When divisional strategies are added up to an overall plan, the result is a low risk, short-term investment and a more conservative approach than is necessary. In his words,

> The traditional scheme for business planning, then, would seem to promote plans that tend to view the company as a collection of independent companies. In terms of risk taking, the advantages of being big are not realized. The division will have to undertake its business strategy analysis in a different way than is now being done so that the corporate/divisional interaction on risk taking can be an orderly part of the planning review procedures.

Lorange's matrix planning method can be used to control divisional planning from the corporate level so as to overcome this problem.

INSTRUCTIONS

Lorange uses a three-dimensional matrix. The dimensions are "Business Attractiveness," "Competitive Strength in Business," and "Consolidation Attractiveness." The first two dimensions are similar to those of the GE matrix and provide a general assessment of the attractiveness of a particular investment from the division's strategic perspective. The third dimension, "Consolidation Attractiveness," adds the corporation's perspective to the model. Each dimension is divided into three categories—high, medium, or low—producing a cube with 27 cells.

Note: Most of us are not particularly good at drawing or thinking in three dimensions and may find this cube a cumbersome visual device. It is not necessary to actually plot a portfolio of products on the three-dimensional matrix—the method uses the three-dimensional model as the backbone of a formal procedure for divisional planning, as outlined in the instructions.

1. The division evaluates its business units and/or product lines on the basis of the attractiveness of the businesses (or markets) they are in. Lorange suggests the following evaluation factors, which may be replaced or added to with company-specific criteria:

DIVISIONAL PLANNING MATRIX

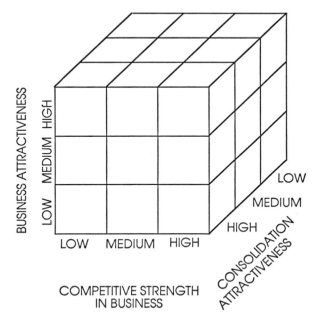

- Market-growth rate
- Frequency of purchase (less frequently purchased products tend to provide higher ROI)
- Concentration of customers (more fragmented is better)
- Barriers to competition
- Size of market
- Structure of competition (concentration of market)

Use the evaluation criteria to develop a qualitative assessment of the attractiveness of each business or market, rating businesses/markets high, medium, or low on the attractiveness scale.

2. Evaluate the divisional portfolio on the second dimension of the matrix—relative competitive strength. Absolute and relative measures of market share may be used, and Lorange also suggests looking at strategic-expenditure level (high investment in R&D, for example, should confer an advantage), product quality, and capacity utilization (high utilization being a positive factor). Rank each divisional business unit high, medium, or low in terms of competitive strength in its market and industry.

3. Now evaluate each of the division's business units or product lines from the perspective of consolidation attractiveness. This is measured according to the following criteria:

Cash Flow. Lorange evaluates the impact of each project on the shape of cash flow, the size of cash flow, the risk of cash flow, and covariance of cash flows.

Timing of cash flows is important from the corporate perspective. For example, even if all of a division's investments make sense from a NPV perspective, their timing could be problematic in light of other divisions' plans or corporate plans.

A balance among cash flows is usually important to the corporation as a whole, but may not be necessary on the divisional level. A collaboration between divisional and corporate management may lead to the division's taking a more exposed position than it would have otherwise, as long as this position is balanced elsewhere in the company.

Covariance of cash flows from different divisional plans is also an issue—a particular investment may be attractive in other ways, but unattractive if it requires a large and risky investment on the same calendar as several existing projects.

Synergy effects. Synergies between strategies of different divisions are an important consideration, but may be overlooked or underexploited in traditional divisional planning. Production synergies may provide cost advantages, for example, when several divisions can produce products in the same facility. Marketing and R&D synergies are also possible.

Substitution opportunities. Decisions to withdraw from or deemphasize a market should be considered in light of opportunities to substitute other business for that which would be lost, either within the division or elsewhere in the company. Competitive advantage, even in an unappealing market, may be worth preserving since it is so much harder to build advantage than give it away. The objective should be to maximize the firm's competitive advantage, not the division's.

Division-level planning. If division managers evaluate opportunities on all three dimensions of the model, they will tend to bring a corporate perspective to their planning. Cooperation between division managers and with corporate planners is clearly necessary to make this model work. Otherwise, divisional managers, who are in the best position to evaluate opportunities, will only present those that meet divisional criteria in their plans. And it will be very difficult for corporate planners and executives to add the consolidation dimension after the fact.

Reference

Peter Lorange. "Divisional Planning: Setting Effective Direction." *Sloan Management Review* (Fall 1975).

MCKINSEY STRATEGY FAILURE CHECKLIST

Applications

- Evaluating strategy in terms of its uniqueness in an industry or market.
- Identifying causes for look-alike strategy and changing the strategy process to make strategy more unique.
- Screening corporate or divisional strategic plans.

Procedures

1. Review strategy to see whether any of the five common failings on the McKinsey Checklist apply.
2. Revise current strategy to make it more unique and adaptable.
3. If necessary, encourage a more independent approach through changes in the process of strategy formulation. Review the questions provided to identify possible changes.

Cross-Reference

Marketing Decisions

This checklist was developed by Loel Bleeke of McKinsey and Company in response to the problem of look-alike strategies. In most industries the strategies of individual companies tend to converge on common elements, forcing direct competition, making strategies less effective, and keeping competitors from developing unique niches. Managers do not usually intend to pursue look-alike or me-too strategies; Bleeke finds that they often fall into this trap through five common failings in the process of strategy formulation.

INSTRUCTIONS

1. The checklist of these strategy failings provides an easy way to test your strategy and the process by which it is developed to anticipate whether it is likely to look too much like the strategies of competitors. Use it for a quick, informal review of your company's strategy or incorporate it into the planning process by assigning responsibility for evaluating your company and each major competitor against each item of the checklist. This is likely to provide insights into competitor weaknesses and strategic opportunities for your company

Checklist of strategy failings

1. *Focus on where to compete*. Strategy often focuses on *where* to compete and not enough on the hows. How a company competes—the ways in which it produces and delivers its products and services—provides more opportunities for developing unique and hard-to-copy strategies.

2. *Low emphasis on uniqueness and adaptability*. Every strategic plan should be evaluated on the basis of uniqueness and adaptability. If these categories are not in the table of contents of the plan, then the plan does not address the issues sufficiently. Questions such as "How different is our strategy from our competitors' strategies?" "Do we target the same customers or markets as our competitors?" and "How can we adapt our strategy if competitors pursue a similar one?" should be built into the planning process.

3. *Low emphasis on when to compete*. *When* a company enters a market is usually more important than where and how it enters the market. This is increasingly true in many technology-driven product and service markets, where product life cycles are shortening. A dominant position is far less likely with late entry, for example, and the specifics of a strategy should reflect the stage of

development of the market. (Product life-cycle analysis should be considered. See ADL Life-Cycle Matrix, this section.) Timing is an increasingly important issue, and it can be used to differentiate strategies that are similar in other dimensions.

4. *Focus on firms and competitors instead of individuals.* Competitive strategy must anticipate the behavior of competitors. Usually assumptions are made about competitor behavior without giving much thought to the personalities of their leaders. But considerable insight into future behavior is provided by information about the individuals, an element of competitor analysis that is often underemphasized. And when competitors are viewed as individuals they often appear more unique, making it easier to develop differentiated strategies. *Example*: A strategy that falls between the areas of responsibility of two strong-willed division heads at a competing company is unlikely to be copied by that competitor in the short term.

5. *Common performance measures.* If companies have different strategic plans but measure success in the same way, their managers will be influenced by the performance criteria to behave in a similar manner despite the strategies. For example, a company which is pursuing a long-range market development strategy on paper but still evaluating its managers on the basis of quarterly and annual ROE may find that its long-term strategy is not achieved. However, if performance is measured in terms of accomplishment of strategic goals it can become a flexible motivator that facilitates differentiated strategies instead of hindering them.

2. A review of current strategic plans often reveals that one or more of these failings may apply. Perhaps most common is the case in which a strategy proves almost identical to a competitor's because both focus on where to compete, glossing over the issues of how and when, which might have been used to differentiate the strategy more effectively. The CEO or division manager can use this checklist as a screen administered to any strategic plans submitted for approval. It is a simple way to focus attention on the conceptual side of strategy; too often review and

approval hinges on internal issues—"Where will the resources come from and how will we get the other divisions to cooperate?"—rather than focusing on the soundness of the underlying concepts.

3. If strategies consistently suffer from one or more of these failings it may be necessary to reexamine the process of strategy formulation. In many cases the basic inputs to strategy decisions do not support generation of unique and adaptable strategy. Review the information your firm uses in developing strategy to see how it measures up to the checklist. As an additional aid, review the following questions:

- Does your staff collect a lot of information about where your competitors compete (geographically and by segment), but very little on how and when?

- Do they know when each competitor typically enters a new market?

- Do they gather statistical information about performance of competitors, but very little about their organization and the personalities of the individuals in charge?

- Do your firm's internal measures of performance provide a clear picture of each manager's achievement of strategic goals?

- Does your staff regularly gather information on competitor strategies and tactics and compare them to your firm's to see how similar they are?

By asking these questions you may stimulate your organization to gather the information required to generate more independent and differentiated strategies.

Reference

"Making Strategy Look Different." *Management Briefing: Marketing* (February–March 1988). The Conference Board.

ORCHARD MATRIX OF MARKET ATTRACTIVENESS

Applications

- Choosing markets for new products or product-line extensions.
- Deciding which markets deserve further product development.

Procedures

1. Estimate each market's sales-growth rate.
2. Estimate each market's concentration.
3. Plot each market on the Orchard Matrix.
4. Interpret. (The markets with the highest growth and lowest concentration are often the most attractive.)

Cross-Reference

Marketing Decisions

The choice of new markets is a difficult one. Companies frequently feel the urge to expand into new markets, either with existing products or through new-product development, and the Orchard Matrix provides a simple way to compare the attractiveness of the alternatives.

INSTRUCTIONS

The Orchard Matrix is a graph whose two axes are sales growth and market concentration. Use the annual growth rate for the market as a whole, if it is known, or the combined growth rate for the top several companies in the market. The simplest way to measure concentration is to use the market share of the leader. *Note*: No data on market shares? Define concentration as the leader's revenues relative to the second and third place competitors' revenues. Divide leaders revenues by the sum of the second and third place competitors' revenues for a measure of relative share.

Now plot each market on the graph. Place growth on the vertical and concentration on the horizontal axis. Let the range of the estimates define the scale of each axis.

If hard numbers are not available on the markets of interest, use your intuition or question industry experts to rank each alternative market relative to the others on the growth and concentration axes. It is not necessary to use hard numbers since the purpose is to rank the available alternatives relative to each other.

The exhibit shows the Orchard Matrix divided into four quadrants, each bearing a different label to indicate its relative attractiveness. A market which has high growth but no strong leader is clearly *ripe*

ORCHARD MATRIX

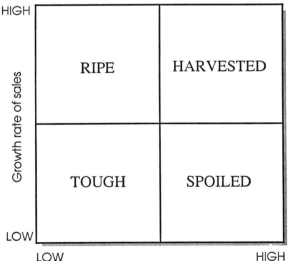

for the picking. A low-growth, low-concentration market may be easy to enter but will probably be *tough* to profit in. A high-growth market that already has a strong industry leader will be difficult to penetrate since another company is already *harvesting* it. A low-growth market with a strong leader is generally the least attractive of the four—it has been *spoiled* by the current competitors.

There is no formula for placing boundaries between the quadrants. Think about the markets under consideration and consider your company's prior experience in defining high versus low market growth and high versus low market concentration. In some industries, growth of less than 20% is low, but in many mature industries 5% growth is a miracle.

The concentration and growth rate of markets do not remain constant over time. Markets will tend to move from tough to ripe when they are young and to harvested and then spoiled as they enter maturity and decline.

Reference

Alexander Hiam & Associates. Project for North Star Computers, 1985.

PORTER VALUE CHAIN ANALYSIS

Applications

- Analyzing business units based on the way they perform key functions.
- Looking for competitive advantages through comparisons of the operations of competitors.
- Providing a formal model and presentation format for competitor research, analysis, and strategies.

Procedures

1. Select the unit of analysis, both for your company and for major competitors.
2. Identify primary value-adding activities (direct, indirect, and quality assurance).
3. Identify support activities (direct, indirect, and quality assurance).
4. Identify linkages between value chain activities.
5. Study the value chains to identify sources of competitive advantage.

Cross-Reference

"Marketing Decisions"—competitor analysis.

Those familar with Michael Porter's work will recognize the basis of his book *Competitive Advantage* in the procedures outlined. Value chain analysis is a complex and rich device for strategic planning. However, the basics of the method can be mastered quite

The exhibit on page 419 is reprinted with permission of the Free Press, a Division of Macmillan Inc. from *Competitive Advantage: Creating and Sustaining Superior Performance* by Michail E. Porter. Copyright © 1980 by Michael E. Porter.

easily, and it is a valuable tool for judgmental analysis of competitors. Use it to evaluate or refine strategies in light of competitor strengths and weaknesses.

The concept behind value chain analysis is simple. The activities of a company add value—increase the price the company can charge for its products—hopefully in excess of the costs of those activities. Value analysis looks at where and how a firm adds value; breaking down activities and assigning a value added to them rather than assigning costs as in the conventional accounting system. The knowledge gained from value analysis is helpful in understanding how competitors differ and where to create additional value that will confer competitive advantage.

INSTRUCTIONS

1. Select the unit of analysis. Use value chain analysis to study individual business units, competing in specific industries. Do not try to analyze an entire industry—the analysis should be competitor by competitor. And do not apply the method to all the activities of a firm if the firm competes in several discrete industries.

2. Identify primary value-adding activities. Primary activities are defined as follows:

Inbound logistics	Receiving, storing, and handling product inputs
Operations	Transforming raw materials and other inputs into the product and creating and maintaining the facilities needed to produce the product
Outbound logistics	Moving the product to buyers, including warehousing and distribution
Marketing and sales	Bringing the product to buyers and inducing them to buy and use it

Service   Installing, maintaining,
                             repairing the product;
                             training, parts, and
                             other services

These activities are generally quite distinct, having different economies and representing significant cost centers within the business unit. For each category of primary activity, prepare a list of the major component activities. For example, direct selling is a component activity in the marketing and sales category.

Porter recognizes three types of activities, all of which can be found in most company's primary activities. *Direct* activities are those activities that most obviously add value— machining is a direct activity under operations. *Indirect* activities are those that are necessary in order to perform the direct activities— overhead and administration included. For example, servicing machining equipment. *Quality Assurance* activities are those that assure that the other activities are performed properly. Example: Testing machined parts for conformance to product specifications.

Look for activities of each type as a way to make sure you are not overlooking any of the activities constituting each primary activity from the preceding list.

3. Identify support activities. Support activities are divided into the following four categories:

Procurement   The support systems and
                             functions associated with
                             inbound logistics

Technology
  development   Research and product
                             development in support
                             of products or processes
                             used to produce them

Human-resource
  management   Finding, training, and
                             keeping the people
                             needed to perform
                             primary and support
                             activities

Firm infrastructure   Management, planning, finance, accounting, and other activities often considered to be overhead

As with the primary activities, look for the specific direct, indirect, and quality-assurance activities that make up each of these four categories of support activities. List the key activities by category, indicating their type.

4. Identify linkages in the value chain. Linkages are defined by Porter (p. 49) as "relationships between the way one activity is performed and the cost or performance of another." For example, parts procurement and assembly are tightly linked in a just-in-time production process. Linkages are often harder to identify than discrete activities—it takes insight into the business to see where the important linkages exist and to see opportunities to create new linkages. JIT production is in fact a good example of how a linkage can be exploited to create competitive advantage.

One way to find linkages is to look at information flows. In general, cooperation, and therefore communication, is needed between different functional groups within the business unit in order to exploit a linkage.

5. Study the value chains to identify sources of competitive advantage. Porter uses a graphic format for presenting value chains. The illustration shows a standard value chain diagram. Use this diagram, adapted to the business unit you are studying, to represent the activities you have identified. Allocate space within the diagram in proportion to the contribution of each activity to value added.

When two competitors' diagrams are compared, differences in primary or support activities are usually noticeable. Even though two companies may produce the same product or service for the same market, each will emphasize different activities in differing proportions. These differences give clues to current competitive positions and also can highlight weaknesses and opportunities that can be exploited in future strategy.

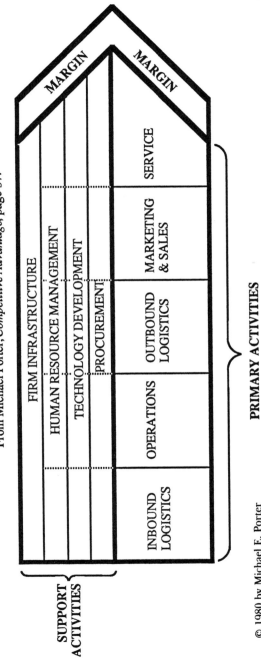

THE GENERIC VALUE CHAIN

From Michael Porter, *Competitive Advantage*, page 37.

© 1980 by Michael E. Porter

Also look closely at the linkages identified and think about opportunities to increase the value added through building additional linkages. An analysis of linkages is often helpful in identifying ways in which to differentiate your company from its competitors.

Reference

Michael Porter. *Competitive Advantage*. New York: Free Press, 1985.

POTLATCH STRATEGIC-PLANNING GUIDELINES

Applications

- Developing realistic, usable strategic plans.
- Evaluating the strategic-planning process to see how it can be made more pragmatic and useful.
- Implementing plans and writing plans that are easier to implement.

Procedures

1. During the strategy development stage, review the first five guidelines for ideas about how to write a successful plan.
2. Use the last five guidelines for ideas about successful implementation of a strategy.
3. Also use all the guidelines to review and improve current planning processes and procedures.

These guidelines for strategy development and implementation come from the director of strategic planning at Potlatch. Their goal is to produce focused, realistic plans that have the support needed for successful implementation. The guidelines are relevant to the planning process regardless of the type of strategy pursued, and they provide an interesting contrast to more academic approaches to strategic planning. Potlatch clearly takes a pragmatic approach, one that other companies could benefit from as well.

INSTRUCTIONS

1. During the strategy development stage the following five guidelines apply:

1. *Homework.* Plans should be based on a detailed study of the constraints, how and where people make money in your business, and what your core businesses are.

2. *Personality.* The plan should be designed to suit the personality of the CEO. An ambitious plan is appropriate for the experienced, aggressive CEO, but not for the CEO who is new or cautious.

3. *Scale.* Strategic planning is an iterative process, so there is no need to start too big. Overly ambitious plans create conflict and unrealistic expectations.

4. *Participation.* Who participates in the planning process is a key consideration. Too many people make it too cumbersome, but enough must be included to ensure quality and support for implementation.

5. *Expectations.* Expectations for strategy should be realistic. For example, good strategy alone cannot always overcome economic problems such as the ones experienced in the lumber and agricultural equipment industries.

2. In the implementation phase of strategy the following guidelines are relevant:

6. *Ego problems.* People not involved in developing a strategy often resent being asked to implement it. It is best to rely more heavily on the people who helped develop the strategy and who are known to be supporters of it.

7. *Authority.* The authority of the planner is often an issue in implementation. Operating managers may not respect the plan's authority unless it comes clearly from the chief executive.

8. *Backsliding.* A new plan can get off to a good start, but when the initial excitement fades there is a tendency, more pronounced in hard times, to return to the old ways of doing things. The plan needs to incorporate milestones and checks to prevent backsliding.

9. *Competitive responses.* Others plan too, which means that your plan may have to be updated to reflect the actions of competitors.

10. *Flexibility.* Management and planners must be flexible and avoid slavish adherence to the plan. Strategy does not always work; failures need to be recognized and corrected early.

Reference

Based on a talk by Charles Neuner of Potlatch Corp. on April 5, 1985 at U. C. Berkeley's business school.

THE RULE OF THREE AND FOUR

Applications

- Developing hypotheses concerning future competitive structure of a market.
- Assessing competitive position.
- Evaluating the attractiveness of a market based on current and anticipated structure.

Procedures

1. Define the market narrowly and gather information on competitor market shares.
2. Apply the Rule of Three and Four to see whether the rule currently holds true in your market and make predictions concerning trends in market structure.
3. Integrate hypotheses based on the rule into future research and planning activities.

Cross-Reference

Marketing Decisions

This is a rule of thumb from the Boston Consulting Group. Although it has not been rigorously tested, it often holds true, providing a good starting point for a quick assessment of competitive structure. Use it to evaluate the stability of your position or a competitor's position and to anticipate long-term structural trends in your markets.

INSTRUCTIONS

The rule appears to hold true in many competitive industries, so anyone in an industry which is entering a more competitive phase, through de-regulation or the entry of new competitors, will find this a useful device for guestimating what future industry structure will be like.

Bruce Henderson of the Boston Consulting Group states the Rule of Three and Four as follows:

> **A stable competitive market never has more than three significant competitors, the largest of which has no more than four times the market share of the smallest.**

The rule is based on the observation that a two-to-one ratio of market shares between two competitors is an equilibrium point at which neither competitor will benefit from changes in relative share. It is also based on the observation that a ratio of four to one is the most the smaller competitor can tolerate. If its relative share falls to less than a quarter it will at best be a marginal business. Taken together, these two statements imply that competitive markets will move toward a stable structure of three competitors, each with a share half as big as the next largest (4:2:1). But note that the rule is only intended to apply to direct competitors in identical markets. A narrow, product-oriented definition of markets is therefore necessary.

The strategic implications of this rule are many, including the following:

- A competitive market with more than three competitors is likely to have a shake-out.

- A position other than leadership or second place is not viable over the long term in a competitive market.

- Rapid relative-share growth should be the objective in the early stages of a market's life cycle.

- If the two market leaders do not have an equilibrium 2:1 share ratio, their competition will make the market less profitable for all other competitors.

The rule is more likely to hold true where the price/experience curve is valid, as in high-capital investment manufacturing industries.

Reference

Bruce D. Henderson. *Henderson on Corporate Strategy*. Cambridge: MA. Abt Books, 1979. (See pages 90–94.)

WORLD BANK STRATEGIC-ISSUE MANAGEMENT

Applications

- Increasing the flexibility and adaptability of the organization in response to changes in the environment and to urgent issues.
- Increasing the length of time between formal strategic-planning sessions.
- Allowing for continuous monitoring and reaction by senior management to strategic issues and problems.
- Responding effectively to challenges that cut across departmental or functional lines.

Procedures

1. Identify and prioritize strategic issues on an ongoing basis.
2. Respond to priority issues through action-oriented task forces capable of crossing organizational boundaries and commanding necessary resources.
3. Follow the progress of issue projects, identify problem issues for follow-up, and integrate strategic-issue management into the organization's routine strategic-planning process.

Cross-Reference

For a related method, see King's Strategic-Issue Analysis in this section.

In a recent study of strategic planning, Nagy Hanna of the World Bank found that large financial and industrial companies encounter several common problems with annual strategic-planning methods:

- Annual revision of plans "overloads manage-ment or deteriorates into ritual"
- Changes in the environment can have strategic implications at any time in the planning cycle, not just annually
- Surprise events can require rapid strategic responses

Merrill Lynch, American Express, Sears, and other firms in the study are responding to these problems by writing detailed strategic plans only every few years and using some form of strategic-issue management to make strategy adaptable in the interim.

Nagy Hanna has identified successful techniques for issue management from these companies and suggests a systematic approach that combines the best features.

INSTRUCTIONS

1. Identification of issues.

Issues are defined as having:

- impact on performance and strategy implemen-tation,
- urgency, or
- impact on other issues.

The goal of monitoring issues is to ensure early identification. Monthly review and revising of an issue list is suggested; it can be prioritized and the priorities reviewed monthly as well. Surveillance of the environment and the organization must be ongo-ing. Executives should be alert for issues of potential importance, and staff can be assigned the task of information gathering and monitoring as well. (See note on staffing under "Staffing for Strategic-Issue Management," next page.)

2. Response.

Once identified, an issue should be responded to rapidly. Use a task-force approach to make response effective and fast. The staff that perform monitoring activities should also be responsible for presenting new issues to upper management "in a standard format that facilitates the examination of options and action." If upper management agrees that the issue is important, a task force is assembled, chaired by one of the issue-management staff, to identify required actions. This task force may need to look closely at interdepartmental issues, since response often involves coordination of multiple departments or functions.

Unless given special authority to act on issues and a clear mandate for action, these task forces will tend to analyze rather than act. Issue-management staff should report to senior executives—at Kodak they are managed by the Executive Management Committee, at Sears by the Planning Committee, and at IBM by the Policy Committee. When a task force decides on a course of action, management needs to assign the necessary resources directly to the task force.

3. Follow-up.

Staff should keep an updated, prioritized list of issues that includes information on the current activities of the task forces assigned to each. In addition, staff should track implementation of projects, making sure they are completed and notifying senior management of any that are not. Special reports on problems encountered by task forces or the organization in dealing with issues should be prepared so upper management cannot lose track of any issues.

In some cases issues will not be resolved, or even fully understood, the first time they are tackled. Many issues are too complex or novel for the task force to deal with fully. These issues should be put back on the issue list and given to another task force as many times as it takes to resolve them to the satisfaction of upper management. According to Nagy Hanna, "In such cases, there is a need to revisit issues and to resolve them in a progressive and persistent manner."

Integrate Strategic-Issue Management into the regular strategic-planning cycle by addressing priority issues in the strategic-plan and by viewing the strategic planning process as a potential source of strategic issues.

Staffing for strategic-issue management

The World Bank study's methodology can be implemented in a variety of ways, depending on the staff resources available and the preferences of management. A lean approach is to use an issue manager who coordinates a committee or task force made up of operational middle managers and staff temporarily assigned to the issue project. Some companies, including Hewlett-Packard and Wang, combine the duties of corporate planning and issue management in a single position reporting directly to the CEO. At the opposite end of the spectrum are companies like Arco and Sears, which have a large, dedicated staff specializing in strategic issue management.

Role of top management

According to the World Bank study, "One common source of difficulty is the refusal of the top management group to submit to the discipline of SIM."

Senior management plays an important role in this method. Without their participation and active support, issue management will degenerate into report writing. Unlike periodic strategic planning, strategic-issue management requires executives' routine participation in planning. Management needs to take an interest in the process and must be willing to accept and act on new issues.

Reference

Nagy Hanna. "Strategic Planning and Management: A Review of Recent Experience." *World Bank Staff Working Papers*, Number 751. The World Bank, 1985.

PART 9

GENERAL DECISION-MAKING TOOLS

ADVANTAGES/DISADVANTAGES TABLE

Applications

- Deciding whether to pursue an opportunity.
- Identifying all the pros and cons of an alternative.

Procedures

1. List the pros and cons in a table.
2. If there is more than one alternative, use separate tables for each.
3. Decide whether the pros outweigh the cons. If there is more than one alternative, choose the best.

Cross-Reference

Strategic Planning Decisions and Financial Decisions

What are the pros and cons of a proposed deal? Everyone has asked this question at least once, for it is probably the oldest form of business analysis. The Advantages/Disadvantages Table formalizes the analysis by laying out pros and cons of a particular choice in an orderly format.

The simplicity of the method is deceptive; it is one of the best ways to think through a difficult issue. Not only is it an excellent method for presenting alternatives in a meeting or memo, but it is also a useful first step in thinking through almost any unfamiliar proposal and is especially well suited to strategic planning, where the choices may be unfamiliar and a subjective approach required.

Idea: Next time you are in a working meeting, try taking to the chalkboard with the Advantages/Disadvantages Table as your scaffolding. With a little practice you will become adept at defining pros and cons and you will learn to use the table as a leadership tool.

INSTRUCTIONS

Lay out a table with two lines forming a "T" to create one column for advantages and a second for disadvantages. Start filling in whichever column is easier. If you favor a proposal, you will have no trouble listing several of its advantages. If you dislike it, the disadvantages will be obvious to you. Once one column has some entries, it is easy to fill in the other.

Tip: Get help. Groups usually generate more pros and cons than do individuals.

Challenge: After the table has been created you must decide whether the project is worthwhile. You may need to study some of the issues before the choice can be made, especially if pros and cons are closely balanced.

In the example shown here, the table is being used to evaluate a proposed retail site for a fresh-baked cookie company. In this case advantages are compelling and management will probably go ahead. The list of disadvantages should be used as an agenda; for example, someone needs to work on the security problems and negotiate storefront design.

ADVANTAGES/DISADVANTAGES TABLE

Advantages	Disadvantages
High-traffic area	Rent is high
Plumbing included	Restrictions on storefront design
No other cookie stores in the mall	Won't give an exclusive
Parking available	Possible security problems at night
Location is near movie theater	

Reference

Kenneth J. Albert. *How to Solve Business Problems.* McGraw Hill, 1978.

CRAWFORD SLIP WRITING

Applications

- Soliciting ideas for problem solving from a large group.
- Polling the members of a department or staff group for their suggestions without including them in the actual decision,
- Generating a large number of creative ideas in a hurry.

Procedures

1. Hand out index cards—20 to 30 for each group member (or fewer if time is limited). The group can be any size.
2. Read a formal problem statement to the group, as in the Nominal Group Technique.
3. Ask group members to write down every idea they can think of that might solve the problem, one to an index card. No discussion allowed.
4. In five or ten minutes collect the index cards.
5. Use a small group of appointed staff or managers to sort and analyze the results, or simply review them yourself for novel ideas.

Cross-Reference

Organization and Human Resources

This method is similar to the Nominal Group Technique. It can be performed quickly and is suitable to very large groups as well as smaller ones. *Note:* It is an easy way to obtain employee input on a problem without group discussion.

It builds employees' sense of participation in the way that a suggestion box does, except that it includes everyone (not just those who voluntarily write suggestions) and it focuses on a single problem that is defined by management. The simplicity of this method, combined with the fact that it does not require managers to give up any decision-making authority, makes it an attractive tool. Use it to make sure you have considered every alternative and looked at a problem from many perspectives before making a decision.

INSTRUCTIONS

As per procedures.

Application ideas

While social scientists apparently have occasion to use this method with groups of thousands, large group gatherings are rare in business. Use the method at annual meetings and training events where large groups of employees are assembled. Otherwise, try modifying it to permit participation through the mail or electronic mail so that you can find out what many people think about an idea *without* having to hold a meeting. If group members participate through the mail, however, it is important to state the rules very clearly so that no collaboration takes place.

References

C.H. Clark. *The Crawford Slip Writing Method.* Kent, OH: Charles H. Clark, 1978.

Arthur B. VanGundy. *Managing Group Productivity: A Modular Approach to Problem Solving.* Amacom (American Management Associations), 1984.

DECISION-TREE ANALYSIS

Applications

- Identifying the options and potential outcomes of a decision or series of related decisions.
- Assigning probabilities to events and calculating the likely returns from alternative decisions.
- Structuring the decision task to identify where and how research should be used.

Procedures

1. Identify decision alternatives and alternative situations or "states of nature."
2. Diagram them on a decision tree.
3. Calculate the possible financial returns and costs and enter these on the diagram. Sum to find the payoffs for each combination of decisions and situations.
4. *Optional.* Estimate the probability of each situation and weight payoffs by probabilities to calculate expected monetary values of each alternative. Select the decision with the highest expected value.

Cross-Reference

Applicable in many areas, including Organization & Human Resources, Strategic Planning Decisions.

This method is helpful in planning a project or making a series of related decisions. It is used to look ahead at the various possible outcomes and map the specific decisions needed and their impact on outcomes. It relies heavily on management judgment, providing structure to the normal judgmental decision process. The method is easily used and, once mastered, is a useful back-of-the-envelope technique. It is also useful in presenting a project or problem to a group in a structured manner in order to get feedback on a decision or the assumptions on which the decision is based.

INSTRUCTIONS

1. Identify all the feasible alternatives—the different decision options available to you. Also identify the different situations that might prevail after the decision, focusing on a variable (or several) of relevance to the ultimate outcome of your decision.

Example: You must decide how much to spend on a new-product launch. Three alternatives are presented by the marketing department: low, medium, and high advertising and sales support. These are your feasible alternatives. You see two likely situations after introduction of the product: No competition and high demand versus a similar product introduction by a competitor and lower demand for your new product.

2. Draw a decision tree illustrating the decision alternatives and the situations. Each decision is illustrated with a square or diamond, and each situation with a circle. Lines connect the decisions and situations and are labeled to explain the diagram (Example 1).

3. To calculate the possible financial returns from each combination of decisions and situations, enter the costs of each decision on the diagram (negative numbers) along with the incomes (positive numbers) from each situation and sum them to calculate the payoffs. Write the payoffs at the right side of the diagram (Example 2).

4. If you want, you can refine the tree by estimating the probability of each situation occurring (probabilities should sum to 1). Then multiply the payoff by the probability to calculate the "expected monetary value" of each alternative. Select the decision that will maximize expected monetary value, as in Example 3.

EXAMPLE 1

Decisions	Situations	Possible Outcomes

A

B

C

a
b
1
2

a
b
3
4

a
b
5
6

A = High support   a = Low sales

B = Medium   b = High sales
     support

C = Low support

EXAMPLE 2

Costs	Returns	($) Payback

A

-1,000,000

-500,000   B

-100,000

C

1,000,000   0

5,000,000   4,000,000

550,000   50,000

250,000   2,000,000

450,000   350,000

2,000,000   1,900,000

EXAMPLE 3

Costs ($ mils)	Returns ($ mils) & Probabilities	Payback ($ mils)	Expected Monetary Value ($ mils)
	1 (P = 0.6)	0.00	**1.60**
-1 (A)	5 (P = 0.4)	4.00	
	.55 (P = 0.6)	0.05	**0.83**
-.5 (B)	2.5 (P = 0.4)	2.00	
	.45 (P = 0.6)	0.35	**0.97**
-.1 (C)	2 (P = 0.4)	1.90	

Calculation: paybacks

EMV (Decision C) = 0.6(0.35) + 0.4(1.90) = **0.97**

probabilities

References

David Anderson, Dennis Sweeney, and Thomas Williams. *Quantitative Methods for Business*, 2nd ed. West, 1983.

Donald D. Lee. *Industrial Marketing Research: Techniques and Practices*, 2nd ed. Van Nostrand Reinhold, 1984.

Charles A. Holloway, *Decision Making Under Uncertainty: Models and Choices.* Englewood Cliffs: Prentice Hall, 1979.

THE GORDON/LITTLE GROUP TECHNIQUE

Applications

- Helping a group come up with fresh ideas and new approaches to a problem.
- Structuring the idea-generation stage of problem solving.
- Encouraging creativity in a group that has run into a roadblock.

Procedures

1. Make a formal statement of the problem, as in Crawford Slip Writing or the Nominal Group Technique. Be as clear and specific as possible.
2. Analyze the problem statement to identify the general tasks or problems that make it up. Write a very general statement of the problem that disassociates it from the context.
3. Give the group the general statement of the problem and ask them to generate general classes of solutions.
4. State the problem a little more specifically, repeating the discussion and generation of solutions.
5. Finally, introduce the problem in its specific form. Discuss and generate ideas guided by the general discussions above.

Cross-Reference

Project Development and Innovation

Most managers have a few problems that crop up repeatedly in one form or another, defying normal efforts to solve them. Management and staff tend to grow tired of these issues and find it difficult to come up with novel approaches to them. In many cases, the failure to solve such problems reflects difficulties of "seeing the forest for the trees" or bringing a novel perspective to an old problem. The Gordon/Little method is useful in these situations. It helps a group look at a problem from new perspectives and can break habitual ways of thinking, leading to creative proposals and solutions.

INSTRUCTIONS

Follow the five steps in "Procedures" carefully. The method requires preparation by the manager or group leader. As "Procedures" indicates, the leader has to take a specific problem and state it in a very general manner. The more generally it is stated, the more successful the group will be at identifying all practical types of solutions.

After the group discusses the problem in a general, unfamiliar form that is independent of the original context, the leader introduces more narrow definitions of the problem until the group is back to the original, specific problem and its familiar context. But having addressed it on other levels, the group is now more likely to see alternative and less obvious approaches.

Example: The original problem statement is, "High employee turnover and a tight labor market at our company-owned fast-food restaurants in the Northeast is hurting the quality of service." (Apologies to Friendly Restaurant Corp.) You have been discussing this problem for several years without making significant inroads. Let's assume that conventional solutions such as higher wages and more training have not made a significant difference and are very costly. General problems within this problem statement include:

- Attracting people to jobs
- Keeping people interested in their work
- Competing with other employers for good employees

Even more generally, these problems boil down to the question of how you get people to make a long-term commitment. So the first statement of the problem might be, "Think of ways to get people to make a long-term commitment."

This is a good starting point because it is so far removed from the original problem that participants can address it without thinking about the original problem at all. After they have proposed general strategies, such as "Offer them something valuable," "Show them how they will benefit in the long term," and "Build a strong personal relationship," you can move to a problem statement that is more specific, like the three listed originally. The group will apply general concepts; for example, by suggesting that a career path with increasing responsibilities might keep people interested in their work (an applied version of "Show them how they will benefit in the long term"). By the end of the meeting, members will probably have a lot of "wild" ideas such as job redesign, offering franchises to successful managers, promotion from within, weekly social activities to build personal relationships, and so forth. These will provide a welcome relief to the original ideas concerning wage and training increases.

References

J. W. Taylor. *How to Create Ideas*. Englewood Cliffs, NJ: Prentice Hall, 1961.

Arthur B. VanGundy. *Managing Group Productivity: A Modular Approach to Problem Solving*. Amacom (American Management Associations), 1984.

_____. *Techniques of Structured Problem Solving*. Van Nostrand Reinhold, 1981.

HARVARD NEGOTIATION PROJECT RULES

Applications

- Negotiating decisions in which both parties benefit and are pleased with the results.
- Establishing guidelines for negotiations.
- Moving from traditional bargaining to "win-win" negotiating techniques.

Procedures

Agree on the four rules of principled negotiations in advance. If negotiations violate the rules at any time, refer back to the rules and try to bring the negotiations back on course.

Cross-Reference

Leadership Skills and Methods

In contrast to traditional bargaining tactics (see Hendon's Negotiating Tactics), principled negotiation is intended to produce creative and beneficial results that leave both parties feeling like they are ahead of the game. Instead of dividing up the pie, they try to make it bigger. This concept is most applicable where the negotiations concern complex issues and there is room for new approaches involving mutual cooperation. It does *not* work well where the parties have an antagonistic or untrusting relationship. But in negotiations between managers of different businesses, for example over terms of joint ventures or major contracts, a cooperative and principled approach is usually successful. These rules can be used informally by one or both parties to maintain a principled stance in the negotiations, or they can be agreed to by both parties in a formal contract.

INSTRUCTIONS

Rules of principled negotiation

1. *Separate the people from the problem.* The objective of this rule is to keep emotions from interfering with the negotiation process. Negotiations can easily become a test of wills. Avoid defining issues in emotionally laden or personal terms. Specific guidelines to follow:

- Identify the emotional significance of the other side's positions so as to be able to avoid inadvertently angering them.

- Acknowledge emotions and recognize them as a legitimate aspect of the negotiating process. Communicate yours clearly. (In traditional negotiations, the "poker-face" approach is usually preferred and emotions are hidden from the opponent.)

- Communicate effectively and clearly. This means listening well—trying to understand the other party's positions and how they reached them, and looking at issues side by side rather than face to face.

2. *Focus on interests, not positions.* In conventional bargaining, you conceal your interests and present positions that you feel will protect your interests. Then you are prepared to be pushed to a fall-back position. But in principled negotiations you should avoid stating a position for the sake of the negotiations and instead communicate your underlying interests. This is difficult to put into practice as it requires a certain amount of trust—you do not want the other party to treat your interests like positions or else you may be forced to a solution that falls short of your interests. So you have to be sure that both parties are expressing their real interests.

When they express interests instead of positions, both parties can collaborate to come up with positions that will be most appealing to both of them. In many cases the parties realize they have common or similar interests which might have been concealed in conventional bargaining.

3. *Invent options for mutual gain.* Both parties should cooperate to come up with ideas in a search for creative solutions that give the most possible to each party. This requires laying aside differences temporarily and brainstorming together to come up with ideas. These ideas cannot be treated as positions or debated at the time, as this will make the parties hesitant to voice whatever ideas come to mind. *After* all possible solutions are on the table, however improbable some may seem, you may express your opinions about which you prefer.

4. *Insist on objective criteria.* Use standard criteria or measures drawn from financial statements or other reliable and clear sources. Avoid making the criteria a cornerstone of your negotiating position and avoid subjective or unconventional criteria. Both parties should work toward the identification of the most reasonable and objective criteria to use, and either party should reject criteria that are not objective and standard.

Warning

This is the method as described in chapters 2–5 of *Getting to Yes.* (It is summarized as "People, Interests, Options, Criteria.") However, in some cases the other party is uncooperative, deceitful, or much more powerful, making the method hard to implement. *Getting to Yes* goes on to define strategies for overcoming these problems (see chapters 6, 7, and 8).

Reference

Based on Roger Fisher and William Ury. *Getting to Yes: Negotiation Without Giving In.* Houghton Mifflin, 1981.

HENDON'S NEGOTIATING TACTICS

Applications

- Reaching decisions through negotiation.
- Selecting tactics to use in negotiations and identifying tactics used by others.
- Negotiating with customers, suppliers, or unions.

Procedures

Use the checklist as a source of tactics for negotiation or consult it to identify the tactics of others.

Cross-Reference

Sales Management Decisions: negotiations with customers. Organizational and Human Resources: salary negotiations and dealing with requests from employees.

Professor Hendon of the University of Hawaii has identified hundreds of negotiating tactics for presentation in his seminars on negotiation. A collection of the most common and effective are discussed here. These tactics are used in distributive bargaining—where the object is to cut up the pie and the question is who will get the biggest piece. Negotiations over prices and wages typically are distributive, making these tactics applicable. If you are engaged in negotiations, it is helpful not only to employ standard negotiating tactics, but also to *recognize* when they are being used against you so that you can respond with an appropriate counter-tactic or call the bluff.

Note: Many negotiations are *not* distributive, or at least are not supposed to be. The Harvard Negotiation Project Rules (also presented in this section) are intended to allow negotiators to reach a win-win situation by making the pie bigger, rather than by quarreling about how to cut it up. But in many principled negotiations, such as those between managers at budget time, someone starts using distributive tactics, pushing the negotiations back into a distributive mode. By recognizing these tactics and objecting to their use, other negotiators or a mediator (sometimes the CEO) can move the negotiations back into a more principled problem-solving style.

INSTRUCTIONS

Negotiation tactics

Acting crazy. Put on a good show by visibly demonstrating your emotional commitment to your position. This increases your credibility and may give the opponent a justification to settle on your terms.

Big plot. Leave yourself a lot of room to negotiate. Make high demands at the beginning. After making concessions, you'll still end up with a larger payoff than if you started too low.

Get a prestigious ally. The ally can be a person or a project that is prestigious. You try to get the opponent to accept less because the person/object he or she will be involved with is considered "prestigious."

The well is dry. Take a stand and tell the opponent you have no more concessions to make.

Limited authority. You negotiate in good faith with the opponent, and when you're ready to sign the deal you say, "I have to check with my boss."

Whipsaw/auction. You let several competitors know you're negotiating with them at the same time. Schedule competitors' appointments with you for the same time and keep them all waiting to see you.

Divide and conquer. If you're negotiating with the opponent's team, sell one member of the team on your proposals. That person will help you sell other members of the team.

Get lost/stall for time. Leave the negotiation completely for a while. Come back when things are getting better to try to renegotiate then. The time period can be long (e.g., when you're out of town) or short (go to the bathroom to think).

Wet noodle. Give no emotional or verbal response to the opponent. Don't respond to his or her force or pressure. Sit there like a wet noodle and keep a "poker face."

Be patient. If you can afford to outwait the opponent, you'll probably win big.

Let's split the difference. The person who suggests this has the least to lose.

Play the devil's advocate. Argue against the opponent's proposal by stating, "Before I say yes or no, let's look at all the bad things that could possibly happen if we did what you want." This lets you show the opponent your better way of achieving his or her objectives without directly opposing the opponent's viewpoint.

Trial balloon. You release your decision through a so-called reliable source before the decision is actually made. This enables you to test the reaction to your decision.

Surprises. Keep the opponent off balance by a drastic, dramatic, sudden shift in your tactics. Never be predictable—keep the opponent from anticipating your moves.

Reference

Reprinted with permission from a list of over 200 tactics prepared by professor Donald W. Hendon of Northern State University, Aberdeen, South Dakota, in his seminar, "How You Can Negotiate to Win."

MINIMAX AND MAXIMAX TABLES

Applications

- Evaluating alternatives given uncertainty about the future.
- Selecting the alternative that will be most profitable under bad conditions or good conditions, depending on the decisionmaker's preference and risk strategy.

Procedures

1. Construct a payoff table identifying the profits from each alternative under various potential scenarios of the future. (Assumes that the cost of each alternative is known.)
2. Apply the minimax and maximax criteria to identify the best alternatives from both a pessimistic and an optimistic perspective.

Cross-Reference

Financial Decisions: Strategic Planning Decisions

This simple decision tool provides an alternative to complex probability-based decision trees and models. It can be used to create a quick, simple model of the decision and identify the preferred alternative based on all the outcomes that management can foresee. It does not require quantitative skills, but it does require the decision-maker to estimate the payoffs or profits from each alternative under different circumstances. This requirement is easily met in investment and budgeting decisions, where it can be a helpful tool.

INSTRUCTIONS

1. Start by constructing a payoff table. Define two or more alternative scenarios or states of nature. For example, high sales, medium sales, low sales; high prices versus low prices; or low, medium, or high interest rates. Limit scenarios by selecting the variable(s) with the greatest potential impact on returns, even if this means simplifying the situation.

Now list the decision alternatives down the left side of a table and the different scenarios across the top. Fill in each cell with your estimate of the payoff or profit from each alternative in each scenario. This will require calculating total returns and costs for each combination. In the following example, the returns are constrained by production capacity and the profits are therefore a factor of cost, capacity, and demand. Demand may be high or low, so payoffs are calculated for the case of $1 million in sales and the case of $10 million in sales.

Alternatives	Cost	Capacity	Payoffs given $1.0 Sales	Payoffs given $10.0 Sales
1. Subcontract Production (volume limited)	0.5	1.2	0.5	0.7
2. Lease an Existing Facility (higher volume and cost)	1.0	2.0	0.0	1.0
3. Build New Production Facilities (highest volume and cost)	2.5	10.0	(1.5)	7.5

(All figures in $ millions)

2. Now apply the minimax and maximax criteria. Minimax is the conservative approach—it maximizes the minimum payoffs from each alternative. Maximax is the optimistic approach—it maximizes the largest possible payoffs from each alternative.

Create a second table, this one listing each alternative on the right like the first, but having two columns for the maximum and minimum payoffs from each alternative. The minimum and maximum figures are used from the preceding payoff table.

Alternatives	Minimum payoff (minimax strategy)	Maximum payoff (maximax strategy)
1. Subcontract Production (volume limited)	0.5*	0.7
2. Lease an Existing Facility (higher volume and cost)	0.0	1.0
3. Build New Production Facilities (highest volume and cost)	(1.5)	7.5*

(All figures in $ millions)

Identify the largest payoff in each column. (They are marked with asterisks in the example.) The alternative giving the highest minimum payoff is the best given a conservative or pessimistic view (#1 in the example). The alternative giving the largest maximum payoff is preferred from an optimist's perspective (alternative #3 in the example).

Reference

D. Anderson, D. Sweeney, and T. Williams. *Quantitative Methods for Business*. West, 1978.

THE NOMINAL GROUP TECHNIQUE

Applications

- Group decision-making with difficult or non-conforming groups and under time pressure.
- Considering problems in staff meetings where political or status issues might reduce the input of some staff whose expertise is relevant.
- Obtaining the input of a group while retaining the authority to make the decision independently.

Procedures

1. Problem is stated and group members generate ideas on paper.
2. Members read ideas to the group; the ideas are numbered and recorded on a chalkboard.
3. Each idea is discussed in turn by group members.
4. Each member selects several ideas, ranks them, and enters their numbers and ranks on index cards. The votes are tallied.
5. If there is an obvious winner, it can be announced. Otherwise clarifying discussion can be held or the leader may make the decision arbitrarily.

Cross-Reference

Broadly applicable.

This method is one of the better known of the formal group decision-making techniques. These techniques arose out of research on group processes that identified problems stemming from the social interaction of group members that often reduces the quality of group decision making and problem solving.

Anyone who has presided over staff meetings will have experienced frustrations with group processes and is well aware of these problems. Some of the proposed solutions are cumbersome and too uncomfortable for most business meetings and work groups. But the Nominal Group Technique is simple to implement and does not lengthen the discussion of a problem or decision—in fact it can shorten the process. It reduces group interaction but does not eliminate all discussion. Often it permits fuller input from all group members and reduces politicking for certain ideas or solutions. It is also a good way to poll staff on a question without actually letting them make the decision, since the leader can calculate the vote tally after the staff meeting and keep the group's consensus to himself if he does not agree with it!

INSTRUCTIONS

1. The senior manager or group leader prepares a formal statement of the problem. After summarizing the procedures to the group, the leader reads the problem statement. Members are asked to generate ideas on paper without collaboration or discussion for five to ten minutes.

2. Members are asked to read their ideas to the group in turn, and without any discussion. Ideas are numbered and recorded on a chalkboard or flip chart by the leader or designated staff. Keep ideas and their numbers posted clearly throughout the process.

3. Now an open discussion of ideas is permitted in order to clarify them, address underlying assumptions, and express opinions. However, the leader should see that each idea is discussed in turn by group members and maintain some control over the direction and length of each discussion. Prevent arguments and make sure members are not put in the position of having to defend their ideas to the group.

4. The leader now requests each member to choose a specific number of favorite ideas (usually

between five and nine). Members write the number of each idea they select on a separate index card, and then rank the cards by numbering their favorite idea "1" and so on until they have assigned each choice a number. Conventionally the votes are tallied at this point and the results summarized on the board. But the leader can also collect the cards now, terminate the discussion, and explain that he or she will make a decision later, after having a chance to review them.

5. If there is an obvious winner, it is usually announced at this stage. Otherwise, clarifying discussion is held to find out why some members ranked ideas low and others high. A second vote can be held, repeating step 4, to see if the group can reach consensus after this discussion.

Note: This method is better for well-defined problems than for open-ended ones. How you state the problem has a big impact on the quality of the results. For example, the problem statement, "We need to improve this unit's financial performance," is going to be harder for the group to deal with than the statement, "The main contributor to reduced performance this year was a drop in margins—what measures should we take to remedy this situation?" Even better, of course, is the statement, "Margins fell because of increased raw materials costs—what should we do to respond to this?" But of course a narrowly defined problem statement requires a clear understanding of the problem.

References

A. L. Debecq and A. H. Van de Ven, "A Group Process Model for Problem Identification and Program Planning." *Journal of Applied Behavioral Science* 7 (1971): 466–492. (This is the original paper on the method, but if you want a practical overview of this and related techniques try one of the other references.)

Arthur B. VanGundy. *Managing Group Productivity: A Modular Approach to Problem Solving*. Amacom (American Management Associations), 1984.

Richard M. Steers, *Introduction to Organizational Behavior*. 2nd ed. Glenview, IL: Scott, Foresman and Company, 1984.

OSBORN'S BRAINSTORMING

Applications

- Generating many ideas in a group setting.
- Producing a long list of creative solutions from which to select the most promising alternatives.
- Helping a group overcome restraints on creative thinking.

Procedures

1. Explain the four rules clearly to the group.
2. Encourage the group to think of as many ideas as possible. (Ideas are recorded but not criticized.)
3. Afterward, review the list with a critical eye and try to develop a solution.

Cross-Reference

This method is useful in numerous applied problems, especially in Strategic Planning, Product Development and Innovation, and Organization and Human Resources.

Many companies incorporate classical brainstorming or a variant of it into some of their problem-solving and innovation tools, and it has been referred to so many times in this book that it has earned its own write-up. Developed in the early 1960s, this is the most popular method for encouraging creative thinking in groups. It is simple and easy for a group to learn and provides immediate results in most cases. Use it to help think of a novel solution to a problem or in any other situation where a fresh idea might be helpful. A brainstorming session can last anywhere from a few minutes to a few hours, depending on the difficulty of the problem and the leader's preference, but usually the sessions are terminated after half an hour.

INSTRUCTIONS

Start with a clear problem statement. Introduce it to your group (traditionally 6 to 12 participants) and explain the brainstorming rules. (If the group members look confused, have them do a simple warm-up exercise, like thinking of uses for a 2 x 4 plank.) Be sure someone records all the ideas, preferably on a large board or flip chart which the whole group can read easily. After the session you can have the group review the list of ideas with a critical eye (it will be in need of exercise by now, having been suppressed during the session). (*Alternatives*: Use a different group to review the list and select an idea, or do the review yourself.)

In addition to explaining the rules to the group and making sure they obey them, the leader should try to maintain a relaxed atmosphere. A group which is on friendly terms and used to working together will produce the best results, especially if it is your first time leading a brainstorming session.

The rules

1. No criticism of any ideas. Save criticisms for the evaluation stage.
2. Wild ideas are encouraged. Say whatever comes to mind.
3. Quantity, not quality. Generate as long a list as possible.
4. No proprietary ideas. Combining ideas or building on someone else's idea is encouraged.

Reference

Osborn, A. F., *Applied Imagination*, 3rd ed. New York: Scribner's, 1963.

QUANTITATIVE RANKING TABLE

Applications

- Evaluating alternatives on the basis of multiple factors.
- Formalizing the choice of alternative options or strategies.
- Helping a group reach a consensus opinion.

Procedures

1. Agree on a number of criteria on which to base the evaluation of multiple alternatives.
2. Assign each criterion a weight by rating its importance on a 1 to 10 scale. Create a quantitative ranking table.
3. Rate each alternative according to its strength on each criteria, using a 1 to 10 scale.
4. Discount the strength scores on each criteria by the importance weight assigned that criteria: Divide the importance weight by 10 and multiply the product by the strength score.
5. Sum the discounted strength scores of each alternative across all criteria and rank the alternatives based on the total scores.

Cross-Reference

Broadly applicable; especially Organization and Human Resources

This method is a quick and easy way to formalize comparison of multiple alternatives. It is useful whenever many alternatives or criteria make the decision too confusing to work out in one's head. It is also especially helpful when a group cannot agree on which of several alternatives to pursue since it can be

| Alternatives | Criteria (importance) | | | | Weighted score |
	Cost (8)	Risk (10)	Time (5)	Resources (7)	
A	4	8	6	5	17.05
B	7	9	8	6	22.80
C	3	6	10	5	16.90

used to force agreement on which criteria to use and how to weight them. Once the decision criteria are established, the choice is more obvious and the group will usually reach consensus.

INSTRUCTIONS

Use this method when you have a set of well-defined alternatives. First, decide which criteria should be used to evaluate the alternatives. List all the criteria across the top of a table and list the alternatives down the left side. Now decide how important each criterion is to the selection and assign an importance rating to each. Use a 1 equals unimportant to 10 equals very important scale.

Once the criteria and their weightings have been decided on, evaluate each alternative on the basis of each criteria. If a group is working on the decision, this step will require considerable discussion. Rate each alternative according to its strength on each criteria, using a 1 equals very weak to 10 equals very strong scale.

When all the alternatives have been rated on each criteria and the table is full, discount these ratings to reflect the importance of each criteria. Divide each criterion rating by 10, then multiply this fraction times each of the alternative ratings in the criteria's column. *Example*: A criterion is given a 5 in importance, and an alternative is given a 10 on this criterion. $^5/_{10}$ = 0.5; 0.5 x 10 = 5. Therefore, the discounted score for this alternative is 5 for the criterion. After every score in the table has been adjusted in the same manner, sum the adjusted totals for each alternative and write the totals to the right. Rank the alternatives based on their scores; in general the highest-scoring alternative is selected.

Reference

Albert, Kenneth J. *How to Solve Business Problems*. McGraw-Hill 1978.

INDEX